CRAVING FOR LOVE

BRIAR WHITEHEAD

D1247891

MONARCH
BOOKS

Mill Hill, London, and Grand Rapids, Michigan

First published by Monarch Books in the UK in 1993.
Revised and reprinted by Whitehead Associates in 2001 and 2002.
Revised and updated edition published in 2003 by Monarch Books,
Concorde House, Grenville Place, Mill Hill, London NW7 3SA.

Distributed by:
UK: STL, PO Box 300, Kingstown Broadway, Carlisle,
Cumbria CA3 0QS;
USA: Kregel Publications, PO Box 2607,
Grand Rapids, Michigan 49501.

ISBN 1 85424 607 0 (UK)
ISBN 0 8254 6213 4 (US)

British Library Cataloguing Data
A catalogue record for this book is available
from the British Library.

Designed and produced for the publisher by
Gazelle Creative Productions,
Concorde House, Grenville Place, Mill Hill, London NW7 3SA.

CONTENTS

116607

FOREWORD

The author of this book has done her research well and, remarkably, has not strayed from the title. As the world becomes increasingly darker, more and more people are finding they are lonely and separated from experiencing intimate relationships. Although technology is bringing us closer together, it seems paradoxically that we are at the same time moving further apart. When neighbours were half a mile down the road, we knew who they were, we could name all their kids and what church they attended. Now our neighbours are a few inches away on the other side of our apartment wall, yet we can know nothing about them at all! We are left feeling isolated, unloved and unwanted. It doesn't help that families no longer gather around the table for dinner, but grab fast food on their way to a meeting or a show. It seems that every ingredient God placed in our lives to bring fulfilment and a sense of belonging has been taken away. Life has become like a landfill site; as the dysfunctional elements of post-modern life interact with each other, a deadly product is created, much like methane gas at a landfill. This deadly product takes the form of separation; separation from the very basics of life God has blessed us with. As a result of separation there are deficits in our lives, and it is these deficits that create the homosexual condition.

The correct response to homosexuality is not condemnation and blame. Homosexual people do not ask to be homosexual: they are the product of a corrupt and dysfunctional culture. This book has a compassionate message to those who take the time to read it. It is our responsibility to make an investment in understanding the condition. Surprisingly, the answer is not in acceptance as our permissive generation would suggest, because that only leads to more sorrow and pain: it exacerbates the problem rather than solving it. Rather than providing connection, a sense of belonging and acceptance, the rejection found in the "gay" world actually far exceeds any rejection from heterosexual society. How can we reach the homosexual community with a Christian message of love and hope, yet at the same time oppose their political agenda that encourages the conditions and deficits contributing to homosexuality? Where is Solomon with his wisdom when we need him? How do we divide this baby in half? God is not willing that any should perish, but he is also not willing that we should live in a sinful condition. The world has changed Jesus' instruction "Go and sin no more" to "Go and sin some more!" As Christians we are called to be salt and light to a darkened world, but how is this possible? The answer is not to take to the streets like the prophets of old, but to use the current tools available.

The search for love and intimacy can become an addiction, a driving force stronger than anything else in life. Often male homosexuality is called a *Father Replacement Search*. The deficits in early life produce driving forces that seek fulfilment and completion. Many are left part adult and part child. The unfulfilled child within creates havoc in the adult life. One important thing that Briar Whitehead explains is that homosexuality is just one of many dysfunctions that can emerge from the same chaotic mix. The followers of Darwin would have us believe that we were created from slime. While this is certainly not what Christians believe, in today's world it is not far from the truth in a metaphorical sense. The "slime" of relational deficits has produced a vast array of dysfunctions: homosexuality, co-dependency, multiple personality disorder, and paedophilia, to name but a few. Almost everyone is looking in the wrong places for love, driven by their unfulfilled needs and making one wrong choice after another.

Briar has overturned many stones. She is one who sifts over and over. As the particles become smaller and more detailed, we find pieces of the puzzle that have answers. From what I know of Briar, she is a woman of courage and determination. She has worked hard to provide answers to those who seek them. It might take years to read all the books, journals and papers she has uncovered, let alone to make sense of everything they contain. Reading this book is almost like having a cheat sheet beside you in a college exam! Yet, amid the flurry of facts and figures is a beautiful description of the nature of God. A strange mix, but one that will encourage us and that we can use to encourage others, even though some of her words are unusual, to say the least, to the American ear (I have yet to find out exactly what a "dolly-bird" is!). This book is exhaustive, but in a good sense: it is not *exhausting* to read, but *exhaustive* in the sense of a biblical concordance. Get out your yellow highlighter, because with this information you will be able to answer almost any question about homosexuality. You can be an instant authority!

There is a major problem in filling deficits. Initially, desensitization was thought to be the answer. It seemed to work with other issues. If you fear flying, you fly, if you are afraid of the outdoors, you go outdoors, a little at a time. But, if your deficit is touch, now we have a problem, because touch is often sexually stimulating. Our touch deficit developed before puberty, before we became sexual and sensual. The early therapies sometimes included bare chest to bare chest hugging which did not produce the desired results. Instead of solving the problem (filling the deficit), it increased and complicated the problem. We also went through a season of reparenting, where someone became a substitute father and offered the love, touch and care that was missing from the natural father. But again, hug therapy was a dismal failure and became the source of several scandals.

The "10% figure" (from Kinsey) is bandied about in almost every article on homosexuality. Kinsey gave us so many percentages that we can almost pick and choose whichever benefits our cause the most. A quote from Kinsey's *Sexual Behavior in the Human Male* reads thus: "10 per cent of males are more or less exclusively homosexual for at least three years... " But Kinsey goes on: "8 per cent of males are exclusively homosexual for at least three years... " The difference here being the "more or less" and "exclusively". The next paragraph is what caught my attention: "4 per cent of white males are exclusively homosexual throughout their lives…" (page 651). Here, we have a more realistic figure. Do homosexuals comprise 4% of the white male population? Many researchers say that figure is still too high, but in recent years estimates are approaching that figure. With the educational system fervently advocating the gay lifestyle, it is possible that the 4% figure will be reached and exceeded.

Chapter 10 reviews the trauma that wives of gay men go through. The pain and grief experienced by wives especially (and other family members) is almost too painful to read. The wife's comment: "It's so unfair" cannot be denied; her husband is wrapped up in the excitement of a new relationship and is anxious to leave wife and family behind. He has no regard for their suffering or ability to survive. Commitment to God and wife mean nothing; lust is in control. There are no winners, all become losers. The book moves on to include the author's thoughts on inner healing and visualization, two controversial issues in the Christian world. If these sound "spooky" to you, then think on the objective of these methods. No one can deny that healing comes through relationship with God. Whatever way you find that will bring that closer walk with Jesus cannot be a bad thing. Healing comes through Christ, and above all, we must have that personal relationship with him.

Let this book cause you to seek the Lord regarding your part in bringing healing to the wounded, whether homosexual or heterosexual. Ask God: "Enlarge my vision, let me see these issues more clearly and show me my part in being your faithful servant." Release any judgment you may be carrying. Many involved in homosexuality were the victims of others' lust, being overpowered and forced into activities at the time they did not understand. They were given little choice. They were also put in a vicious dilemma. They knew what had occurred was wrong, but they also experienced an intimacy they had sought since birth. It was water to a person dying of thirst, but it seemed the world was saying, "It's wrong to give that person water." Yes, we all know that what they needed wasn't sex, but care, concern and affirmation. However, the cold facts are that sex became the vehicle to obtain these life-giving gifts. It is our calling to find a way to affirm the unaffirmed, to show the way to a fulfilling life without taking advantage of the wounded. Can we? Do we care enough?

Love in him

Frank Worthen
January 2003

INTRODUCTION

Craving for Love was first published in 1993 to help people understand homosexuality and other dependent relationships. It was in trying to understand homosexuality that I gained the self-understanding that made me realize the homosexual and I – a person who tended to get stuck in absorbing relationships with older men – were next-of-kin.

The book was published in the UK and distributed internationally. It slowly became recognized in the Christian community as something of a classic among those who wanted out of homosexuality, those who helped them and those who wanted to know what homosexuality was. But the book also spoke to people who were stuck in similar sorts of holes and didn't know why or how to get out either.

Craving for Love drew initially on about 100 personal interviews that I travelled more than 16,000 miles to collect: with gays and lesbians, many ex-gays, wives of gays and leaders in the ex-gay movement, and I read scores of books, did a lot of listening and made a lot of observations.

Since 1993 my involvement with people who are attracted to others of the same sex has continued and so has the research. Since 1993 there have been two more books, one of them: *My Genes Made Me Do It! A scientific look at sexual orientation*, Neil and Briar Whitehead, Huntington House, USA, 1999. But demand for *Craving for Love* has continued and women particularly have begged for a reprint.

I should say a little about the term "ex-gay". It is used in this book to cover people at all stages of transition who are seeking to become heterosexual in orientation and practice. There

9

are hundreds of them. Ex-gay support groups are beginning to prefer to talk about themselves as gender-affirming groups rather than ex-gay groups. This is not a renunciation of genuine healing, it's an attempt to avoid giving misleading messages about the process. The term ex-gay can create the impression of a change that is sudden, swift and complete, instead of the process it more often is.

I also want to make it clear that I am not saying the homosexual orientation in itself is an addiction. The orientation is a symptom of unmet emotional and gender needs. But the deeper these needs, the more likely it is that we will get into addictive relationships and behaviours in our attempts to assuage them.

I have changed many names to protect individuals. Testimonies are only as current as the day they were told me, as are names and activities of some support groups.

My grateful thanks first of all to Neil, my scientist husband and best friend, without whom I would have drowned in the scientific literature. The "interstitial nucleus of the anterior hypothalamus-3" and psychoneuroendocrinological studies didn't daunt him.

Thanks also to Dr Elizabeth Moberly, Cambridge developmental research psychologist, to Frank Worthen, now over 30 years an ex-gay and one of the founding fathers of the ex-gay movement, his wife Anita and the team at San Rafael; to Alan Medinger, Baltimore, another ex-gay and pioneer of the ex-gay movement, and Willa his wife, whose understanding of relationship dependency is comprehensive and compassionate; to Andy and Annette Comiskey; to "Carrie" who let me into her private diary; to Jeff Collins, an ex-gay, and gifted minister to people with AIDS; to Leanne Payne, whose books have been a personal inspiration; to the hundred or so people I have interviewed – and the scores I haven't – like Sy Rogers – but have come to know through cassette tapes and videos and boxes of paper and personal testimony. Thank you.

PROLOGUE

People were so shocked that I soon heard about the incident even though I was 12,000 miles away, and the voices of those who passed the news on quivered with outrage.

At 4am on a chilly spring morning a hooded man carrying a long, sharp knife had hacked one of the area's best-loved pastors to within minutes of his life – in his own home. Pastor Jon Fletcher had woken to answer the doorbell – something he did during the night from time to time. But this time the caller wasn't seeking a shoulder to cry on.

The details began to emerge several hours later in a small interview room in the city police station and the interviewing officer was gagging as he asked the questions: in eleven years of police work he had never seen a man so covered with the blood of another, or so unrepentant about his actions. The assailant's only regret was that he hadn't been able to get a "decent swing at the bastard". The following morning he still showed no remorse. "Fletcher told me I'd go to hell for eternity. That guy has killed me six times over – he's a murderer with words," he told a psychiatrist. But he felt he had gained a moral victory: he had struck back at the fundamentalist Christians: "bastards, who ruined people's lives".

Pastor Fletcher's life hovered in the balance, but he recovered, and many called it a miracle. If any one of five deep lacerations had been only millimetres deeper or slightly differently located, said the surgeons, Jon Fletcher would have died instantly.

Love and sympathy poured into the Fletcher household in the following weeks from all over the globe, and as he recovered

Jon Fletcher talked of supernatural protection and a new identification with those who suffered. The church's prayer meetings
burgeoned and the big, busy church united in overflowing
thanksgiving, mixed with anger and indignation. Descriptions of
the incident took on the tones of the cosmic struggle between
darkness and light: Satan had tried to annihilate Jon Fletcher and
had failed. The attacker became an extension of Satan's evil
desire – possibly a reprobate, maybe a "son of perdition". A few
felt compassion for the attacker, many were just bewildered,
struggling with the "whys".

The Fletchers and the church made warm overtures
towards the man's family and it was quite clear that Jon Fletcher
had forgiven his attacker. Early on a few people visited him in
prison and later at the city's psychiatric institution – but to all
intents and purposes a year after the stabbing the assailant was
remembered mainly as Satan's failed plot, a dark shape and
shadow to be pushed out of mind while the church got on with
the important task of evangelizing and discipling.

The man, X, was found not guilty by reason of insanity. He
was diagnosed paranoid schizophrenic and said to be living in a
frightening and threatening world in which he felt he had to
defend himself. But that was only part of the diagnosis. The
young man was also homosexual, and what is clear about paranoid schizophrenia is that it expresses itself around significant
conflicts in the sufferer's history and people associated with the
conflict. For X his homosexuality was a major conflict.

The church leaders continued to treat the man's homosexuality confidentially and sought to keep mention of it out of
media reports. Gradually church members developed a theology
around the assault which incorporated satanic attack, miraculous
preservation, suffering, providence and paranoia.

But the attacker's feelings about the fundamentalist stance
on homosexuality and about his own sexual orientation came
up frequently in the first police interviews and in the psychiatric
court reports, which noted an earlier hospital admission specifically to "look at the question of his sexual orientation". They
painted a picture of an isolated boy, who felt remote from his
adoptive father and unable to confide in his mother, who lacked

confidence at school and ran away at fifteen "to be a hermit and to find God", who always felt self-conscious of his body and had been aware of homosexual feelings for as far back as he could remember.

Fifteen years earlier, he had come to believe that Christ was his Saviour, and begun attending Hope Tabernacle in the hope that the church would help him change his homosexual orientation. He soon confided his homosexuality to Jon Fletcher, asking him not to make it known in case he was ostracized by the church, which had a clear moral stance on the issue. Fletcher kept the confidence. He worshipped Fletcher from afar, wouldn't hear a word against him, "renounced" homosexuality and for two years had no homosexual relationships. But he "fell", and felt "tremendous guilt". He attended the Tabernacle for seven years, until he met a local minister who told him that it was OK to be homosexual. From this man he sensed "kindness", and he left the Tabernacle. As he did, an "obsession of hate" developed towards "Christian fundamentalists and Jon Fletcher in particular".

In X's case, the hostility was severe: paranoid. When he awoke in the small hours that spring morning, intensely anxious, wanting "to strike back at society", his first thought was to "get" Jon Fletcher – the pinnacle of a group of fundamentalist Christians whom he hated. "If I hit him I would hit them all," he told his psychiatrist. When Jon Fletcher answered the door, he "snapped", and lunged, but not before feeling weak at the sight of a couple of Fletcher's male relatives appearing in their briefs.

It is not hard to reconstruct what happened in X's encounter with evangelical Christianity because many homosexuals tell the same story. For years he tried – but failed – to eradicate feelings and behaviour that he knew the church rejected. He knew the conservative manifesto on homosexuality: homosexuality was sin; people could turn up a list of scriptures to prove it. It disgusted people. Homosexuals went to hell. Badly wanting acceptance from his peers he felt rejected by them. As a boy who had rejected his father, he attached himself to Fletcher as a surrogate, sought his approval, hung on his words, and wouldn't hear a thing against him. Remote from his father, he had made God over in the image of his father and felt remote from God, rejected by him for his homosexual sin. He desperately wanted to be free of his homosexuality, but, no matter how much he tried, he could not get rid of the hunger for the closeness and touch of other men and his fantasies pierced him with guilt. The bright promise of deliverance became a cruel joke, his Christian life a sort of desperate charade, and pentecostals and evangelicals a righteous bunch of people who espoused a theology that rejected homosexuals. It didn't help of course that for a whole year before he rang Pastor Fletcher's doorbell, fundamentalist and evangelical Christians, including the Tabernacle group of churches, had slugged it out with the homosexual and liberal lobby against proposed legislation granting new rights to homosexuals. He would have felt the sharp edge of fundamentalist indignation. And as his paranoia flared, Pastor Fletcher, senior figure in the Tabernacle movement and his one-time hero and father figure, became the target of his homosexual hostility – even though the Tabernacle churches were not callous or indifferent and Jon Fletcher was a warm-hearted man, not a sanctimonious bigot.

Really there were two victims that chilly spring morning: Pastor Fletcher and a lonely, hooded homosexual man with a long, sharp knife who had stopped taking his medication and made too many wrong choices for too long.

In X the rejection that is one side of the homosexual condition had developed to paranoid proportions. The church did not know how to deal with either his homosexuality or his paranoia. When it comes to healing the soul of deep-seated unconscious pain, the church often abdicates to the psychologists.

I start with this story, because, although it is complicated by paranoia, I have seen its pain repeated over and over as I have spoken at length with homosexuals and lesbians and Christians of all shades over the past 14 years. Conservative churches often bog down in the moral issue and their aversion to homosexuality, combined with their sincere belief in the scriptural statements against homosexual practice, dominate their response. They do want to help but usually they haven't known how. They haven't known what causes homosexuality – things that would arouse compassion if they did know: loss of trust, loss of love, fear, loneliness, rejection and deep gender insecurity. They certainly don't appreciate the guilt and deep discouragement of the homosexual struggling alone in an unfriendly milieu to get the upper hand over same-sex attraction. Ignorance, confusion, aversion, and lack of correct teaching in the church toughen the hearts of good conservative Christian people towards the homosexual. Moral righteousness militates against compassion.

Pastor Jon Fletcher is not to blame any more than the church at large is to blame. In fact, he is less to blame. Most churches offer no hope of change to homosexuals: if they don't ordain them and bless their unions in their determination to be accepting, they openly reject them or aren't quite sure what to do about them. At least the Tabernacle – and other churches like it – promised hope, but they didn't really know how to deliver. In the conservative church the promised deliverance has tended to come as a formula: you're a new creature in Christ, confess it and believe it, pray and read the Bible, worship the Lord, resist the devil, come to the services and get a bit of counselling – all fine in themselves but inadequate where deep-seated pain and powerful addictive cycles are concerned, and quite self-defeating in a judgmental and generally rejecting moral context.

But let's not be unreasonable – all of us are in the learning process. The keys to the healing of homosexuality are only now being understood, so that pastors and counsellors cannot be held responsible for what they have not known or understood. True! But it is also very clear that there is some resistance in the church to the learning process. We can't identify with the homosexual person if we think our sins are holier. We don't realize that some of our own well-entrenched, unhealthy behaviour patterns and habitual responses come from similar needy places in ourselves. We don't know ourselves, or don't want to (often don't know how to) do anything about these compulsive or obsessive little or large behaviours and responses that go on in secret. We end up thinking we are better than the homosexual because – well – because he's homosexual and we're not. It's easier to take a moral stand against homosexuality, than it is to take an honest inside look and discover we are like him.

I was one of the ignorant. Homosexuality left a bad taste in my mouth. As a young Christian of the conservative variety I used to believe that God could change the orientation of gay people, but over the years I saw no evidence of it. Those very few I did hear about were soon on a circuit of Christian public platforms to proclaim the miracle, but a couple of years later I heard they were back in the gay scene. Slowly, like so many other Christians, I became confused, a victim of the noisy, pervasive propaganda that has largely persuaded the West, and the liberal church, that homosexuality is somehow innate and merely an expression of a different and innocent sort of loving. In the liberal church new doctrines of love and acceptance were replacing the cornerstones: the Divinity of Christ, the Resurrection and doctrines of sin and redemption. There was nothing wrong with homosexuality. Practising homosexuals should be accepted and incorporated, not helped to change!

I had a lot of questions but no answers. If God said homosexuality was sin and gave power over sin, why weren't there more former homosexuals in the church? If God said homosexuality was wrong, why did he seem so reluctant to give any homosexuals a hand out? If homosexuals couldn't help it but were unable to enter the kingdom of heaven (as the Bible seemed to say they were), then they were damned before they had started, and God wouldn't be that unjust! Or would he? After all, he had made "objects of… wrath, prepared for destruction". Nothing added up. Homosexuality was in my too-hard basket, and obviously in the church's too-hard basket, because no one I spoke to in the church could give me any answers either. Rather, the church was in confusion, and becoming polarized. The psychological literature was complex, contradictory and inconclusive. In fact research had stopped, the result of a reasonable enough decision by US psychiatrists in the seventies to declassify homosexuality as a mental disorder. In the new human rights era, political correctness (read: acceptance) rather than research, began to drive the response of the health professions to homosexuality, and seemed to spread everywhere else as well.

I badly wanted to believe that Jesus Christ was able to do

the impossible – restore the homosexual – just as I badly wanted to believe that he could still reach into my own chronic and painful struggle. But I was desperately disillusioned. This I had in common with homosexuals: God seemed about as interested in my predicament as he was in theirs. He had dumped me in a desert and disappeared, leaving me to struggle on alone. God was Love, so they said, but I no longer knew what that meant. God had removed himself far from our struggles and sat indifferently down in a lofty place in total disregard of our pain – while he continued to give the orders.

Then I met Noel – a huge, aggressive man with a big heart – who told me he was ex-gay. I was instantly interested, particularly when he told me a mental institution had once diagnosed him paranoiac and that he had also once run at a man with a knife. I spent weeks with him hearing his story. A rabid gay activist, he had been a founding member of the first gay church in New Zealand, and a member of the advance guard in the seventies' crusade to promote gays into top policy-making offices round the country and to legalize homosexual acts: he used to invent cases of discrimination to help the cause along. Adopted, remote from his father, molested by a Roman Catholic priest when he was seven, and homosexually active from the age of 12, he had tried for years to find acceptance and answers in the church but the attempt left him bruised and homosexually used by leaders and laymen alike. Homosexual aversion therapy at a psychiatric institution failed and he was homosexually raped by several members of staff in the process. On discharge he bitterly renounced the church and threw himself with a vengeance into gay activism and prostitution. He was running from the law in Britain when he took the first plane out to Tunisia and wound up – of all the unlikely places – in an Anglican vicarage in Tunis. He says he was thrown on his face in the church gardens by a vision of Jesus descending from the cross, walking over to him, and putting his arms around him. He heard his voice say, "I love you, Noel." This turned everything upside down for him: God didn't hate him, God loved him. He made himself accountable to the Anglican chaplain – a former Royal Navy commander who understood men – burned his porn and his gay clothes, cut contact with his gay friends and everything that associated him with his gay past, and began the uphill journey out. It took some years, but Noel, now married for 15 years, says he is no longer homosexual. His wife agrees. He has since given years of his life to helping other homosexuals make the same journey.

As I began to meet people with same-sex attraction and attend group meetings where lesbians and gay men shared their successes and failures in the transition to heterosexuality, I began to identify strongly with them. As they discovered and discussed the reasons for their homosexuality, I found I shared the same painful and empty relationship with my father that many of the men had experienced. I could identify with the loneliness and struggle of their teenage years, their sense of abandonment by God, and I knew, only too well, the desperate craving for that indefinable but imperative "something" that drives the homosexual person into a same-sex relationship to try to quench it. I was not driven into lesbianism to satisfy my craving; mine had expressed itself in quite another way, but it became obvious to me that the dynamics that had shaped me were so similar to what had shaped the homosexual that I was no different in essence. As I slowly realized that I had made God over in the image of my father – so that he seemed unpredictable, critical, indifferent, emotionally cruel, demanding – I began to gain insight into my own pain, fear and hopelessness. Slowly, at the pace I could accept and assimilate it, I realized that the sum total of the emotional deprivation and rejection of my childhood and teenage years, in which I stammered painfully and isolated myself, was a craving for love that was buried too deep for me to know anything about, but which motivated me – the adult woman – at a level beyond conscious awareness.

Like lesbians and gay men who sought love, affection and affirmation in someone of the same sex to assuage their craving, I also sought love in relationships. But my unconscious drive was specifically directed at men old enough to be my father, men who were what I had never known my father to be, who were gentle, approachable, who would spend time with me and talk to me, advise me, accept me, and think I was special – and who were Christian. Just like a gay person, I responded only to a certain "type" and never others. And once I had found him, I hung on for dear life, and nothing, but nothing, would prise me away – certainly not my own will-power. I couldn't do without it. I fed off the love I received like a leech draws its life from the blood it sucks, and I quickly lost interest in all other friendships. I gritted my teeth through enforced absences and counted the days till return. The only thing that ever ended these completely inordinate affections (I can call them that now; I couldn't then) was geographical relocation of some kind. But, as surely as night followed day I would start another one the minute the right person came along, and I knew I would, as I had done for 20 years, but I never knew why. I seemed powerless to prevent it. I spiritualized these relationships: he was the spiritual mentor and I was the protégée; I didn't know how else to explain them to myself. And each relationship seemed more intense than the last and in each case the size of my world would shrink down to the size of the person I could not do without. And I hid it very well; no one ever knew anything about it but me (and my husband with whom I shared everything, and who was as puzzled about it as I was). In some of the relationships I would be frightened by occasional incursions of sexual imagery that would flash unbidden onto an interior screen in my mind. Frightened because I was married and loved my husband, frightened because I didn't want them, and because I couldn't understand them. Frightened because I thought I must be secretly adulterous.

I was staggered when I realized what it was. I was 20 years a committed Christian. I loved God, even though I believed he had dumped me in an excruciating desert for his own unfathomable reasons. As the pieces fell into place and I realized the extent of the emotional damage I had sustained over the first half of my life, God began to show me why I felt he had deserted me, and why I clung like a limpet to gentle, loving older men. It took a long time before I could see that my total and exclusive focus on one older man who would love me and think I was special was idolatry. But God was gentle with me: at the same time as I realized that idolatry inevitably pushes God out of the picture and creates an absence out of his presence, he showed me he understood why I had replaced him and that he did not condemn me: I had a deep craving for the male love and attention I had never received as a child, adolescent and young woman. For the rest of my life I was on an expedition – although I never knew it – to stuff the pain with love from a substitute father. And flesh and blood was a lot more tangible than a remote God fashioned after the image of my father.[1]

And as I realized all this for the first time in my life and began to make confession of my idolatry, and allow God to use my imaginative faculty – the language of my heart – he began to heal me of the desolation in which my soul had lived for years. I shed buckets of tears. God baptized me with love: for weeks and months he said little else to me except that I had ravished his heart. My need to be special to an older man was displaced by burning images of God's tenderest love for me. For days I felt like a trembling bride amazed and overwhelmed by the intense, adoring gaze of Christ, my lover. In all the years of relationship addictions my mind had never succeeded in conveying to my heart images of divine love such as these – though I was well acquainted with my Bible. Now they were flooding in. The distant God who was indifferent to my pain was replaced by a God who suffered whenever and because I suffered, and who personally and intimately experienced and identified with, and grieved over, the pain of the smallest child and longed to comfort. It overwhelmed me and healed me.

And as I stabilized and began to look about me – and particularly about the church – I saw my own story and the homosexual's looking back at me in different ways from the faces and lives of people everywhere. People who had been Christians a long time, caught in compulsive behaviours they couldn't even own, let alone understand; disillusioned and feeling out of touch with God, but keeping up a good act for appearances' sake. Women dependent on food, work, men, on spending money, helping people, other women. Men addicted to sex and porn and denying it, men seeking power, status and success, but camouflaging it in acceptable Christian ways: focused on church growth, winning souls, building ministries. Women needing men, doing anything to get them and keep them, excusing their abuse and anger; women marrying men to "help" and "fix" them and so gain and keep their love (it never worked, but they kept trying); Christian women attaching to and marrying the wrong men – often men like their fathers – but calling it God; possessive relationships between women that blew apart leaving bitterness and gossip in their wake; possessive relationships between mothers and sons because husbands and fathers weren't there, and between pastors' wives and other men because pastors were too busy. I saw Christian men secretly abusing their wives, abusing their authority; sexually abusing their kids. I saw a lot of people who were as trapped in their behaviours as the homosexual was in his – and for similar reasons. All caught somewhere on the continuum of unmet need, trying to meet their needs their own way.

And I saw a lot of denial and justification in the middle of it all. People did not want to know they had a problem. The gratification they obtained from their unhealthy relationship, or porn, or recognition, or work, or food, was better than calling it a problem. Better than admitting a big hole where God was meant to be, and other people thought he was. Better than the God who wasn't there.

And these dear people – who populate the church in millions – are the same people who can shrink from homosexuals as if homosexuality were a plague that could be caught. Homosexuals are seeking nothing more or less than any of us who craves value, identity, love and comfort, and gets addictively involved in searching for it in another human being – or in anything from sex to success. It is the same search, gone awry, except that in the homosexual person the dynamics of early deprivation make it inevitable that the emotional deficit is made up in a person of the same sex. A "straight" woman turns to a man; a homosexual man turns to a man. So what! Both sexualize their need, because they don't understand its origins. A man may turn to sex, power and status. There is no difference.

To the person with homosexual desires and the Christian heterosexual relationship addict, and any who struggle with deep-seated compulsions – for there is little difference – I dedicate this book. My prayer (for men) is that you will discover your extraordinary and unique value to God and (for women) the staggering dimensions of God's intense and passionate love for "only you", and in so doing find the strength to leave lesser loves. To the homosexual I say with ardent empathy, God does not hate you. He is your best friend, most faithful lover, and the father you always wanted to have. He can profoundly meet your deepest needs for acceptance, love and significance.

Note

1. My father was not an ogre. He was simply, to me, a child and teenager, someone I admired but someone who seemed indifferent, demanding and emotionally callous. I sought his love and approval for years but because it seemed to me in the end that I didn't matter to him, I finally shut him out of my life. But the end result was emotional starvation and relationship dependency.

PART ONE:
ADDICTIONS

CHAPTER ONE

SEX, POWER, STATUS – THE MALE ADDICTIONS

"People who believe in God," he said with a derisive smirk, "are people who can't get through life without a crutch."

"Oh," I said. "What's your crutch then? What do you need to keep you going? Recognition? Admiration? Success? A-passes? Got to have a challenge to keep you stimulated? Sex? Bit of porn perhaps? Sport? Exercise? Gambling? Nicotine? Alcohol... I could go on if you wanted me to."

He looked at me as if I were mad.

"I don't have any crutch," he repeated.

"You're either bluffing, or you don't know yourself," I said.

"I learned that all people are addicts, and that addictions to alcohol and other drugs are simply more obvious and tragic addictions than others have. To be alive is to be addicted, and to be alive and addicted is to stand in need of grace." (Addiction and Grace, Gerald May.)

WHAT IS ADDICTION?

An addiction is a compulsive habitual behaviour, something we can't stop – though we think we can; or something we can stop briefly – only to resume later. A true addiction is characterized by five things: wanting more of it, a stress reaction when we can't have it, self-deception in order to perpetuate it (it's not a problem, or I'm doing this *because...*), a belief in the power of the will to stop it, and the way it absorbs more and more of our thinking. Even when the negative consequences outweigh the kick we get out of it we still keep on.

In *Addiction and Grace*, psychiatrist Gerald May comes up with 182 things he has found people become addicted to. Here are some of them: anger, approval, being right, being loved, being good, chocolate, computers, causes, eating, exercise, fishing, golf, gardening, housekeeping, lying, money, movies, music, neatness, performance, pets, power, relationships, responsibility, status, the stock market, sex, sports, stress, television, winning, work. The point is not so much what we become addicted to, but that we become addicted because of what our attachment does for us. The reason we choose one addiction rather than another is complex but it happens this way, as Dr Larry Crabb says in *Inside Out*: "Sinful habits become compulsively attractive when the pleasure they give relieves deep disappointment in the soul better than anything else one can imagine."

Our addictions distract, comfort, gratify, stimulate, relieve and stroke us – and we need them most when we're feeling insecure or bad about ourselves. "Regardless of how an addiction starts the longer it lasts the more powerful it becomes," says May.

Let's have a look at six different "male" addictions, bearing in mind that although ours may be different or not as severe, we often have our own secret habits for similar reasons.

PHILIP (SUCCESS, ACTION, WORKAHOLISM)

Everything Philip did had to be "top stream". He was a performer. He was only happy when he was busy and always guilty whenever he relaxed. Every obstacle to success was a barrier to be smashed through; he pictured himself as "the biggest, strongest, fastest car on the motorway" that motored through anything in the way. "I got the approval I wanted from achieving and doing. And I did it to please people, especially males."

Whatever he did – in the church, with youth, in the community – he ended up leading. In business he was a corporate high flyer, heading irresistibly for top management. But he gave it all away for "a vocation in Christian ministry". He joined a national Christian organization and worked seven-day weeks to transform it. What he did was innovative and successful. Then he crashed with a total breakdown. It's taken him five years to understand what was going on.

Philip's father was not only an alcoholic, but obsessed with the idea that his sons should have all the opportunities he lacked and succeed where he had failed. He pushed his boys along and when they succeeded they were "paraded round like prize peacocks". Philip's achievements were his only emotional link with his father, the only time he ever heard anything personally affirming out of him. His dad usually spent every night and weekends incommunicado in front of the TV with gallons of beer, slowly getting sloshed. The only chance for conversation was at evening's end, when he was very argumentative.

His father "ruled the roost", his mother anxiously keeping the peace and begging the boys not to say anything to upset their father. "We always had to please him. If we didn't he would punish us. We were stifled, never allowed to express our own views. I was scared of him." There is one expression above any that he associates with his father: If a job's worth doing it's worth doing well.

His boss, the national general secretary at the Christian organization he restructured, was very like his father in temperament: and Philip felt that nothing he did was good enough, though he bent over backwards trying. God seemed "judgmental, dominating, angry. I had to please. If I stepped out of line, Bingo!" He felt the same about his boss and the organization. He began driving "like a maniac", half hopeful of killing himself. Until his nervous system exploded.

Philip realizes now how much his drive to achieve was rooted in his need to please his father and how much he had made God over in the image of his father. But he is still struggling with oppressive images of God, guilty when he is not doing something, tired all the time, his body breaking out in bad eczema attacks when the stress is high. He is no longer as driven as he was, but still feels he is only worth something if he succeeds. Although he knows it mentally, he cannot accept that God loves or approves of him. He has difficulty with intimacy.

RALPH (SEX, PORN)

Some of Ralph's clearest memories of his childhood are his alcoholic father's often repeated words to him: "You'll never amount to anything." They crushed him, he says. His father "verbally and emotionally abused everyone", including his mother, "a sweet Christian woman", and sexually abused his young sister. He grew up with a craving for attention that stopped at nothing. "I did all sorts of daring things just to get people to notice me." At 15 he was sent to a correctional institution after multiple suspensions from school and drug abuse. He quickly became one of the ringleaders, and was arrested several times for stealing to support his drug habit.

His next big discovery was girls. "I seduced girls one after the other, it was my way of yelling out to the world, 'See what a great man I am.'" Girlie magazines progressed to hard-core porn, till "I just couldn't quit. Porn gave me a high and I craved it every day, just as people crave alcohol or drugs."

He married "but even as a married man I couldn't stop seducing other women. I even got into male sex just for the sexual release as I watched dirty movies." By this time Ralph was a deputy sheriff, with the nickname: Maniac. His wife left him "but I always told myself I could get more women. I'd be juggling three at a time."

Ralph left this life behind him six years ago after he came close to blowing his brains out. He now directs an organization helping others out of sexual addiction. "Sexual addicts are into self-gratification in every possible way," he says. "Whatever its roots, sexual addicts develop a very strong pride and arrogance – which starts from the feeling of trying to make something of yourself, because you've always felt so small."

TRENT (VOYEUR)

Trent looks and sounds thoroughly male: tall, rugged, good-looking.

But Trent never felt that way about himself when he was growing up. He felt "different, weird, ugly", and convinced none of the girls could possibly like him.

Trent reckons three things contributed to the feeling he had about himself.

- When he was ten he was repeatedly sexually molested by a next-door neighbour who beat him up if he didn't co-operate, and paid him if he did.

- Sex was something dirty that was not talked about at all in the family.
- He felt too alienated from his father to ever confide in him. His father was emotionally aloof, always angry and upset with him over something, a strict disciplinarian who was "right, always right" and would allow no explanations. He said he always felt in the wrong, unacceptable and put down by his father.

Sexually abused, he felt cheap and deeply ashamed. But he gained a guilty enjoyment from it – which increased his feelings of shame. To tell his father was to ask for the rod and long, cold, disapproving stares and silences that withered his insides. Trent had nowhere to go; he disappeared into his shell.

He was very aware of girls, but he felt dirty, and ashamed, unattractive, "unworthy of them", so he didn't date. From the age of twelve he became a voyeur.

Until he was 40 he spent three or four hours at it each night, "following people home and waiting in back yards for hours until a bedroom light came on or something started to happen. I'd masturbate while I was watching. I knew it was wrong and I felt sick and perverted. But it was my way of feeling good, of getting sex. I got very good at it. I was never caught, though I did it thousands of times."

Intimacy with a woman terrified him, he only went to bed with a woman when he was drunk, "drunk enough to talk to a woman".

Trent is now making a real effort to break the addiction and so far he's been celibate for six months. He says his greatest breakthrough was the discovery (in experiences that almost "broke his heart") that God was not like his father. "It always seemed God was always angry and upset with me and hard to please. I wasn't allowed to fail. It made it so hard. I had no idea. I wanted to be affirmed and loved and thought of as important, and accepted, and we all look for that everywhere but at the source. I tried to feel good through sex; other people look through drugs. What I'm understanding now is that it's God I've been looking for. Now I know I'm able to get intimacy, closeness and acceptance from him."

KEITH (PERFECTIONISM, CONTROL, RELATIONSHIP ADDICTION, SEXUAL ADDICTION)

Keith, 45, a church-going Baptist and accountant, was extremely generous to his fiancée, Karen, and her two children by her first marriage. During their courtship he bought her a new wardrobe of clothes, took her and the kids on outings, mowed her lawns, paid her bills, repaired the kids' bicycles, personally nursed her through several months of painful recovery from back surgery. Abused in her first marriage, Karen was overwhelmed by his care. When he asked her to marry him she said "Yes", because he was a Christian.

The stunning reversal happened in the first week back home, immediately after the honeymoon. He refused to share the marriage bed, and began to dictate every detail of Karen's life from her spelling, grammar and manners to her dress, hobbies and personal interest. He told her what to say and what not to say around his friends, controlled who she saw, who she talked to, eavesdropped on her telephone conversations, rationed her petrol money, bitterly criticized her friends. If she went out for the night he whimpered like a child, "My mother never went out, why should you", or retreated into black silences that lasted for days or literally shook with rage. He often called her "Mother", and when they went out together on rare social occasions he held onto her skirt.

He allowed no criticism of his parents and reminded Karen frequently that his upbringing had been perfect. He wanted her to use his mother's recipes, sweep the floor, fold the linen, iron his shirts as his mother did. If she didn't do it the right way, he was up at 4am re-ironing them. He wanted the cleanest house in the suburb, like his mother's, and often rose in the night to polish finger marks off glass and furniture.

Marital intimacy was practically non-existent, though he freely and frequently masturbated in front of the television and as he walked round the house. To help their sexual relationship along Karen invested in a therapy manual. It didn't work. "When he was supposed to be caressing me, he would knead me like dough, serve me up a lot of family history, then disappear." But he had a prurient interest in little girls and some odd nocturnal habits – like jogging (for hours) in the small hours of the morning. He tried to entice Karen's teenage daughter to swim naked with him.

He was contemptuous of Karen's opinions whenever she disagreed with him – often telling her she didn't have "a brain between her ears". He blamed her for his lack of business success, his tension, and his bad back. If she challenged him he accused her of not loving him, or of being a poor wife. "He would thump the table with his fists and tell me he was the head of the house and I had to obey him. Everything was rules and regulations."

Karen's children, fourteen and ten, began crying and locking themselves in their bedrooms when he came home from work. He constantly found fault with their schoolwork, criticized them until they cried, and then scorned them for being babies. The eldest – a daughter – left home after two years, the second, a boy, needed counselling.

But if Karen threatened to leave him he would go into uncontrollable rages, threaten her, run away and sulk, or plead desperately that he loved her.

Although Keith protected his parents from criticism, his "Christian" father was rigidly opinionated, perfectionist and cruel: Keith still remembers him standing by while Keith nearly drowned at the age of five, refusing to help because Keith was calling for his mother. During his father's frequent four-month absences his misdemeanours were listed and he would be thrashed for each when his father got home: no explanations allowed. His mother's life centred round placating and pleasing her husband, who freely disparaged and overrode her. She worked overtime keeping the house the way he liked it. When she went away once for several months it was for a quiet nervous breakdown; no one talked about it and when she came back nothing was any different. Keith feared his father and was close to his mother who leaned on him heavily for emotional support.

Frightened of his father – who he said had sexually abused him – and focused around his mother, Keith's masculinity was unaffirmed: intimacy with a woman was beyond him. To conceal the frightening black hole in his manhood Keith denied anything was wrong. He came to believe what he told himself: that he was powerful, invulnerable, in charge, unemotional, respectable, Christian.

Keith was a relationship addict, terrified his wife would leave him, binding her to him by stripping her of her confidence, identity and independence, using anger to cow her and get his own way. He was also sexually addicted: the sexual excitement of visual stimulation, fantasy and compulsive masturbation.

TERRY (PEDERAST)

Terry is mild, affable, and pleasant. But he served a gaol sentence of 16 months several years ago for sexually molesting three young boys.

His upbringing was rural conservative; his parents were kind but very emotionally distant. "I just remember this huge emotional distance between myself and particularly my father; I was closer to my mother. Dad just wasn't active in our upbringing." As a child he remembers being constantly on the hunt for older boys who would be a "source of strength to me somehow": someone either physically strong and good at sports, or his "special friend", or "friendly and attractive". "They were always someone I wanted to look like or be like, always everything I wasn't."

When he was 18 he switched. Attracted to thirteen to sixteen-year-olds for strength when he was younger, he now found he wanted to be a source of strength to them: he wanted to protect and care for "kids with a look of openness and innocence, who were young and carefree". The focus was still on what he never had and never was. "I was never open and vulnerable because I wasn't strong enough to be, I didn't have the strength in my home. And I never felt innocent, or young and carefree. I felt isolated and uncared for."

Terry's fantasies slowly became sexual, particularly in his

early twenties when he and a male friend had been drinking heavily and his friend made sexual advances during the night. It was another 16 years before his fantasies were acted out – with three boys. Then he was so horrified at what he had done he took a gun and was about to kill himself when a Christian friend walked in. Terry became a Christian and was wondering what to do about his crime when one of the boys informed the police. He made a full confession of all three incidents and was gaoled.

Terry doesn't lay all the blame at his parents' door. No one but he made the choices he made, he said. "I let it happen to me; I never took the risk of getting for myself the things that I needed. And I was so isolated I never talked to anyone about it." But he is quite sure that his fantasies took root in the emotional isolation of his home life, especially in the hunger for the close, strong, male figure that he never found in his father.

WALTER (HOMOSEXUAL)

Walter was adopted at six months. As he grew up in a family of five he became convinced his father loved his blood children more than him, and his relationship with his hard-working father became more and more testy, argumentative, difficult – "like two he-goats butting heads", his mother said. He was over-weight, adopted, he felt rejected by his father, the family was poor, he was bad at sports, and his peer group rejected him.

At the age of seven he was sexually molested by a priest, an incident that both frightened and attracted him: he was frightened by the man's actions, but responded hungrily to the attention and touch. And down at the toilets behind the timber mill he found that some men who used the place would touch him in the same way.

Starved of normal affectionate interaction with his father, other male figures and his peers, he grew up associating male acceptance and affection with sexual contact.

ARE YOU ADDICTED?

"But my addictions aren't as bad as any of these," you may say.

Quite probably.

But many people do secretly struggle with addictions as

severe as those described above. And though many men would object strongly to being compared with homosexuals, the homosexual often has much the same story to tell as anyone caught in addictive behaviour: a tale of unhappy relationships at home and in peer groups, feelings of shame and difference, rejection and isolation.

The difference between a strong desire for something and being addicted is our freedom to choose. A good test for the presence of an addiction is simply to stop doing it for some time. If you can, you're OK. If you can't, some sort of addiction is present.

Another good test for the presence of an addiction is your own reaction: How defensive are you? As someone said: Touch an addiction, get a reaction.

Chapter Two

ABSORBING RELATION-SHIPS – THE WOMAN'S TENDENCY

Absorbing friendships

In China in 1918, an unusual man addressed a group of more than 200 senior political advisors, military leaders, and leading bishops, pastors and missionaries.

The man was Frank Buchman, initiator of the Oxford Group, later known worldwide as Moral Rearmament. The Prime Minister of China, Sun Yat Sen once said of Buchman, "He is the only man who tells me the truth about myself." Buchman was a boat-rocker. The people who resisted him most fiercely were often the Christians. It was no different at the conference in Kuling, China.

China's deputy Prime Minister, Hsu Ch'ien, also addressed the conference. Christians were powerless in China, he said, because of their private sins. Buchman agreed and in the twelve days that followed he dug into them, and stirred up indignation and antagonism – as he had anticipated. But nothing erupted over his head as furiously as the storm that broke over one *unassuming paragraph* in his third address in a series of nine. He told the conference:

> When I first came to China last year, a man who is an old tried physician of souls came to my room and said, "I believe God has sent you to China for a certain purpose." He told me of one of the bandages which bind… He said, *"Do give a strong message wherever you go on 'absorbing friendships'… "* (my italics). On these hilltops I have seen "absorbing friendships". I can't judge, I can only say this,

they may be unhealthful. He knew far more than I do. He asked me to be faithful in passing on that message.

The reaction was explosive and the bishop, Logan Roots, was inundated with protests. He complained to Buchman and Buchman responded that people who were offended had obviously missed the love behind the criticism, which was meant to liberate not oppress. But Bishop Roots and one Harry Blackstone, conference financier, collaborated in forcing Buchman out of China on grounds of his physical and emotional health, which, on the contrary was quite sound. Buchman went seven months later but confided to a friend at the time that there were clearly other reasons behind his dismissal.

Blackstone was the ringleader of the backlash and it turned out had more to hide than many of the others. A few years later his secret predilection for female Eurasian secretaries spilled into the open; the church dismissed him and he went into business. Interestingly Blackstone almost immediately owned up to Buchman and asked for help. Roots too, wrote asking Buchman's forgiveness.

The "old, tried physician of souls" was right on target, and not much has changed. What he said then provokes the same reaction amongst Christians today. Some of us are relating in unhealthy ways but get very defensive if anyone says anything about it. Buchman used the phrase, "absorbing friendships". Today we are hearing phrases like: love addiction, emotional dependency, women who love too much, relationship addiction. A woman who latches on to a man and can't let go is relating addictively.

WHAT IS RELATIONSHIP ADDICTION?

The alcoholic, the drug addict, the gambler, the compulsive eater: these provide us with our images of addiction. But us, adults, *our relationships*?

An addictive relationship is an adult relationship with a person of the same sex or the opposite sex that we can't give up. Often we don't understand the reason for the powerful attraction the person holds for us, but we become preoccupied with them and the relationship, jealous of others who might mean as much or more to them. Our life begins to revolve in diminishing circles round them, and the prospect of living without them fills us with desperation and pain. Other relationships become empty in comparison.

A good general test of relationship addiction is your reaction, as an adult, to giving up right now any relationship that is vital to you and is taking up a lot of your time and emotional energy. If you already find yourself saying indignantly, "Excuse me! There's nothing wrong with my relationships", or "What right do you have to tell me... ", you may already be caught. How do we know that a relationship addiction is developing? Here are some clues. But before you read the list, remember this. Nothing about you is new to God though it might be new to you. If what you read upsets you, God knew all about it anyway and loved you regardless and will love you now not one bit less.

Relationship addiction is developing when you

- are frequently jealous, possessive, and protective of the relationship: keeping others out.
- want to spend time alone with this friend and become impatient when it does not happen.
- become irrationally angry or depressed when your friend withdraws slightly.
- lose interest in all other friendships.
- have romantic or sexual feelings leading to fantasy about this person.
- become preoccupied with your friend's appearance, personality, problems and interests.
- are unwilling to make short or long-term plans that do not include your friend.
- are unable to see the other's faults realistically.
- become defensive about the relationship when asked about it.
- show physical affection beyond that which is appropriate for a friendship.
- refer frequently to the other in conversation, feeling free to speak for the other.

- exhibit an intimacy and familiarity with this friend that causes others to feel uncomfortable or embarrassed in their presence.[1]

In reference to the list, you may be free of sexual fantasy or romantic feelings, you may not act familiarly or intimately, you may not even presume to speak for the other – your personal standards may have put that sort of behaviour off-limits – but if all or most of the other factors are present you have already crossed the line into an addictive way of relating. But don't be discouraged. There is a way out and the first step is simply to own up to it.

BINDING OTHERS TO US

Let's have a look at another list, and see if it strikes any chords. This shows common ways in which addictive relationships begin and are maintained. Some of the behaviours are perfectly innocent in themselves. It is the motivation behind the behaviour that matters. *Is it manipulative: to bind another to you?*

- giving gifts and cards regularly for no special occasion, such as flowers, jewellery, baked goods and gifts symbolic of the relationship.
- using poetry, music or other romanticisms to provoke an emotional response.
- physical affection: body language, frequent hugging, touching, rough-housing, back and neck rubs.
- eye contact: staring, giving meaningful or seductive looks, refusing to make eye contact as a means of punishment.
- flattery and praise: You're the only one who understands me. I don't know what I'd do without you.
- flirting, teasing. In the company of others using language that excludes by creating a secret conversation that only the two of you understand.
- failing to be honest: repressing negative feelings or differing opinions.
- needing "help": creating or exaggerating problems to gain attention and sympathy.

- making the other feel guilty over unmet expectations: "If you love me then... ", "I was going to call you last night, but I know you're probably too busy to bother with me."
- threats: of suicide and backsliding. These can be manipulative.
- pouting, brooding, cold silences; when asked, "What's wrong?" replying by sighing and saying, "Nothing."
- undermining your partner's other relationships: convincing him others do not care about him, making friends with your partner's friends in order to control the situation.
- provoking insecurity: withholding approval, picking on your partner's weak points, threatening to end the relationship.
- keeping the other's time occupied so as not to allow for separate activities.[1]

If you can see yourself in the lists, are flushing with embarrassment and are trying, not very successfully, to convince yourself that the relationship you are in is really far more beautiful and more spiritual than the list would make it appear, congratulations struggler! Join the club. You are just like many of the rest of us. Really all you want is to be known, accepted, loved and affirmed but you're going about it the wrong way.

There is a broad continuum in relationship addiction, as there is in any addiction. The more intense the emotional entanglement, the deeper the underlying unmet needs for affirmation. The most significant and common kind of relationship addiction is codependency; the other is emotional dependency.

For grammatical simplicity we will use the more common scenario in what follows: the female dependent and codependent. Codependent men certainly exist but they are a rarer species.

CODEPENDENCY

Codependency is when he's got the problem and she helps him keep it. Codependency is *her* problem.

Codependent is the name given to those women who are regularly attracted to problem men: men of the kind described in Chapter One. For the codependent *to be needed is to be loved.*

The codependent has no sense of her intrinsic worth: she finds it in doing things for others. While she can *help* she feels worthwhile. Because her self-esteem comes from taking others' problems on board, helping and fixing, she feels bad when things get worse. To stop things getting worse she becomes controlling, the more so the more the chaos deepens, e.g. controlling access to his drink, to his drinking friends and activities. But she continues to try to please him too to keep the relationship: telling the boss he's sick today, borrowing money to pay his bills because he's spent it all on alcohol, getting a job to "help". She is out of touch with how she really feels, how the kids feel, she tries to hide the problem from outsiders, tries to hold the family together. She tells herself everything's OK.

Never confronts

But she never confronts the addiction in her mate – for at least four reasons:

- The most important: he might leave her
- Women with low self-esteem don't have the courage to confront
- She easily believes that his continuing problem is her fault
- She needs him to keep needing her. So she nags and placates

Nagging sounds like confrontation but isn't: it only creates the comforting illusion that progress is being made. To keep the relationship together she makes excuses for him, mops up the messes, takes the abuse, and keeps the secret. In the end, he, his problem, her relationship with him becomes the centre around which her life and everything else revolves. And if she stops focusing on him, he accuses her of not caring.

The man she is involved with is married to his addiction, not her. He may have no intention of giving it up. As long as she alternately nags and placates him he is safe. He has the relationship and his addiction too.

I quote an excerpt from a letter from a recovered male alcoholic.

... I have long wondered, "Where in the world have all the women gone?" I am now fifty-six years old. In past years women flocked around me. The worse shape I was in, the more blighted I appeared, the more they came to cuddle me. I *always* had women in my life, nurturing me, attempting to make me all better. That was years ago when I abused alcohol, was a chauvinist about women, prejudiced against Blacks and Jews, and you name it. I was very popular!! Women came forth from all directions to be with me. But now I have no women interested in me, no women bubbling around me, seeing it as their duty to "help" me. ... I had many women interested in me when I was a sick alcoholic, prejudiced and obnoxious (but) now I'm healthier there are very few... I changed my life, rid myself of much blight but at the same time I lost my charm.[2]

I use alcoholism as the example but the nature of the addiction is irrelevant.

The games: manipulation and control

The games played between a codependent and a problem partner are well documented in the psychotherapeutic literature: the rescuer (trying to help), persecutor (accusing and blaming), and victim (blameless and helpless). They are played in the complex interaction between their personal self-gratification and the survival of the relationship. Both play all the roles, switching when each has gone too far and the relationship appears to be at risk. The games? Displays of affection, helping, listening and encouraging, giving advice, praising, managing, pleading, cajoling, bribing, nagging, undermining, coercing, bullying, battering, raging, ladling on guilt, accusing of not caring or not loving; threatening violence or suicide or divorce, "repenting", buying forgiveness, promising to reform, making up.

Willa – a former codependent – says Alan, a practising homosexual at the time, would "come home hating himself, ashamed, hanging his head. It would always break my heart. I just wanted to make it better. I would say, 'But you're a good person, you do good things.'" But she would undermine Alan by talking in superior terms whenever he asked her advice "just to keep him feeling inferior and incompetent and depending on me".

Perfectionism

Willa says:

> To be saviour you've got to be the all in all, the best cook, the best lover, the best party-giver, the best dresser, the best wife; you're mother – a good mother, everything his own mother wasn't – you're brother, you're his buddy, everything, because you still have the blind hope that you can make this person happier.

Willa remembers feeling wretched all day if one corner of her house had not been cleaned.

You exist for him

> Both of your eyes are upon his needs, on what will make him happy. What I needed or wanted had no importance to me. I gave them up gladly in pursuit of making him happy. I believed that if I gave up enough, and served him enough that he might love me. You're driven, to please him. You concentrate so hard on him that you don't have to deal with how you really feel deep down inside. You work so hard that you can't think how you feel.

The fantasy

> Seventy-five percent of the time I lived in this dream world of happy home and lovely family and loving husband – the life I wanted – terrified of facing the reality and that awful mess. Many women are in relationships with men who are being cruel and abusive to them and they don't see it, because they are living in a dream world. They also repress any information from the unconscious that might hint something is wrong: They tell themselves: "I'm not angry", "I love him", "he didn't really mean what he said", "I'm not upset".

EMOTIONAL DEPENDENCY

Where the codependent says, "You need me", the emotional dependent says, "I need you". She is not motivated to fix or rescue the person to whom she attaches: she simply clings. Where the codependent boosts her self-esteem by doing for others, the emotional dependent finds hers by being in relationship – sometimes any relationship, depending on the level of self-esteem. She moulds her identity around what he wants because she wants his love and approval so much; she doesn't have an identity otherwise. Like codependency, emotional dependency runs the gamut from mild to severe. The emotional dependent may also be a victim who attracts (and manipulates) the codependent man (the more unusual case).

THE ADDICTIVE CYCLE

Relationship addicts follow the same cycle as those caught in substance addiction – or any addiction: tolerance increase (more and more of his company to get the same effect); obsessive thoughts (preoccupation with him, the details of his life, his problems); compulsive behaviour (not, I *choose* to, but I *have* to be with him); protection of the supply (possessiveness); withdrawal symptoms (pain at separation from him).

The relationship addict thinks the intense highs and lows of the addictive cycle are love, but they are more accurately the emotional swings that accompany addiction: anticipation, excitement, euphoria, jealousy, anxiety, fear, insecurity, panic, depression. Conditioned for years to believe that these emotions define love, she thinks that where she doesn't feel them, love is not present. A "healthy" relationship is therefore not attractive.

The relationship finally breaks up because what underlies it is not love but needs for love and value that each has got into the habit of gratifying the wrong way. It breaks up when the pain wins over the need.

WHY A PREDOMINANTLY FEMALE ADDICTION?

Relationship addiction tends to be a female phenomenon, though men also relate addictively, like Keith (Chapter 1). In their review of the scientific literature on relationship dependency, Schreurs and Schreurs, writing in the last decade, found women were much more likely than men to form dependent relationships and that men had much higher levels of autonomy in relationships. There are reasons for this. In her book *You Just Don't Understand*, researcher, Deborah Tannen, says women see life as relationships and tend to seek intimacy and avoid isolation in a world of connection, whereas men tend to see life as a contest in which they struggle to prevail and achieve mastery, preserve independence and avoid failure. So women tend to use relationships to meet their needs. Men, on the other hand, tend to turn to activities or things to meet needs, often in ways that prove mastery. Relationship addiction in men may involve expressions of power therefore, e.g. mastery, in attempts to rescue through codependency; or control, to maintain possession.

REPETITION

They say Elizabeth Taylor has found the right man this time… this time… this time… this time.

The relationship addict goes from one relationship to another – and although each relationship may appear to be different, there will often be a common thread. Why?

Habit! Habits start at home, then are reinforced outside home. Our upbringing and our response to it, goes a long way towards making us the kind of people we are. The kind of people we are, we take with us wherever we go, continuing to use the certain kinds of behaviour that "worked" in our families. We also tend to gravitate to people who allow us to continue behaving and relating that way, largely because it's familiar, it fits. So it feels secure. And strangely, for the relationship addict, if home life has starved her emotionally, she will tend to go for men who will starve her emotionally. If home life abused her, she will gravitate towards abusers.

Come on now, we wouldn't be so silly! We'd run a mile the other way! Once bitten, twice shy! But it's not so. The statistics bear it out, and therapists are familiar with the phenomenon. "My father was an alcoholic and I married an alcoholic." "My father sexually abused me, and I married a man who's abusing my kids − or abuses me." "My father was a workaholic and I vowed I would never get involved with anyone like that. But I did. He's never home." Claudia Black even wrote a book about it called, *It Will Never Happen to Me!* But often it still does.

If the codependent does avoid hooking up with the man with the type of addiction she declares she will never tolerate, she often finds herself with a man with a different but still powerful addiction.

Addiction match

In relationship addiction there is an interesting "addiction intensity" match. The lower the sense of self-worth in the dependent person the more serious or numerous the problems in the person she is attracted to. Psychologists have even set up technical scales measuring it. "It's every time a beeline," say psychologists at the Minirth-Meier clinic. "They'll always find each other − even in a crowded room." There is a swift commitment. They light each other up; it's something in the eyes, in a glance, in the manner. The conscious mind is totally fooled: it interprets the sudden surge of interest as love's awakening.

What's going on?

Codependency

Each case is as different as one person is from another, but, for the codependent, for instance, something like this is happening. The oldest girl who stands in for an alcoholic mother shoulders responsibility past her years: she keeps the household running, the family together, and often sacrifices her own plans and career. For her, love, appreciation and approval become linked with being strong for others in a needy household: responsible and indispensable; focusing on other people's needs, not her own; pleasing people, peace-making, hiding the problem from the outside world. It gradually becomes ingrained in her: people depend on me, I mustn't let them down, to be needed is to be loved, good appearances matter. But buried deeper than any of this is the powerful fear that was implicit in the chaos: this is all the love I know and I might lose it.

Along comes a good-looking man with an alcohol problem.

They fall for each other. At the conscious level she has vowed never to marry an alcoholic – not after her home life. But her conscious mind is not what is answering for her. Her unconscious needs for love are, and her definition of love was something she picked up in an alcoholic home: being loved is all tied up with being indispensable and strong and making things better, and his particular problem is familiar territory. She knows all about it. He no doubt disguised or excused his drinking to get her and she no doubt minimized and made excuses for the drinking she did see – as she did at home. And so she got involved. And her underlying fear of loss of love will ensure that although she might nag and despair she will also placate and rescue him from the consequences of his behaviour rather than seriously confront it.

He had grown up learning to fill the hole in his self-esteem with alcohol. He wanted a strong, mothering type of woman: strong enough for him to lean on but not strong enough to confront his addiction, so facing him up with his need to deal with it. Strong enough to feel responsible for him, to carry him, try to help, take the blame, but not strong enough to live without him. He got what he wanted, not what he needed. She wanted love, and she didn't get it – and won't – though she may try until she is a wreck.

Emotional dependency

As mentioned, the emotionally dependent woman is not trying to fix anybody. She simply clings. If a woman was abused in childhood she may seek relationships in which she will be cared for, often going for a strong man, but ending up with a man who is merely dominant and aggressive. When he abuses her it's normal enough: no different from the way she and her mother were treated at home. Or she may attach to emotionally inaccessible men because it's normal for her: her father was remote or rejecting. Or in flight from a harsh, unloving father, she may fall into the opposite trap: get involved with a sensitive man who proves to be passive or ineffectual: maybe homosexual or sexually addicted.

But whether it's codependency or emotional dependency

This is what, for most of us, constitutes love. We feel at home, comfortable, exquisitely "right" with the person with whom we can make all our familiar moves and feel all our familiar feelings. *Even if the moves have never worked out and the feelings are uncomfortable,* they are what we know best. We feel that special sense of belonging with the man who allows us, as his partner, to dance the steps we already know. It is with him that we decide to try to make a relationship work...

says Robin Norwood in *Letters from Women Who Love Too Much.*[3]

But it's not just that a woman can slip easily into the patterns of relating that she knows well. If there is also a promise that *this time* she will succeed in gaining the love she longs for, she will find it very hard to resist, she says.

In relationship addiction, the greater her need for love the more tenacious her attachment will tend to be, the more troubled the man she will tend to gravitate to, and the more manipulative and unhealthy the relationship. As someone once said: hungry people make poor shoppers.

But the tragedy in addictive relationships is that when they break down, the parties simply go their separate ways to repeat a similar scenario with someone else, because no causes have been understood. Or in codependency the partnership may stagger on for years in an exhausting mutual manipulation that is better than no relationship at all.

Dr Elizabeth Moberly, research psychologist, comments, "This sort of person who has not resolved the past will either marry a problem partner, or become a problem partner. That is why it is important for people to resolve their past issues, consciously, with help, rather than act them out on other people, time and time again."

SEX IN RELATIONSHIP ADDICTION

We relate addictively because we are trying to fill a crying inner void that stretches back to childhood with a person, someone to whom we matter more than anyone else in the world, someone who will need us so much that he/she can't do without us.

Romans 1: 23–25 comments on the implications for our sexuality when we seek to make someone else an "all-in-all". When we "worship the creature" rather than the Creator – which is what happens in the intense enmeshment of relationship addiction – our sexuality becomes involved, and "sexual impurity" (v24) can be one of the outcomes.

If it is allowed its head, relationship addiction will frequently express itself sexually, simply because it is so hungry for connection. Relationship addiction can cause adultery. Or if sex is not one of the ways a woman will allow her longing for love to be expressed: emotional adultery. At any rate the emotional pressure she can apply may find a weak point in the man she worships. She may become sexually involved if she thinks it might win her the love she is wanting. It won't, but she may still try.

"In adult life whatever a person's deepest emotional need is, will be prone to be eroticized," says Dr Moberly.

It is ridiculous to think that emotional-psychological wounds sustained in early years can be healed in a sex act, but this is what our behaviour presumes and our culture encourages. The relationship addict who has sex in a bid to meet her need for love, lacks understanding of the true nature of her need.

HEALING THE RELATIONSHIP ADDICT

We relationship addicts, wherever we are on the continuum, will resist the idea that our relationships are unhealthy, simply because we cannot do without them: they are our source of life and love. Without realizing it we have developed elaborate – even scriptural – justifications for them. We cannot stop our manner of relating anyway, no matter how much we try. All we're probably aware of is the all-absorbing, compulsive nature of our relationships with certain kinds of people, and a high level of pain. We will be troubled by them if we're married to someone else, puzzled at the way one relationship follows another; while God seems far off. The Christian relationship addict has probably done everything she knows to rid her life of "sin" – in the absence of any understanding of the true nature of the pain.

"The roots of addictive relating can inevitably be traced to emotional trauma in childhood – loss, pain, abuse and abandonment – and the patterns of relating developed in consequence of those traumas," says Robin Norwood. Much of this lies buried in the unconscious.

When the process that God instituted for meeting childhood need fails, no person can meet that need in the adult, save the Real Parent: God. As adults, we are unable to return home and repeat the growth process the right way. Significant unmet childhood need becomes an emotional black hole in the adult: the hole that fuels repetitive relationship addiction. It places impossible demands on another adult to expect him or her to meet unmet dependency needs, but that is what the relationship addict does.

The relationship addict is caught. Her relationship *appears* to be meeting her need and her inner imagery of God is often distorted and frightening. How can she find, in the arms of a God she fears and cannot trust, all she has ever wanted?

There will be much more on healing in Section Three, but the relationship addict must have an encounter with God, the tenderest Parent and Lover of her soul. He must pick up and comfort the heartbroken child, and reach into the desolation. When he appears to her in this way – not as the harsh God of her inner imagery – her relationship addictions will begin to lose their hold. She will no longer need to go after idols because his love for her will be meeting her deep need and winning her heart. She will not need other lovers.

Relationship addicts are often cynics. An end to the endless round of obsessive relationships? An end to the God who doesn't seem to care? An end to the pain? It seems just another cloud without rain over the desert in her soul.

Just another mirage? No! Reality.

OTHER ADDICTIONS

Although relationship addiction is common in women it is certainly not the only way unmet need is expressed. Women, like men, can be workaholics. They can be chemically dependent, or dependent on food: overeating, anorexic, bulimic. Women can have several addictions at once.

Carrie

Food only became a problem for Carrie when her marriage to a homosexual man, Tait, fell apart after 18 years. Over the worst part of the break-up the weight fell off: seven kilos a week, but as she recovered Carrie found food was a comfort. When she felt bad she ate. The weight began stacking back on in spite of the rate at which she burned calories. She rapidly gained all she had lost and kilos more.

Carrie was not only codependent but she found she couldn't stop eating. It was as she discovered the causes of her rescuing behaviour that she also found out a few things about her relationship to food. I quote from her diary:

> My emotional attachment to food started at a very young age. Mum was a great cook and the biscuit tins were always full. But I see now that food was my substitute for love. I got my love and comfort from the food she cooked, not from her, because she was not available. She was too busy. Of all the kids (7) I always felt the most unloved by her. I eat to feel better, especially if I am lonely, angry, anxious or depressed, so the grief process has certainly not helped. I also used it to hide, mask and tranquilize the pain of my relationship with Tait. Now, of course, Mum is critical of my weight so it is probably an act of defiance to keep it on, saying I am OK as I am.

Pauline

Pauline was raised in a household where emotional needs were not recognized or talked about. Her parents were good citizens, but no one ever touched anybody else: she never remembers being hugged or kissed. She remembers crying a lot in her room and no-one ever coming. There is one saying she associates with her father, particularly when emotional demands were being made on him: "O well, I must get back to work." By the age of 38 Pauline had had relationships with fourteen different men, most of which had started out promising closeness, gentleness, warmth, and emotional interaction. But they all fell apart, and whenever the danger signals appeared, Pauline would withdraw and begin to work obsessively. Until another relationship came along.

RELATIONSHIP DEPENDENCY BETWEEN WOMEN

Jane was a pastor's wife, and Sandra a young married woman in her husband's congregation. Jane was an unostentatious caregiver, there for others. Sandra's relationship with Jane began innocently enough but Sandra became thoroughly monopolising: spending two or three days a week at Jane's for months on end. The relationship blew apart when Jane returned from a conference of pastors' wives and told her friend that they really should see each other less often. Sandra turned nasty. She filled the ears of other women in the church with poisonous tales about Jane's husband that produced kickbacks in the life of the church that kept board members occupied for months. About a year later the woman returned overseas with her husband and family and the matter lapsed. Unfortunately no-one identified what was happening: unhealthy dependency in the lives of two women with unmet emotional needs – one who needed to be needed, the other who wanted her needs met. The relationship happened, blew up, caused damage but left no one much the wiser or anybody the better because of it.

A missionary friend told me recently of two single missionary women on her station who had formed such an exclusive relationship that no-one else was able to penetrate it. Those trying to make either of them a friend, or to involve the pair in a wider social circle met a fierce resistance – as Frank Buchman found when he warned against "absorbing friendships".

At its extreme such mutual dependency between two women becomes lesbianism when it finds erotic expression – as it often does.

THE LESBIAN

The lesbian is no different from any relationship addict – it is just that the particular dynamics of her emotional history mean she is drawn to *women* for the same reasons women are drawn to *men* – for affirmation and love. And like the relationship addict she will be drawn only to certain types not others. As much as the dependency test-list (pp 36) applies to heterosexuals who are relating addictively, it also applies to lesbians. Intense emotional involvement will often be eroticized and it's no different in lesbianism. One relationship will follow another. Like the heterosexual relationship addict, lesbian needs for love and connection will be so strong she will seek to justify her relationships, and will probably be unable to stop them even if she tries. Overt lesbianism is a complex interplay of need that – in the absence of healing – becomes a lifestyle.

We will look at lesbianism in more detail in Section Two.

Notes

1. Lori Rentzel *Emotional Dependency*, pp 8–9; 14–16 (1990). Copyright 1984, 1987, 1990 by Lori Thorkelson Rentzel. Used by permission of InterVarsity Press, PO Box 1400, Downers Grove, IL 60515, USA.

2. Robin Norwood, *Letters from Women Who Love Too Much*, Arrow Books Ltd, pp 301–2.

3. Robin Norwood, *Women Who Love Too Much*, Arrow Books Ltd, pp 77–78.

Chapter Three

THE ORIGINS OF UNMET NEED

We saw them gazing at us on our screens and they captured the hearts of the West and led to a scramble for adoptions. Little pinched faces some of them. Big brown eyes looking out from behind bars. Children holding onto the bars and peering out, shaking the bars and crying, reaching out through the bars. Children sitting inside their bars and rocking endlessly and obliviously to and fro. The bars were the bars of their cots, but really they were the very beginnings of their emotional prisons and possibly their future addictions. The plight of the Romanian orphans deeply distressed millions of us. What were we reacting to? The awful effects of abandonment on innocent children, children without parents. We cried because we realized it all over again in those starved faces: none of us can survive without love and a sense of significance: it is our birthright and without it we languish, waste and die.

Behind addictions lies the story of our lives: what happened and our reactions to what happened. We will look at the "dysfunctional" family, conditional love and lack of self-esteem as contributors to addictive behaviours. In particular we will look at fathers and the skewed image of God that results when fathers fail children and children reject fathers. We will look at damage to our masculinity and femininity and see how that contributes to compensating addictions. And we will look briefly at the influence of the peer group and our culture in reinforcing addictive behaviours.

THE FAMILY

The family pre-dates man. It existed before the world was created, a family of three: the Father, the Son and the Holy Spirit. It was an intimate, powerful, gentle, holy, joyful, deferential, kind, loving, peaceful and secure circle of total and mutual trust. God commanded the first humans on the planet to be fruitful and multiply because he wanted "godly offspring" (Malachi 2:15): millions of replicas of the Original Family, fathered by fathers who were replicas of him... from whom all fatherhood... derives its name (Ephesians 3:14–15).

UNCONDITIONAL LOVE

This is the way God loves us. He loves us while we hate him, ignore him, defy him, and reject him. What we do or don't do makes no difference to the way he feels about us. We can't earn his love, we can't stop it. He simply loves us. As the Original Father, he models the way parents he has made in his image might love their children. As Dr Ross Campbell says in *How to really love your child*, "Unconditional love is loving a child no matter what... Unconditional love means we love the child even when at times we may detest his behaviour."

SELF-ESTEEM

Psychologists at the Minirth-Meier Clinic have invented a concept of "love-tanks" which helps us picture self-esteem. Over everything is God's tank, continually full of unconditional love, meant to feed into parents' tanks and through those into their children's. Parents also replenish each other's tanks through mutual love and respect. At birth our love tanks are running on empty. If Dad and Mother are agnostic and if Dad is an alcoholic abusing his wife and kids and Mother is preoccupied with Dad, Suzy's love tank will remain low. Dad and Mother may even drain Suzy's love tank. Typically Suzy will grow up trying to "suck, pull, shove" something into her love-tank in other ways: often through relationship addiction, or else through other addictions, all in the attempt to satisfy her heart hunger.

But that is not all there is to self-esteem. Our self-esteem problem really starts before the cradle, in our human legacy.

When the human race tumbled from perfection at the start of history – from unclouded, close companionship with God – it was because our forefathers wanted to prove they could go it alone. We have the same hereditary streak. We make the breach, God doesn't. He tries to close the breach, but we have already found substitutes for a relationship with him. Our egos and our ignorance are soon in the way. We kick against the love that created us, wants us, and has great plans for us. The result is guilt and dissatisfaction – deep-seated and unconscious but ever-present – because it's not the way we were destined to live. Destined to know God's unconditional love and our great value to him, many of us grow up knowing him only as an expletive. Without him we have a hungry hole in our insides that grows larger all our lives: hungry for approval, significance, attention, and love. Without him we live with a sense of insecurity and inadequacy that we seek to assuage. If our family life conspires to make the hole larger – through anything from conditional love to constant abuse – our negative self-image grows: we view ourselves as anything from "only loveable if… " to loathsome. If we get into self-gratifying behaviours in our search for love or comfort or attention we can begin to despise ourselves more, and the more the further addicted we become. We can end up hating ourselves.

Christians are allowed to have self-esteem. Lack of self-esteem is not humility. Self-esteem is not pride or self-centredness. It is the person who does not have self-esteem who becomes self-centred. Self-esteem is the warm and appreciative respect and regard I have for myself as a person made in the image of God. We are meant to love ourselves: the second great command is that we love others *as we love ourselves*. If we do not love ourselves the right way we cannot love others. Lack of self-love fuels compensating behaviours.

THE "DYSFUNCTIONAL" FAMILY

Therapists have come up with the term "dysfunctional family". Broadly speaking it is a family life that leaves us to some degree or another with unfilled love-tanks, leaving us vulnerable to addiction as we attempt to fill our own. The Greek prefix, *dys*, means pain, ill, bad. The dysfunctional family is a family that functions, but painfully or badly. It is an unhealthy organism.

All families are unhealthy to some degree because none is perfect. Some are unhealthier than others. Many families cluster round the low end of the continuum, parents dishing out what has come to be known as passive abuse: stinting on time, attention and affection for their kids. At the far end of the spectrum some homes are violently abusive: sexually, physically, psychologically, ruled by the tyranny of the "olics and isms".

No family is healthy by virtue of the label "Christian". Many "Christian" families are unhealthy because they are religious rather than Christian: the Christianity they profess has never gained access to the roots of the family's unhealthiness.

In the book *Love is a Choice*[1], Minirth Meier have put together a definition of what they call the unhealthy family, one designed to produce "an addiction to people, behaviours or things". It is a family in which:

- One parent is mentally ill or holds eccentric or odd opinions about the world, or is continually preoccupied, or frustrated. Or in which the parent not having these problems is preoccupied with the one who does.
- Parents are addicted to alcohol, drugs, work; consumed by rage or obsessions; or compulsive about things healthy people are casual about.
- Parents draw their emotional support from their children leaning heavily on them for advice, help and ego boosting.
- Parents have a poor opinion of themselves.
- Parents are atheist or agnostic or in an "uncomfortable" relationship with God.
- Parents are "intensely religious" but live by rules: (if you act right, look right and think right, God will accept you), or are extremely rigid in their theology and impose it on their kids.
- Parents divorce, separate, fight viciously, feel bitter toward each other or toward marriage in general.
- Parents remain together in a hostile relationship "for the sake of the kids".

The *California Lawyer* describing the family most likely to produce the codependent said it had these characteristics: a parent exercising inflexible control; secrecy (problems and emotions are not talked about); denial (problems and emotions do not exist); appearances (look good at all costs); isolation (emotional – though sometimes physical) from "outsiders" and each other. Members of these families learn to live by three commandments: thou shalt not talk (about problems or emotions), thou shalt not trust, thou shalt not feel.

What all unhealthy families have in common, says Robin Norwood in *Women Who Love Too Much*, is their inability to discuss root problems:

> There may be other problems that are discussed, often ad nauseam, but these often cover up the underlying secrets that make the family dysfunctional. It is the degree of secrecy – the inability to talk about the problems – rather than their severity, that defines both how dysfunctional a family becomes and how severely its members are damaged.

Therapists Subby and Friel have come up with a few other attributes of the dysfunctional family: do as I say not as I do, don't rock the boat, and indirect communication (through a third person).

Donald Sloat, a practising psychologist, has written a book, *The Dangers of Growing Up in a Christian Home*. According to Sloat the dangers are:

- Instilling a fear of God rather than a love for him, so that the Christian life becomes an exercise in avoiding demerit points or punishment.
- Using guilt and shame to produce good behaviour. (What would Jesus say if... ?)
- Discouraging honest questions and doubts, thus destroying exploration and discovery and genuine title to faith. Good Christian families can have other bad habits. The first four in particular tend to produce the codependent – the "strong", responsible, need-meeter.

- Imposing unrealistic expectations on kids: be strong, be good, be right, be perfect and make us proud.
- Making approval and love appear dependent on good behaviour, i.e. I love you when you do good things (conditional love).
- Discouraging expression of negative emotions – because Christians are not meant to have them.
- Don't be selfish. (Christians are only meant to think about others.) It is amazing how widespread this notion is, and how wrong. Each of you should look not only to your own interests, but also to the interests of others (Philippians 2:4).
- Using scripture in a manipulative way to control another. ("Children, obey your parents", "I am the head of this home.")

"If being a Christian does not make one an awful lot better it can make one an awful lot worse," says Leanne Payne, in *The Healing Presence*, paraphrasing C.S. Lewis. "Such a one becomes a religious tyrant, who, in the name of a religious cause has a great deal of power to do harm."

It's a rare family that won't show up somewhere in this catalogue of dysfunction. Dysfunctional homes can hide behind a lot of religious humbug. "Good Christian homes" can leave a lot of love-tanks empty. When our love-tanks are empty we start to go on searches to fill them.

MASCULINITY AND FEMININITY

In his book *Inside Out*, Dr Larry Crabb comments: "… an inside look that gets to the bottom of things will expose our doubts about our ability to function as men and women." Leanne Payne remarks in her book *Crisis in Masculinity*: "Much that is called emotional illness or instability today, as I continually discover in prayer and counselling sessions, is merely the masculine and/or the feminine unaffirmed and out of balance within the personality."

God wanted the men and women he had made to be male and female in his image (Genesis 1:27). Our gender is not just incidental. It goes right to the heart of what we are. He made us to be men and women.

But God also wants each man to be masculine and feminine, and each woman to be feminine and masculine – because he is both masculine and feminine. He is a "mothering" Father. One of the names of God – El Shaddai – has a root meaning: many breasted God. God is primarily Father (AB as in Abba, meaning he who decides) but is both mother and father. "As a mother comforts her child, so I will comfort you" (Isaiah 66:13). "Can a mother forget the baby at her breast and have no compassion on the child she has borne? Though she may forget I will not forget you" (Isaiah 49:15).

God initiates (masculine) and he responds (feminine). He is a creator and nurturer. He breaks down and he builds up. He smites and he heals. He disciplines and comforts. He judges and forgives. He is full of justice and compassion. He is strong and tender, mighty and gentle. He makes the mountains shake and he rests in his love. We see it in Jesus. Whipping the money-changers out of his father's house and verbally flagellating the Pharisees he was masculine. But weeping at Lazarus' grave and filled with compassion for the crowds who came to him he was feminine. The fruit of the Spirit (Galatians 5:22) is traditionally feminine virtues: love, joy, peace, patience, kindness, goodness, faithfulness, gentleness and self-control, but both men and women are meant to develop and display them.

Men are more masculine than feminine, women more feminine than masculine, but as C. S. Lewis remarked: there ought to be a man in every woman and a woman in every man. The further away we are from a healthy inward balance of masculinity and femininity the more likely we are to suffer from low self-esteem and to seek to compensate ourselves in some way. Secure, balanced gender identity is not something we are born with – despite our sexual anatomy. We grow into it steadily over two decades – and life in the family contributes significantly towards its development.

WHAT ARE MASCULINITY AND FEMININITY?

Gordon Dalbey in his book *Healing the Masculine Soul*, searching for a definition of masculinity, quotes the unexpectedly un-Rambo responses of a group of Army Green Berets who were asked to define the qualities of the ideal warrior. This is what they came up with: loyalty, patience, intensity, calmness, compassion, will, self-mastery, and taking calculated risks. Dalbey also asked a group of male college students to describe qualities in common between a sportsman and a soldier. They cited courage, righteousness, camaraderie, fellowship, discipline, determination, strength, action and energy... anger rightly focused and an enemy overcome.

Dr Larry Crabb in *Inside Out* defines masculinity and femininity in this way: "Men are designed to enter their worlds strongly, providing for their families, leading them (through servanthood) towards God, moving towards others with sacrificing powerful love." Women, he says are "designed to courageously give all they have (intellect, talents, wisdom, kindness) to others in warm vulnerability, allowing themselves to be entered, wrapping themselves with supportive strength around those with whom they relate".

Another scriptural study of masculinity and femininity came up with this: Masculinity is mastery tempered with kindness, compassion and love. Femininity is caring tempered with truth, justice and independence.

Gender researchers, Brad Sargent and Bob Hendrick in their sophisticated development of Professor Larry Crabb's "Threatened Sexuality Scale" put it this way. God's ideal for intimate relationships between the sexes is a self-sacrificial, open, intimate, faithful, life-long, sexual relationship with one equally mature member of the opposite sex. A real man – the man with a "strong masculine identity" is the man who can come closest to fulfilling that ideal – though he may be challenged by it he will not be threatened by it. The weaker a man's masculine identity the less he will be capable of this sort of relationship with one woman. The weaker his masculine identity, say Sargent and Hendrick, the further out on the continuum he will be found – the continuum moving out through bisexuality to homosexuality to transsexuality and autosexuality (sex only ever with oneself).

Initiation and response

"The *essence* of masculinity is initiation and the *essence* of femininity is response" is how proverbial wisdom puts it.

Women who have suffered at the hands of men can close down their "feminine side" and over-develop their "masculine" side. They can decide never to be vulnerable again. Women unaffirmed by men may become determined to show they can make their way in life without men or achieve as much as any man. To over-simplify, a woman who has learned it doesn't pay to be responsive, trusting and open can begin to develop an over-concentration of masculine traits: she may become competitive, goal-oriented, independent, over-assertive, over-functioning, over-achieving, over-rational. Women hurt by significant men in their lives can become controlling, angry, disdainful, even hostile towards men. Or, in an opposite move, women can make themselves over in the way they think will make them desirable to men or into a faithful representation of the negative way they have been treated. Neither is a woman with a developed feminine side.

Men respond too, of course, to the things that hurt them. They too can over-develop their masculine side to compensate for feelings of inadequacy, or they can simply fail to develop their masculine power to initiate, and remain passive, their feminine side overdeveloped by default.

If a man over-develops his masculine side (his power to initiate) or fails to develop it, or a woman shuts down her feminine side (her trust and openness) and over-develops her masculine side, both remain inwardly out of balance and vulnerable to compensating comforts and relationships.

THE ROLE OF THE FATHER IN AFFIRMING MASCULINITY AND FEMININITY

Only the father can *finally* affirm his children, "tell his son that he is a man, and his daughter that she is a woman," says Payne in *Crisis in Masculinity*. To affirm means to ratify, to confirm, to formally declare.

Very few men are adequately affirmed as men today… The father who is unaffirmed in his own masculinity cannot adequately affirm the son in his, or his daughter in her femininity. An automatic and serious consequence of a man's failure to be affirmed in his masculine side is that he will suffer from low self-esteem. He will be unable to accept himself. Men who are unable to fully accept themselves lose to one degree or another the power to act as *father, husband and leader*. (My italics.)

The father is key particularly just after puberty in the step to self-acceptance. A father in possession of a secure masculine identity has the power to kiss to life the woman in his daughter, to "appreciate and affirm the beauty and the giftedness of the feminine". The masculine in a "whole" father "strikes" the masculine in his son, allowing it to "flame to life", says Payne. "When the father's strong hand of love and affirmation does not rest on his son or daughter's shoulder, tragedy results… "

But the role of the father is important well before the age of puberty. It is essential in the separation of mother and child after at least a good year of emotional and physical maternal nurture. Simply by being present and actively involved he encourages the development of personal identity and independence in the child. A father who is "not there" emotionally or physically injures the development of "accrued confidence" in the child: insecurity, rejection, attention-seeking, lack of confidence, maternal over-attachment and difficulty in relationships can be the result, says Mary Pytches in *Yesterday's Child*. At age three to four the child's core gender identity is more or less decided: he is aware "he belongs on Daddy's side of the line, opposite to his mother and she on mother's side of the line; the opposite to her father". The daughter continues to identify with her mother as her gender model; the son seeks to identify with his father. "Every man is a son in search of his father's affection and approval, longing for his Daddy's embrace, even as his mother embraced him in the womb," says Gordon Dalbey in *Healing the Masculine Soul*. If father is "not there", particularly for his son; if he is unaffirmed and passive himself, or abusive, or sexually abusive – the process of gaining personal and gender identity can be disturbed.

Mothers

This is not to say mother's role is not absolutely essential. Children who have been unwanted and inadequately nurtured can grow up with irrational fears, depression and painful dependency needs, says Mary Pytches, echoing current psychological opinion. Although father is vital in affirming his daughter's feminine identity, mother is also vital as her feminine gender model. A severe breakdown in the mother-daughter relationship can disrupt the gender-modelling process sufficiently that lesbianism can be an outcome (see Chapter 9).

ROLE MODELLING

God was Jesus' role model. Jesus said he did everything he saw his Father do. So, often, do children; except that parents represent both the mothering and fathering sides of God, and children imitate their parents. In the addictions that develop in compensation for low self-esteem, adults will sometimes be found imitating parents. Between 50% and 60% of children of alcoholic parents grow up addicted to alcohol; between 60% and 80% of parents who sexually abuse their children were sexually abused as children.

UNAFFIRMED FEMININITY

The kind of relationship a daughter has with her father – *and the way she sees him treat her mother* – will determine the way she views men – as authority figures, and as a sex that she wants to be intimate with, or does not. It will certainly influence the kind of wife she will be.

The girl who has had good relationships with her parents and watched them relate affectionately and considerately, and who has had no traumatic brushes with men, stands a good chance of growing up comfortable with her femininity: open, trusting enough, giving and responsive. Almost as a matter of course she will go on to develop her masculine side: initiating, planning, deciding, acting, and will be a balanced woman. She will probably make a good choice of mate.

She won't relate needily. But if male neglect or abuse has entered the picture her feminine side may have shrivelled, not grown, and she may have become tough, protecting herself against more pain with a bullet-proof exterior, seeking refuge in food, work, alcohol. Or she may have become a dolly-bird, cultivating the femininity promoted by the image makers, throwing herself at men to get the love and attention she missed out on. If her femininity is not affirmed she may remain weakly passive, manipulatively and obsessively seeking fulfilment in her husband and children.

Unaffirmed masculinity

A man unaffirmed in his masculinity may be passive, his power to initiate impaired. He may be stuck in a timid, sensitive mode, unadventurous, insecure, lacking confidence and initiative, hungry for male attention and affirmation. Many homosexuals fall into this category. Or he may compensate for an inner sense of inferiority and inadequacy by swinging into pseudo (macho) masculinity: becoming competitive, seeking attention, visibility, and power, fuelled by the need to prove and heal himself. "One may act," says Leanne Payne,

> as a Don Juan, a compulsive seducer of women, another as a compulsive liar and boaster in order to prove himself, a third may chronically fear to step out and lead as he is gifted to lead, to speak or act the truth. Another may be caught in the mire of an uncreative, passive loneliness, suffering from a sensitive but overly developed feminine side.

The boy who has developed a secure-enough masculine identity also feels secure enough to begin to own the feminine traits also found in God: kindness, gentleness, responsiveness, sensitivity, compassion. Here will be a balanced male.

The kind of relationship a growing son has with his father – *and the way he has seen him treat his mother* – will have a great deal to do with the kind of husband he will be to his wife. The secure male will not fear being rejected by a woman, nor will he be dominated, controlled or manipulated by her. His relationship with his father will influence the kind of role model he will be to his own sons – who will also grow up and marry.

In summary: the father-son link is crucial because sons become fathers – fathers capable of affirming the masculinity of their sons and femininity of their daughters or of failing to; capable therefore of leaving a positive or negative imprint on future husbands and wives. Sons and daughters unaffirmed in their masculinity and femininity have low self-esteem, may develop compensating behaviours that can become addictive, often make poor partner choices, do not know how to affirm their own children and are inadequate role models. There is a curse upon the land when the hearts of the fathers are turned away from the children and the children's from their fathers (Malachi 4:6).

SEXUAL ADDICTION

Sexual addiction is one of the most common expressions of unaffirmed masculinity and it covers the spectrum. Remember Sargent's and Hendrick's definition of the "real man" – a man capable of need for, and of long-term faithful intimacy with, one woman. The further a man is from that place the more likely it is that the expressions of his sexuality will be compensations for low self-esteem that may become addictive and even aberrant the more they are performed.

Although a man might think exotic sexual activity and erotic images in his head and before his eyes make him a "real man", they only reveal an insecure man. Affairs, sexual abuse, regular sex with girlfriends, a string of relationships, porn, prostitutes, sexual fantasy and regular masturbation are common addictive uses of sexuality, widely reflected in the statistics.

Seven men in ten attempt sex with a woman before they are married; most of these succeed, and more than one quarter of them manage it with between ten and 50 different women, says the Kinsey Institute in its latest survey, *Sex and Morality in the US* (1989). It also said that eight men in ten "know men" who have committed adultery against their wives not just several times but up to ten or more times.

In their book, *Child Sexual Abuse*, Hancock and Mains,

echoing other researchers, say around one girl in six is sexually abused (sexual contact) usually by a family member. Figures for non-contact abuse are higher. In 2000, Birchard, looking at clergy misconduct in the UK found 24% of clergy had done "something sexually inappropriate with someone other than their spouse"[2] (compared with 38% of secular people holding doctorates). Nothing appeared to have changed since 1988 when the journal *Leadership* published the results of a *Christianity Today* survey of North American pastors in which one in four of those who responded admitted to "sexually inappropriate" behaviour in the course of their pastoral duties, and one in five to "passionate kissing" and "mutual masturbation". One in five also fantasized at least weekly of sex with someone other than their wives. In another survey of lay people (subscribers to *Christianity Today*), the figures were about double. Commenting on the two surveys (of 1000 pastors and 1000 lay people, only one third of whom responded), author and psychiatrist, Dr John White, said he suspected the figures were conservative. Dr Stephen Olford told the story of a US convention of evangelical pastors that broke all the hosting venue's previous records for weekend guest-hire of X-rated videos. Fundamentalist church teens are no different from teens in the wider community: they have just as much pre-marital sex, the latest Kinsey Institute survey shows.

THREE CHEERS FOR FATHERS

Fathers have come in for a clobbering in this chapter. Let's state the obvious. Low self-esteem in children is not to be blamed on fathers. Adam and Eve had the perfect Father but still managed to mess everything up all by themselves. Parents do not set out to create problem children: children are born with temperaments that make them easy children or difficult children; they can misperceive and misinterpret many things and by burying the injury deep they can separate themselves from loving parents; they can be provocative in the extreme; they can defensively detach. Some tragedies are circumstantial in nature. The environment outside home can play a significant part. Nothing is all anyone's fault. We are talking of principles.

But how did the Perfect Father and the Perfect Son relate? It's here we find clues to healthy self-esteem.

THE FATHER AND THE SON

- The Father often called his Son "beloved", which means much loved and very dear.
- The Father was pleased with his Son and let him and others know his approval. He encouraged his Son. "And a voice from heaven said: This is my son, whom I love; with him I am well pleased" (Matthew 3:17).
- The Son sought his Father's approval. "... I seek not to please myself but him who sent me" (John 5:30).
- They enjoyed being together. "I was filled with delight day after day, rejoicing always in his presence" (Proverbs 8:30b).
- He was a help to his Father. They worked together: Dad worked, son helped. "I was the craftsman at his side" (Proverbs 8:30a).
- The Father taught his Son, "I tell (you) the things which I have... learned at my father's side," Jesus said (John 8:38, Amplified Bible).
- The Father disciplined his Son: "Although he was a son he learned obedience from what he suffered... " (Hebrews 5:8).
- The Son knew his Father would not desert or abandon him. "Do you think I cannot call on my Father, and he will at once put at my disposal more than twelve legions of angels?" (Matthew 26:53)
- He knew his Father would always be there for him. "... I am not alone because my father is with me" (John 16:32b).
- He trusted his Father with the trust of a child. The adult Jesus called his Father, Abba, Daddy. It was an intimate term used in the home and signified absolute, unquestioning trust. Jesus even used it as he faced the cross.
- They communicated. "Everything that I learned from my Father I have made known to you" (John 15:15).
- The Father was his role model. "... Whatever the Father does the Son also does" (John 5:19).

- The Son was obedient but clearly had a mind of his own. He laid down his life *of his own accord* (John 10:18).

A picture emerges of close communication. The Father was available, supportive, affirming. He taught his Son and disciplined him. The Son sought his Father's approval, trusted his Father implicitly, and knew he could call on him for help, strength and understanding.

THE FATHER'S NATURE

A mere skimming from a portion of Psalms, shows something of the true nature of God the Father – that side of him those who have had inadequate fathering never seem to see. He hears my cry, will not disappoint me, he offers me his companionship and unfailing love, adopts me as his child, hides me from trouble, considers all my doings, never wants me to blush with shame or be confused, is close when I am broken-hearted, grants the desires and secret requests of my heart, grasps my hand, occupies himself with my every step, lifts my head, hears and answers me, looses my bonds and frees me, gives me irrepressible joy. He speaks to me, protects me, takes pleasure in me, will not forsake or reject me, puts a song in my heart, binds up my wounds and heals my inner self, picks me up and carries me, is my ally, puts my tears in his bottle, knows when I sit down and get up and watches over me as I come and go, formed me in the womb and delivered me into the world. He hides me in the shadow of his wings, wants me to pour out my heart to him, goes before me, restores me, is full of loving compassion towards me, gives angels special charge over me, comforts me, wants to carry my burdens, loves and pities me, satisfies my longing soul, is committed to me, fills my mouth with laughter and singing, gives me sleep, knows when I am overwhelmed and rescues me, is gracious and full of compassion towards me, slow to anger, kind and full of mercy. He understands my weakness, teaches me, gives me good things, recompenses me, is gentle with me, avenges me, maintains my cause, strengthens my heart, counsels me with his eye upon me, heeds me, refreshes and supports me, fulfils my plans, fills me with irrepressible joy.

THE SKEWED IMAGE OF GOD

When things go wrong in relationships between fathers and families it has bad repercussions on our relationship with God. As the ultimate Father, God – who is invisible – is someone whom we tend to make over in the image of the fathers we know.

Vaughan, a Christian man, described his father as someone he didn't know at all, "emotionally dead, cold, distant, angry, he would never discuss anything, he just gave orders; everything revolved around him; he was impossible to please, unsupportive, critical, never encouraging. He put me down. My thoughts and feelings had no value." When Vaughan thinks of God he thinks first of a total vacuum, a nothingness, a void: like his father. "I just don't know who he is at all." His next picture is of someone he has to please but can't. "Nothing I do is good enough." He can't believe God is "concerned" about him.

Janet described her father as kind, caring, compassionate, fun, loving, and merciful. She felt her father's love came without conditions attached. She felt happy in his company. For Janet God is like her father: approachable, forgiving, supportive, caring. "So many have suffered hurt and rejection by their families it is hard for them to see God as He really is," says John Dawson in a magnificent little pamphlet, *The Father Heart of God*:

> Many of us are unable to receive God's love and approval. We are trapped by the harsh God of our imagination. We have to get to know God for who He really is – not who we think He is. He is the Perfect Parent. He loves you and longs to spend time with you... He is a broken-hearted Father who yearns to heal you... He pursues you with His love from your first breathing moment until the day you die... He was there when you first walked as a child. Some of His greatest treasures are the memories of your childhood laughter. He was overjoyed with your every success. When Daddy never looked, never appreciated, God did. Father God always looked, always took delight in the work of your hands... You don't have to get His attention, He's already listening. Don't worry about taking His time – it's

all yours... He always disciplines in love. He delights to forgive you; we just have to be honest with Him... He is faithful, generous, kind and just. He is fussy, doting, generous, extravagant... He is your real Father, always will be. Don't ever resent the failings of your human parents. They are just kids who grew up and had kids. Rather rejoice in the wonderful love of your Father God.

Those who struggle with addictions often carry an inner image of a hard, judgmental, unapproachable, angry, unsympathetic God, which has to change if healing is to take place.

OTHER FACTORS IN ADDICTION

The peer group

To a large extent the peer group reinforces what has gone wrong at home, it rarely reverses it – though may. The peer group – particularly the male – is ruthless in picking on and ostracizing kids whose self-esteem is already low, who are troubled, and withdrawn. In a bid for acceptance a teenager may adopt a tough behaviour that can become ingrained. If rejected, he may take refuge in a behaviour that will deliver comfort or significance. The more these behaviours are used for pain relief the more likely they are to become addictive. As adults with established addictions we tend to choose peer groups that don't challenge them.

The cultural endorsement of addiction

Our culture continually teaches us how to boost our low self-esteem. In only a few hours in front of the television set we will be urged to consume all we want of almost anything. We will be compelled to improve our image, to buy a bigger house, a bigger car, get a bigger bank balance, get to the top, look better, dress better, be better than anyone else. Companies promote the image of the highly motivated, totally committed, bright, career-minded, aggressive employee. To measure up we are pushed to perform, succeed and (implied) be admired.

To an addicted man love means, accommodate my addiction, let me live the way that makes me feel good. Come on baby, light my fire! The man who wants a woman for the night and the man who takes a wife both say the same thing: I love you. Love is... when you can't get her out of your mind. (She wouldn't want to be in there if she knew what love really was.)

Relationship addiction

In our media-shaped culture true love means that men and women are meant to be infatuated with each other. Crown Prince Rudolph of Austria killed his mistress, then himself in a suicide pact because neither could bear the thought of living without the other. "Good stuff for the gullible public," said the filmmakers, "Let's make a movie," and paid large sums to a contemporary heartthrob to play the smitten prince. Predictably the women sighed, "How passionately they loved." Really? Let's call it what it is: mutual possessiveness leading to death. The greatest romances of all time – take Tzar Nicholas II and his Empress Alexandra of Russia – at a closer look often reveal themselves to be horribly unhealthy affairs: Nicholas was an unaffirmed male, weakly dependent on his wife, to whom he could never say "No", while she was infatuated with a mad, debauched monk called Rasputin, who was deeply addicted to lechery and power. How nice! Or Romeo and Juliet, another infatuated couple who do themselves in while we touch our hearts and say, "How idealistic young love is." Or Antony and Cleopatra, who both killed themselves for love. Shakespeare knew how to pull in a crowd.

Why do so many "love stories" end in death or suicide? If we want someone to love us so much that he would die for us – God did. But his sacrifice doesn't move us. If we want someone to think the world of us – God does. If we want someone to love us so much that he is constantly jealous – God is. The love of God for the human race is the most passionate love affair in history. But it's not enough for us. We reject his passion and re-educate ourselves to believe that pain, infatuation, jealousy, sex, possessiveness, exploitation, revenge, violence, despair, manipulation, threatening, coercion is the true love we are all searching for.

Hertz Rental Cars once ran a TV ad showing a beautiful woman. The ad ended with a facial close-up showing her eyes awash with tears. "Love Hertz!" said the music, and the woman. If he hasn't hurt you you're not in love. When the movies show her in anguish after the lovers' bust-up, or when she attempts an overdose, it is because she is in love – never because she's relating unhealthily. The media promotes and romanticizes unhealthy relationships and makes a bundle out of it.

In the TV advertisement promoting perfume, the all-together, perfectly groomed, handsome, aloof male leans back against a tree, his jacket slung over his shoulder, his hazel eyes coolly appraising the slim, stunning brunette appearing to his left. His look says, "I want you, and I'll have you." Her look says, "I can't resist you. I was made to be with you. How can I help but yield to you?" It's sick – but it sells litres of perfume.

So why addictions?

When we are inadequately fathered – or mothered – when there is abuse in homes, or they break up, when parents do not love each other, when children reject their parents, when our masculinity or femininity is not affirmed, when much of the time we feel insecure and alone we will have empty love tanks and poor self-esteem. Unaffirmed sons make inadequate husbands and fathers. Emotionally starved daughters grow into emotionally starved wives and mothers who lean on their children or partners. None can fill his child's love-tank. The love our Heavenly Father planned to drench us with through the human family so that we grew up toward him and flourished, is something many of us know very little about.

It is trite but true. God's love was meant to fill us and without it we go on consuming searches for substitutes: people, things and reputations that will fill our love-tanks and comfort us. The more love-starved we are, the more we are addiction-prone.

In our pain and starvation we reach through our bars like the Romanian orphans – seeking we know not what. Seeking to meet our needs for love and value we go on sprees to fill the inner void, not even aware that there is a void or that we are on a spree. We can become relationship junkies, hungrily seeking in person after person the love and significance we crave. Or we may addictively hook into being good, being liked, power, work and success, sexual conquest, pleasure, or become sports fanatics in our search for gratification. We have acceptable addictions: taking responsibility, helping others, getting A passes, winning high-achiever and sportsman-of-the-year awards, growing Christian ministries and churches – while our children never see us and their love-tanks languish. We create special identities for ourselves in our headlong flight from being a nobody. We turn to other things that will bring comfort or diversion: alcohol and drugs, compulsive spending, gambling.

Many of us are addicted creatures to one degree or another, depending on our experiences in our families and peer groups, and the ways in which we reacted.

As people caught in self-gratifying habits we can't break, we not only become good at rationalising our addictions, but we become good at classifying one addiction as worse than another. Alcoholics say, "At least we aren't junkies", and narcotic addicts say, "At least we aren't winos." And the average heterosexual male, whatever his addiction, sees no resemblance between himself and a homosexual. The female relationship addict looks alarmed at the thought that she could easily have been lesbian if some relationship dynamics had been a little different.

Homosexuality

The person who is sexually attracted to the same sex is very similar to the rest of us. Many male homosexuals talk of dysfunctional homes: absentee or emotionally remote or abusive fathers, of emotionally demanding or smothering mothers and rejecting male teenage peer groups. The deficits send him on a search for affection, gender affirmation and acceptance from other men just as straight men search for acceptance, affirmation, and worth in their activities. Any of the men in Chapter 1 could have been homosexual, if things had been just a little different. But the deficits weren't of the kind, or severe enough to propel them on the search the homosexual makes. Instead they found refuge in the more "acceptable" male activities often linked to status and sex – which can become addictive when they become linked to the relief of emotional pain. In the woman who finally takes on a "lesbian" identity, unmet needs have left her searching for love from women, as some heterosexual women search for it from men. The deeper the need the more compelling the attachment. It's really no different in principle.

Addictive relationships between members of the same sex can become eroticized, just as they can in heterosexual relationships for similar reasons. heterosexual relationships for similar reasons. As in heterosexual relationship dependency, one relationship usually follows another, and certain types attract, sometimes in the same rescuer/needy, strong/weak configuration.

But, a lot more about homosexuality in the next section.

Notes

1. Hemfelt, Minirth & Meier, *Love is a Choice*, Thomas Nelson, Inc, 1989; Monarch Books, 2002.
2. Birchard T., "Clergy sexual misconduct: frequency and causation". *Sexual Relations Therapy*, 15, pp 127–39, UK.

Chapter Four
ADDICTION AS A MASK

Addiction is idolatry. "The objects of our addictions become our false gods," says May in *Addiction and Grace*. "These are what we worship, what we attend to, where we give our time and energy." Addictions get in the way of God's love for us, and our love for God.

We were made to love and desire God. But "psychologically addiction uses up desire. It is like a psychic malignancy, sucking our life energy into specific obsessions and compulsions, leaving less and less energy available for other people and other pursuits." Addiction has been called a "counterfeit of religious presence". Addictions make an absence out of his presence; we lose the sense of his desire for us, of his nearness.

God wants to heal us of our addictions because addictions are our false saviours that keep the real Saviour out. They are our pacifiers, but Jesus came as the Great Physician. They are our idols that become tyrants that rule our lives and those of our families. In this chapter we will discuss the way addictions develop and our attempts to avoid facing the pain behind them.

ADDICTION AS A DISGUISE

When we use something to cover up something else it becomes a cloak, a disguise. Addiction masks the real problem: unmet need; the pain that God wants to heal. It also helps deaden the pain; in that sense addiction is self-protective. But while we hang on to our addictions God cannot heal us.

This poem, adapted slightly, author unknown, shows the classic self-protective function of the mask and of the "real me" behind it.

I keep my mask with me everywhere I go
In case I need to wear it, so ME doesn't show.
I'm so afraid to show you ME, afraid of what you'll do
You might laugh at ME, or say mean things
Or I might lose you.
I'd like to take my mask off, to let you look at ME
I want you to try to understand
And please love what you see.
So if you'll be patient and close your eyes
I'll pull it off real slow
Please understand how much it hurts
To let the real ME show.
Now my mask is taken off. I feel naked! bare! so cold!
If you can still love all you see,
You're my friend, pure as gold.
I want to save my mask and hold it in my hand
I need to keep it handy if someone doesn't understand
Please protect ME my new friend, thank you for loving
    ME true,
But please let me keep my mask with me, until I love
    ME too.[1]

Without the mask we fear people will see into "the core of our soul's ugliness, pierce into the darkness of something hideous, despicable and utterly undesirable", says an ex-gay group, Regeneration, in an article on shame.

THE GROWTH OF THE MASK

Fig 1[2] was originally drawn to describe the growth of codependency: the development of a nice, helping, strong persona to gain love. But it holds good for the way we try to mask our pain behind any addiction or cultivated persona. The small white figure is the "real me"; the black figure can be the addiction we develop, or the persona we cultivate (our public face), and/or the person we come to believe we are.

It's very lonely behind the mask. Fashioned in the first place to insulate us from pain, it slowly increases our pain by

Figure 1   **ADULTHOOD**

EARLY CHILDHOOD

separating us from genuine satisfying human contact. We cannot give and receive love through it.

THE SURVIVAL KIT

The mask becomes our survival kit. We refuse to let anyone remove it, not only because we have invested so many years in it, but because without it we have to face up again to the pain behind it. Psychiatrist, Frank Lake, is talking specifically about the paranoid personality in the following excerpt, but it is so true in principle of our refusal to surrender the mask that I repeat it here:

> His inmost being... is identified with emptiness, meaning-
> lessness, inferiority, low self-esteem, emasculated powers, a

weak and sickly human spirit… Until he can deflate his defensive pride (mask) by coming to terms with the pain of his initial humiliation, nothing can reach him. (He) cannot surrender this defence without encountering… pain of great emptiness.

Most of us would not have to face "the naked terror of emptiness", but many of us would have to face the pain of abusive homes, abandonment, rejection, humiliation. "These 'survival kits' constructed and fashioned over the years are the real problems people have to grapple with," says Mary Pytches, in *Child No More*, who has struck them for many years in the course of counselling. "They will block a person's growth indefinitely unless the difficult work of laying them down is accomplished."

FUSION WITH THE MASK

Eventually we come to believe completely in the mask – to accept that our addictive behaviour, our coping persona, is normal – just us. We think people are odd if they suggest to us that we don't know who we are. In Bruce Courtenay's book, *The Power of One*, the main character, Peekay, describes the process by which we fuse with the mask, though Peekay was able to recognize what was happening and tear the mask off before it deceived him totally.

> I had become an expert at camouflage. I had come to identify with my camouflage to the point where the masquerade had become more important than the truth. While this posturing was so finely tuned it was no longer deliberate, it had nevertheless been born out of a compulsion to hide. My camouflage, begun so many years before… was now threatening to become the complete man. It was time to slough the mottled and cunningly contrived outer skin and emerge as myself, to face the risk of exposure.

When we have fused with the mask we no longer know the difference between who we really are and who we pretend to be. The mask is who we believe we are.

Kit

Kit gradually fashioned a mask to hide the shame of being sexually molested at five by a family member, creating "an overriding breach of trust with people he loved"; the pain of being a disappointment to his parents because he didn't behave "like a healthy young boy should", and the pain of being rejected and bullied by peers. By the time he was a teenager his family had withdrawn from him thinking he was "weird and on drugs", and Kit came to the realization he would have to change if he was to be acceptable to them and to his peers. I quote from *Living Waters*, a course manual used by a group called Desert Stream.

> In order to become acceptable I had to hide more of my real self and create a more desirable, socially acceptable person. This entailed a change in appearance and in my personality as well. Over a period of time I dropped mannerisms and speech patterns then adopted new ones. I became a cold, calculating but very composed and well-packaged person. Very few traces of my real self were left, as soon as one of them was spotted it was modified. I completely shut off and repressed my real self. What I had now was a creation. I hoped my real unloved self was dead and gone forever. I hated him. He was weak and vulnerable and people were always hurting him.
>
> Even my romantic and sexual life was different. Relationships and lovers were out of the question. I wanted sex, I wanted people to see and adore me as a new polished creation. Cold, hard, untouchable and unattainable. My seductive talents were honed into powerful tools to get the worshippers I so desperately needed to keep up my new creation. But the façade began to rot from the inside.

Kit developed a sophisticated veneer to hide who he was, but in so doing became sexually addicted. When repressed pain continues unhealed we begin to find that some of the things we do relieve our pain temporarily, though we don't always know how or why. When this happens the behaviours can become addictive.

REPRESSED PAIN

Dr Geoffrey Satinover, a New York psychiatrist, remarks that the human race has a tremendous desire to avoid pain: the pain of loss or absence of love, diminished self-worth or a sense of meaninglessness.

While animals will take action to get out of a place where they are experiencing pain, human beings take up other kinds of activity to get out, he says. We tend to make symbolic substitutions of one thing for another – typically using appetitive drives like food or sex. Hunger, for example, can be substituted for emotional need and then we eat to satisfy our hunger. In other words, a higher thing – a spiritual need – is replaced by an appetitive drive which we attempt to slake and it makes us temporarily feel better. Animals don't do this, he said.

But what happens when the original distress is temporarily blocked by another instinct? It not only comes back, but gets progressively worse. It also turns the instinct away from its proper use.

Addiction is misapplied, good, acceptable, neutral and normal activity that gets used for pain relief, Satinover says. People get trapped in it because they want to feel better and it doesn't feel dangerous for a start. But after a repetitive process they find it doesn't work as well as it did, the original pain is still there, and the appetitive drive, originally a guest in the house, has become not just master but tyrant.[3]

Come on now! I might have a bit of an addiction – if you want to call it that – but all this talk about pain. I don't have any pain and besides, the past is in the past!

It may be that you don't have any addictions to speak of, but there is no question that we do try to eliminate past painful experiences: that is, our conscious mind does. But our unconscious, that 80–90% of our mind that is not conscious, remembers a great deal about them.

The experiments of a neurosurgeon, Dr Wilder Penfield, in the fifties, showed that a vast amount of experience was stored in the brain, out of reach of the conscious mind. Under electrical stimulus to specific points of the cerebral cortex, Penfield's patients spontaneously recalled clear and remarkably detailed incidents from early life – recollections that stopped immediately the electrode was withdrawn. Over two years of experimentation Penfield had this to say: that the memory of the event and the feelings associated with it were "inextricably locked together in the brain". It was actually more accurate to say that his patients relived these memories rather than recalled them, he said.[4]

JUSTIFICATION AND DENIAL

When our addiction is helping or comforting us in some way, we have no wish to revisit our distress and find a more effective solution. Rather we develop ways of avoiding the issue. We simply tell ourselves our addiction is not an addiction, or that no distress exists. We don't want to think about it, or talk about it. Or if we do concede a problem might exist, we rationalize.

Christians are no different. The workaholic says he is "building the Kingdom", the man striving for his A pass says God only wants the best, the man spending a lot of time making money promises to spend it on missions and charitable causes. The food addict says she is just large-boned with slow metabolism, and that if weight doesn't get her in the end, cancer or drowning or pollution will. "But," says a person hooked into another, "he needs me."

THE HOMOSEXUAL

Like the rest of us homosexuals may also deny there is a problem, and justify, sometimes even parade, the "homosexual" persona. Homosexuality has evolved a highly developed justification that its activists have promoted with skill and energy: I was born this way: for me this is normal, everyone should have the freedom to express the sexuality that is normal for him; legitimate minorities should be legally protected; homosexual couples are entitled to marry and adopt just like straight couples.

God does not love the mask. He loves the real person hiding his pain behind addiction and denial and justification – the one he died for. Our survival kit finally becomes a cruel prison, a hardened sheath around our hearts. Our denials and elaborate justifications resist the truth. Ultimately the Truth is Jesus Christ who wants to change our lives and futures. Jesus came to speak a healing word to the real person crouching in pain behind the mask and to raise him/her to life. He commands us with great love to lay the mask down.

Notes

1. Quoted in *Fresh Elastic for Stretched-out Moms*, by Barbara Johnson, F.H.Revell. 1986.
2. Robert Subby and John Friel. Reprinted with the permission of the publishers Health Communications, Inc., Deerfield Beach, Florida, USA from *Codependency:An Emerging Issue*, by various authors, copyright 1984.
3. From a lecture given at the Seattle Conference of Exodus International in 1998.
4. W. Penfield, "Memory Mechanisms" AMA Archives of Neurology and Psychiatry, 67 (1952).

PART TWO:
HOMOSEXUALITY

Chapter Five

WHAT'S SO DIFFERENT?

It's time to look in more detail at homosexuality, what it is and why it is. I have argued that homosexuals and lesbians are little different in essence from the rest of us.

Homosexuality in men is a story of unaffirmed masculinity and in women, of unaffirmed femininity. Those who become homosexual have found the process of acquiring a psychological gender identity consistent with their biological gender to be too difficult, or too unattractive or too frightening.

This frequently has its origins in breakdowns and difficulties in the relationships that help create gender identity – that is, mainly between parents and children of the same sex, and between these children and their same-sex peer groups. Generally speaking, children form their gender identities through bonding with the same-sex parent, wanting to be like them, and copying them. They get another good dose from their same-sex peer groups. If these relationships are significantly difficult, gender acquisition can suffer. The literature abundantly documents the breaches between homosexuals and their same-sex parents. They are much more frequent among homosexuals than among heterosexuals, and often start early.

Gender deficits increase when boys particularly are excluded from boy peer groups, mainly because they already lack the gender characteristics that make them fit. Girls are not so cruelly excluded from girl peer groups but commonly experience themselves as different from other girls. In fact "childhood gender non-conformity" is one of the strongest predictors of later homosexuality.

These emotional deficits fuel a yearning for acceptance. A person who is very thirsty drinks copiously. Someone who is healthily famished will eat a large meal. People with gender deficits have a longing to belong to their gender group at the same time as they have detached themselves because of the rejection they have learned to expect. Typically the yearning will take the form of silent idealisation and admiration of an older person or a contemporary who represents what they would love to be or have, but aren't, and don't have.

If a pre-pubertal child with these sorts of needs for acceptance and attention is sexually approached by someone of the same sex who offers attention, affection and touch, the need for gender connection links itself easily to erotic gratification.

But even without sexual abuse, at puberty and in the years following, this strong focus on people of the same sex, in an attempt to gain the crucial love and acceptance – understandably so – can become eroticized, not because it is erotic in its essence, but because, unfortunately, our culture can only understand such intense needs for connection in erotic terms. It also eroticizes because our sexual responses often attach themselves to our strongest emotional drive. With the passage of time – gaining power from cultural acceptance, repetition, fear and shame – the erotic association can begin to ingrain itself. A same-sex sexual relationship at this point is a powerful reinforcer. The person begins to slowly identify himself or herself as "homosexual".

So, in many ways people who identify themselves eventually as homosexual share experiences common to many heterosexuals.

- Often, breaches between fathers and sons, mothers and daughters and siblings, and between parents.
- Unhappy or rejecting peer group experiences.
- Sexual abuse.
- Wrong, but understandable reactions on the part of the child: fear, loss of trust, withdrawal of dependency, resistance to role modelling, isolation and insecurity: low self-esteem.

- The compensating search for comfort, connection, security, love in certain kinds of people – those who have that indefinable something that promises it.
- A continuing pattern of these sorts of responses and their growing power. The more we respond that way, the more powerful the response becomes.

In other words, homosexuality is a tale of unmet need, low self-esteem and the attempt to make things better in ways that can become addictive. It's not so very different from the stories told by many heterosexuals caught in addictive behaviours.

Homosexuality is almost inevitably about absorbing relationships – no different from the kind straight men and women get into. Just as compulsive heterosexual relationships with people and things are an attempt to fill empty "love tanks", so it is with homosexual relating and sexual contact. They share the same characteristics: one relationship follows another, and certain types will attract.

These relationships are usually eroticized in the same way that heterosexual dependency is usually eroticized, and, in men particularly, can become sexually addictive – in the same way that many heterosexual male addictions are also sexual in nature.

The male peer group has a lot of influence in the development of homosexual love and gender needs by its taunting and rejection of "sissy" boys – as it does in the way peer group behaviour can shape the deficits that heterosexual men seek to fill.

Homosexual activity follows the usual swings of the addictive cycle: the sense of loss and emptiness, the search for relief, comfort or stimulation, the release, the recurring sense of emptiness and so on.

Homosexuals often manipulate others so they can continue to keep doing what they do – like most people caught in addictive behaviours. The general acceptance of homosexuality in large swathes of Western society today is testament to gay activism's success in convincing the public that there is no problem.

The homosexually oriented often have a skewed image of God, a God who rejects them for their sexual orientation and is generally distant and condemning – such image is often based on their experiences of their own fathers and of the church.

Like anyone caught in a deep-rooted compulsive behaviour, the homosexually active person will generally be unable to stop acting out without outside support.

The causes of homosexuality, like the causes of most of our addictive behaviours, cannot be pinned on any one person or thing in particular, but some people are more culpable and some experiences more causative than others.

Society doesn't understand homosexuality. People either have a gut-reaction against it, or tolerate, accept or welcome it with little to no understanding of what created it. A typical range of responses is seen in the small poem that follows:

THE PIT

(Dedicated to those who struggle homosexually.)

A man fell into a pit and couldn't get himself out.

Respectable people came along and said:
"We don't associate with pit-dwellers."

An empathist came along and said:
"I really feel for you in that pit."

A sociobiologist came along and said:
"You were born in your pit."

A psychiatrist came along and said:
"It can be very destructive to remove people
from pits they were born in."

A psychologist came along and said:
"Accept your pit, that way you'll be happy."

A gay activist came along and said:
"Fight for the right to stay in your pit."

A politician came along and said:
"Discrimination against pits is illegal."

A researcher came along and said:
"What an interesting pit."

A religious fundamentalist came along and said:
"You deserve your pit."

A religious liberal came along and said:
"Your pit is God's beautiful gift to you."

A charismatic came along and said:
"Just confess you're not in that pit."

His mother came along and said:
"It's your father's fault you're in that pit."

His father came along and said:
"It's your mother's fault you're in that pit."

His wife came along and said:
"It's all my fault you're in that pit."

But Jesus, seeing the man, loved him,
and reaching into the pit
put his arms around him and pulled him out.

(Developed from an idea in the book, *Pain is Inevitable but Misery is Optional*, by Barbara Johnson, Word Publishing, 1990.)

Before we begin to look more closely at homosexuality let's enter the life of a Christian struggling with homosexuality and see what it tells us.

Chapter Six

CHAD

Chad says he was just any typical Christian kid – "came to the Lord at nine" and knew when he was twelve that God wanted him in "full-time ministry". But he was not a typical student or young man: he was a young man with outstanding leadership gifts who held all top student offices at school and university and carried away all the top honours – including coveted model student and President's Award distinctions; finally making it into the prestigious *Who's Who among Students in American Colleges and Universities*. He was also a "soul-winner" par excellence. At weekend youth rallies he directed in Atlanta "hundreds and hundreds of teenagers came to know the Lord". A rising star in the evangelical firmament, he had his heart set on Christian ministry in Eastern Europe and was studying Russian in Florida, when he met two men having lunch together in a park in central Orlando, who changed his life because he was able to tell them what he had never been able to tell a soul before: that he was sexually attracted to men and didn't know what to do about it.

All through his education as a model student at the country's finest Christian colleges Chad had been unable to confide his sexual conflict to anyone. "I have an unspoken request," was all he could screw up the courage to say at dormitory prayers. The shame and ostracism he knew he would face after such a disclosure was more than he could face. He didn't know where to go for help.

The two men in the park were homosexual lovers and Chad came upon them because he was witnessing and handing out tracts. They were very sympathetic. "They said to me, 'Look, you need to be with people who understand, who won't reject you, where you can open up and talk and get help.'" Chad agreed to go with them to a professional counsellor the following night. The counsellor turned out to be gay and the interview was at a local gay bar. It was the beginning of "six and a half years of pure hell" for Chad. Able to share for the first time in his life with people who understood, but in an atmosphere that encouraged him to express his sexuality, Chad's years of repressed longing for intimacy with men found an outlet.

And so the double life began – while everything Chad touched continued to turn to gold. He went through seminary and became an assistant pastor and under his leadership the church youth group burgeoned from five to 50, 45 of them becoming candidates for full-time ministry. The church grew from 300 to 700 – over half of them under the age of twelve. But three or four nights a week Chad was in gay bars, going home with a different man each night and no one knew.

Plagued with guilt he decided to leave the church. "I knew my life was out of control and that I desperately needed help." He sought out a minister at the State University.

> He told me, "I can help you live as a homosexual without guilt, and I can help you learn to accept your homosexuality as a gracious gift from God." But I knew if Jesus were Lord and Saviour and the Bible were true there had to be a way out of this mess.

He finally found the courage to open up to a few Christian friends, and they began to pray for him daily.

A year and a half later – far too soon – Chad was married. But together he and his wife, Emi, began a year of counselling. Emi opened up for the first time about early sexual abuse that had made sexual intimacy frightening and Chad began to understand the origins of his attraction to men: the early loss of his father, the sexual molestation as a child, and his early aversion to female sexual anatomy.

Chad's father died when he was three leaving him "desperately looking for a father in older guys". His school recesses were spent, not with kids his own age, six and seven; but rough-housing with older boys, and "eventually I found some guys who would not only play with me and touch me, but, for about a year and a half fondle me sexually, one of them the Baptist minister's son". In counselling another significant incident emerged: lying with his head in his mother's lap one day at the age of seven he smelt her menstruation odour. "She was very poor and she couldn't afford modern sanitary products." For Chad from that time, female sexual anatomy became "dirty and repulsive and disgusting", at the same time as he was "learning sexual gratification in a different way". By the time he was twelve Chad knew there was something different about him: when the boys in the scout troop talked sexually about girls he could only think about what had happened to him when he was six and seven.

In 1983 Chad was appointed to a post on Capitol Hill, and travelled widely with congressmen, senators and British MPs. This was the time of the AIDS outbreak, and flicking through medical journals one day Chad panicked to discover that anyone who had been sexually active up to seven years earlier – when he was promiscuous in the gay bar scene – was a candidate for AIDS.

He couldn't bring himself to take an HIV test, because in Washington DC at the time, people testing positive were losing their health insurance, and his bosses would be informed. "What Christian ministry would want to keep me?" But the real heartbreak was closer to home. He was unable to tell his wife, Emi, afraid she would leave him, taking their little daughter. For two years there was no sexual relationship.

> Every time Emi reached out and touched me in bed at night I would panic. I would break down and cry and she wouldn't know what was wrong. I didn't know if I had already infected her. I didn't know if the next act of love was going to infect her. I didn't know if our beautiful little daughter was infected. I caught the flu – my joints ached, I suffered from sudden sweats, my glands were swollen; I had the symptoms of a man suffering from a weak immune system.

After two years of this, and one homosexual encounter in a weak moment, his marriage was in pieces. He and Emi separated for a while.

He confided in a few friends and they began avoiding him.

> I would call Bob up and say, "Let's go out for lunch some place", and there would be this pregnant pause on the other end of the phone – about 30 seconds. Then he would say, "Well, do you mind if Steve comes too?" He didn't want to be seen alone with me.

Then the ministry found his marriage was in tatters and asked him to resign his directorship. He never heard from them again.

He tried to be honest at church about his problem and asked if he could share something of his struggle and progress with the church. The pastor told him to write out his testimony, then checked the text. "He took his pen and every word that read "homosexuality" or "homosexual", he put a line through and said, 'You can't say that.'" Reduced to non-specifics the testimony was robbed of force. Chad decided to share more specifically with the elders, who had been very friendly to him, inviting him to preach from time to time. "But when I did, all of a sudden their attitude changed: they began making excuses not to see me, and if they saw me coming any place they would change direction. These were people who had been hugging me before."

He only realized how desperate he was when he found himself sitting late one night on the American Legion Bridge, Washington DC,

> with one foot on the gas and one foot on the clutch trying to figure out a way to get the car off the bridge and into the Potomac River so that Emi could collect my life insurance. But God stopped me from doing anything so stupid. He spoke to me from a verse of scripture I had never noticed before: "Forget the former things, don't dwell on the past. See I am doing a new thing. Don't you understand it? I am making a way in the desert."

Five days after he read the verse Chad had a nervous breakdown.

> I was in the supermarket and I couldn't work out whether
> the five things on the list were in the shopping cart or not.
> I broke down completely and ran out of the supermarket.
> Everyone was staring at me. I couldn't find my car in the
> parking lot. I finally made it home and I sat there in the
> middle of the living room floor and I just cried and I said,
> "God, I want to die."

Chad was admitted to the local hospital for psychiatric evalua-
tion and diagnosed as situationally depressed, "basically because
of my fear of what other people might think of me". He was
admitted to a psychiatric hospital in California and on the way
to the airport he opened his Bible to read again the verse: Forget
the former things... "and here I was going to a psychiatric
hospital!"

After three days of observation Chad was allowed out and
began going for long walks into the desert with his hymn book
and Bible. He usually made for one hill about a mile from the
hospital, where he sat in 120°F heat under a Joshua tree, on a
towel.

> I would sing and I would pray. The first week was mainly
> self-pity, "O God please help me. This person doesn't like
> me, and if that person finds out they won't love me, and I
> don't know whether my wife is going to stay with me or
> not, and I don't know whether I can support my family
> because I can't think. And God, what am I going to do?"

After about a week God broke in.

> The Lord came to me in a very strong way. I felt his love
> and his holiness and his presence, and all I could do was fall
> on my face there in the dirt, and I cried out, "O God, you
> know what a hell of a son-of-a-bitch I've been." And I felt
> his love and compassion for me, I felt him lift me up and
> hug me and he said, "Yes I know all about that – that's the

bad news. But the good news is I love sons-of-bitches very, very much and this is what I have to say to you. The very thing that you thought would disqualify you from serving me is going to be the very thing that will bring me glory and honour and that I will use in your life to serve me. I want you to go back and start working with people who have AIDS and who are bound by compulsive behaviours, sex and drugs, helping them to overcome, and helping my people to understand. And you're going to go back to your family and friends and let it all hang out, and let people know who you are and what you struggle with, and they will support you. And if they can't handle it, it's not your problem, it's theirs.

Chad returned to the East Coast and began to help people with AIDS. The group he founded, *Love and Action*, sprouted into an organisation that has trained thousands of volunteers – members of hundreds of churches in the north-eastern states – to give unconditional care and hope to the growing number of people with AIDS. Chad found that more than half of those he contacted had been members of evangelical churches, or were when they found they were HIV positive. In the ministry's first three years, about 95% of the 500 people that volunteers cared for became Christian or re-dedicated their lives to Christ.

As he began to share his story and speak about homosexuality and AIDS in churches, Christian high schools and universities, staff, pastors and students began to disclose homosexual struggles they had never revealed to anyone. At each of the first three churches he spoke, three pastoral staff confided their struggle with sexual attraction to other men.

Chad finally found a local church with a reputation for helping people from problem backgrounds. Encouraged to share, he "told everyone everything". This time the church gathered around him. He screwed up the courage to take an HIV test, and found he was negative – twice. He began attending an ex-gay group in Baltimore, and made more progress out of homosexuality. He and Emi are still working towards reconciliation.

Chad does not believe AIDS is the judgment of God on

homosexuals; he sees it as the outcome of behaviours that orig-inate in a lot of pain. To go with Chad and helpers to a local hospital is to watch him put his arms around these dying men, and say hoarsely and tearfully, "Bill, God wants you to know that he loves you very, very much and he wants to help you."

Chad shows us that

- Homosexuality is found in the conservative church and among its leaders: among the best, most gifted and most promising.
- Homosexuals in the conservative church practise secretly, living guilty double lives, not daring to admit their homo-sexual struggle for fear they will be ostracized.
- Small boys looking for father replacements or for attention and affection from males are vulnerable to men or older boys who approach them sexually. Often this behaviour in boys is exploratory only, but boys like Chad can be con-fused and programmed by it. People who sexually fondle young boys like Chad also attend churches.
- Homosexual despair can lead to the verge of suicide.
- Homosexuals do not know they can change, nor does the church.
- The church deals summarily and judgmentally with homosexuals rather than compassionately, or else urges homosexuals to accept their homosexuality as God's good gift.
- The homosexual who cannot find help in the church will turn to the gay scene for the acceptance he longs for.
- Fear of loss of reputation will prevent a Christian man or woman from befriending a known homosexual in case people think he is one too.
- The church that finally helped Chad was made up of people who didn't think Chad was any different from them.

CHAPTER SEVEN

MALE HOMOSEXUALITY

"There is no such thing, strictly speaking, as a homosexual or a lesbian. There are only people who need healing of old rejections and deprivations" (Leanne Payne).

This chapter will look at what homosexual men say they are *really* wanting in a relationship, look more closely at father-son and peer relationships, see what homosexuality is not and why some heterosexual men fear they might be homosexual.

WHAT IS HOMOSEXUALITY?

Frank Worthen – who lived for years as a gay man but left the lifestyle about 30 years ago and founded one of the world's first "ex-gay" groups, puts it this way: If a person has a visual sexual response coupled with active same-sex oriented fantasy, then even without sex acts, a homosexual problem exists. Other definitions of homosexuality require the preferential attraction to be an adult pattern "over a significant period of time". Teenage sexuality is still fluid and forming.

SEX IS NOT WHAT HE'S WANTING

Michael Saia, who has counselled a lot of homosexual men, has asked many of them what they were looking for when they first had a sexual relationship. He says he never once heard the word: sex. He lists their answers: strength (usually emotional), security, acceptance, understanding, sensitivity, comfort, friendship, companionship, identity, a sense of completeness. Saia summarizes,

> Gay men enter relationships with other men to try to meet two major human needs: the need for identity (value, significance, competence, self-worth) and the need for love (security, affection, friendship, companionship).

Prior to puberty, homosexuality remains only a problem of feeling inadequate and of admiration for others, says Frank.

> All the deep roots of homosexuality are non-sexual: lack of affirmation, lack of a sense of belonging and a great river of insecurity. If the cause had to be summed up in one simple statement, it would be: lack of affirmation ... a large part of male homosexuality is simply father replacement.

"God has allowed parents to fulfil all the small child's needs," he says. "That carries a person through life. When that foundation is lacking, the immature needs of the child dominate the adult."

In his experience strength and power are the qualities gay men admire most and look for in their partners – "the qualities that should have been associated with the father figure". The ingredients of homosexuality, says Frank,

> are the lack of unconditional love, unmet need, the lack of a gender identity transfer, a search for fulfilment, a longing for acceptance and attention, wrong choices, a large dose of self-pity, rebellion, admiration, envy and isolation.

"In most instances the attraction for the same sex begins before the age of ten," says Andy Comiskey, formerly a gay man. "It is emotional, non-sexual and involuntary. With sexual maturity these needs become eroticized; sexual intimacy becomes a primary means for feeling loved and affirmed."

Few homosexuals enjoy their first sexual encounter; it is often painful and they have to drive over a bump in their conscience to do it, says Frank.

> The first experience of sex is painful, unpleasant, repugnant. It's a dichotomy. It's everything you ever wanted in

touch and affirmation. It's the best and worst moment of your life – because the sexual acting out is not what you're after. For many homosexuals their first sex acts were unfulfilling and for some even repulsive, but because of great emotional voids you're willing to make the trade-off, sex for emotional fulfilment. Many gay men treasure the skin-to-skin contact and being held far more than fleeting sexual encounters. Sex is the key to unlock the door of relationship.

"I was starved for affection," said Bob. "I didn't like the sex at first, I just wanted someone to really love me. I told myself, OK, if this is what I have to do to get the touch, I'll do it – then it got to where I liked it, so… "

Once the line is crossed into homosexual sex, the statistics bear it out, it will happen again very quickly – and the act itself will slowly become pleasurable – or at least the memories of it will. Whenever his need for love, acceptance, and significance overwhelms him he will try to meet it in the embrace of another male. As addiction takes over, the personal nature of the act can become superfluous – all that is necessary is sexual release even if the parties are unable to see each other in some dark cubicle. And when the habitual palls, novelty beckons.

ENVY AND THE "CANNIBAL COMPULSION"

There is widespread use in the ex-gay movement of a term – the "cannibal-compulsion" – an expression coined by Leanne Payne, author and founder of Pastoral Care Ministries, which specializes in emotional healing. It resonates with men and women seeking to understand their same-sex attractions. A missionary once told Payne that cannibals ate those they admired to get their traits, and often in homosexuality people find themselves attracted to others who have particular qualities (physical or psychological) that they believe they lack and wish they had. By uniting with the person with these characteristics, the homosexual attempts to incorporate in himself what he is lacking. "It's the idea that I will be complete and secure if I have what you have," says Frank. One former gay man remarked that homosexuality was the attempt to take in externally the sense of masculinity that he needed internally. Nicolosi, a psychologist specializing in gender re-orientation therapy mentions one client who commented, "I realized I didn't want another man, I wanted a manly me."

WHAT CAUSES HOMOSEXUALITY?

This chapter focuses particularly on relationships of sons and fathers, though it goes without saying that the father-son relationship alone is not the cause of homosexual attraction and behaviour. It is often a major factor. But there are many contributing factors and it is the cumulative effect of them, without counterbalancing factors, that make homosexual orientation a likely result.

There have been some weird and wonderful attempts to explain homosexuality. The Lepchas of the Himalayas believe homosexuality comes from eating the flesh of an uncastrated pig. Plato believed Zeus split every man and woman in two, then felt sorry for them but reassembled them in such a way that they were either attracted to the same sex or the opposite sex. Some of the earliest scientific research into causes focused on the genes, sociobiological theories, brain structure and hormones, but to date no causal connection has been established. (For a full discussion see *My Genes Made Me Do It! – a scientific look at sexual orientation*, Neil and Briar Whitehead, Huntington House, 233pp, 1999.) Psychology has focused on environment and behaviour.

In the last two decades thousands of people have made substantial progress towards a heterosexual orientation with the help of "ex-gay" support groups and counsellors. Ex-gay groups – former homosexuals helping other homosexuals out – have proliferated in the last decade: now upwards of several hundreds in the Western world. They have focused strongly on environmental factors and found particularly helpful the research conclusions of Dr Elizabeth Moberly, who applied the psychological notion of "defensive detachment" specifically to homosexuality.

"Defensive detachment"

After seven years of exhaustive assessment of the existing psychoanalytic data on gender identity, which she believed had been "insufficiently assessed hitherto", Dr Moberly had this to say:

> From amidst a welter of details, one constant underlying principle suggests itself: that the homosexual – whether man or woman – has suffered from some deficit in the relationship with the parent of the same sex; and that there is a corresponding drive to make good this deficit – through the medium of same-sex or "homosexual" relationships.

Dr Moberly argues that a tug of war between a deep emotional repudiation of the parent of the same-sex, and an equally strong drive to recover love and gender identity missed out on through the disrupted attachment, is the foundation stone of homosexuality. She calls this tug of war "same-sex ambivalence" and says it structures itself into the personality and finally expresses itself in homosexual orientation and behaviour.

Something occurs early in the life of the child – or consistently through it – that causes the child to inwardly repudiate, or defensively detach from the parent of the same sex at a significant level in a long-term way, says Moberly. It is not necessarily the fault of the parent, but it disrupts the essential dependency, bonding and identification processes that foster gender role modelling. The child self-protectively withdraws from the process to some degree or another.

Growth of an inward sense of gender identity (I am on Dad's side of the line not Mum's, and I belong to boys and not girls) is something that usually takes place steadily and almost invisibly day-in, day-out in the "good-enough" relationship of a child with the parent of the same sex and it takes a strong counteracting influence to disrupt it.

> In detaching from a parent, says Dr Moberly, the child actively resists the normal gender identification process. Defensive detachment from the parent of the same sex is detachment from gender… The significant thing about

defensive detachment is that it is not just a failure to identify, but *a reaction against identification* (my italics)... When
the same-sex deficit is particularly severe the effects on
(gender) identity may well be marked.

However, where there has been a disruption, the urge to connect to others of the same gender doesn't disappear. It goes on
– naturally enough in the attempt to belong to the boy groups
around. But boy groups are notoriously hard on soft, sissy, inadequate boys, and a boy whose initiatives to belong are constantly
rebuffed fails to find reinforcement there either. It can become
too difficult or threatening to belong. Being "a boy" becomes
problematic.

Bancroft in *Homosexuality/Heterosexuality* (OUP) says gender non-conformity in childhood is "the only characteristic that
has repeatedly distinguished between the childhoods of homosexual and heterosexual men".

But the search goes on, with the boy becoming more and
more vulnerable because the need to connect increases in
urgency in spite of his detachment. If he is sexually approached
at this point by a man who also shows him affection and attention or if he gets into frequent sex play with other pre-pubertal
boys (at least half play round briefly out of curiosity but take it
no further), he is almost set up for later homosexuality. At any
rate he will envy and admire boys who look like he wished he
did, who are confident, maybe good at sports. His orientation,
appropriately so, is towards men – he is still trying to make up
the increasing gender deficit – but the testosterone surges of
puberty will now be getting in the way. If he really admires and
envies a certain boy and finds erotic feelings intruding, he is
going to be confused and frightened. He may find fantasies
involving the boy he admires come up when he masturbates and
a pattern may start that continues. This is where the long, lonely
struggle begins with feelings and habitual responses he doesn't
understand. When he finally emerges from it, it could well be to
self-identify as "homosexual" because he can find no other
explanation for the way he feels. His attempts to form his gender identity were impeded in the family and in his male peer

group but they haven't gone away. The powerful urge to bond is still there, and now it has linked with his sex drive. He is still focused on men but particularly on those who promise to return his interest as intensely as he feels it. Not surprisingly there are often high levels of dependency, though in male homosexuality, if emotional needs have been flooded by the sex drive, sexual release can become over-riding, and relationship secondary. Whenever the emotional need becomes overwhelming he mis-reads the signals and thinks he needs sex. Some homosexual men are deeply sexually addicted.

Homosexuality is a psychological incompletion that is contrary to God's intention, says Dr Moberly. She believes homosexuals are men and women who are still capable of reaching heterosexual psychological maturity.

SO WHY AREN'T WE ALL HOMOSEXUALS?

But haven't many of us had problems with our fathers? Absentee fatherhood has been called the modern disease. A lot of hetero-sexual men were bullied at school by their peer groups. A lot of us have felt rejected and insecure. Why aren't we all homosexual?

A lot of things are circumstantial. The drive to connect is very strong. Particularly in extended families a grandfather, or uncle or even older brother can become the surrogate connecting point if a father-son bond breaks down. Some boys have made a father out of a teacher, a pastor, a youth mentor, a sports coach – and it has saved the day. They developed enough gender confidence to weather the rough waters of the peer group.

It depends a lot on the temperament of the child: a lot of children have the resilience to genuinely get over a hurtful situation or to go out and get what they need. The sensitive, intro-verted child is more vulnerable than the child with an extroverted and hardier temperament.

A child's peer group may be accepting enough that the boy feels he is one of the group. Or he may team up with one or two close friends, boys who may be a little out of the main-stream but with "acceptable" specialist interests – computers, hiking, music. It may be enough to make him feel he belongs as a male.

THE FATHER-SON RELATIONSHIP

Blame is not the issue

Before we explore what is behind the breach that occurs between a son and his father it is very important to establish that it takes two to cause a breach. Andy Comiskey, formerly a gay man:

> Both parties – the parent and the child – are involved in that process of defensive detachment. The parent is not necessarily malicious and unloving; the child is not just a victim, as he or she develops a pattern of defensive reaction to the parent... in fact... the child's disdainful reaction to the parent can affect the parent's reaction to the child.

Children are immature, properly so, and egocentric, they are not objective. They are excellent recorders but poor interpreters. If they detach defensively it can be because they have misperceived the situation.

The wound

The wound behind homosexuality – whatever it is – is always traumatic enough to interrupt the instinctive process of gender acquisition. This does not always imply wilful maltreatment, though it may. It may result from unintentional and accidental hurt: marital separation, death, divorce, placement of the child in foster care, illness or hospitalisation. Father can be away from home a lot simply because he is doing his best to make ends meet. He can be absent through no fault of his own: military service may have claimed him for a year. Maybe he is workaholic – not because the family needs the money but because he is more concerned with success or making money than with making a family. Maybe the boy's father, a good enough man – relates more easily with the boy's brothers. Or a parent can be present but emotionally inaccessible. "In homosexuality the key word is separation – either physical or emotional – between the child and the parent," says Dr Moberly.

If the incident that causes "defensive detachment" is so important why isn't the incident and the child's detachment obvious to everyone?

Partly because the incident often happens too early for the child to understand or be able to explain it and because the memory of the incident is soon repressed, partly because the parent knows the child has misread or exaggerated the incident, and fails to see the effect it has had.

Inwardly the child is saying something like, "You did this to me, I can't trust you now", "You do not love me, I do not love you either", or "You are never here, I do not need you either", or "I don't matter to you, you don't matter to me either". It may have been a single traumatic event, or it may be the cumulative general tone of the relationship. "As daily life goes on, adjustments may be made that leave few or even no signs of disturbance," says Dr Moberly, "but that may mask repression. The family relationships may seem to be good, indeed are good at a certain level... But it can be a superficial adjustment" – such as quiet, compliant behaviour. Mothers can be incredulous when they learn of their sons' homosexuality. "But he was always so good – he gave me the least trouble of any of them," they often say.

THE EMOTIONALLY ABSENT FATHER

Father can be home but too busy, or emotionally remote.

It is very common to hear these sorts of comments from gay men. David: "My father? I never knew him"; Michael: "I was never close to my father"; Les: "I can't remember Dad ever being around"; Mark: "I had very little contact with him, I couldn't call him a father"; John: "Physically he was there, but emotionally I did not feel loved by him – nothing I did was good enough"; Bud: "My dad wasn't home much, and there was no physical affection".

A study by Richard Pillard, in *Homosexuality/Hetero-sexuality* found fathers of gay men to be twice as distant as those of heterosexual men – backing up many research reports of fathers of gay men being cold, psychologically remote, and less "fatherly". Pillard also found that the more distant the father, the greater likelihood of several gay sons.

Saghir and Robins in their book, *Male and Female Homosexuality* said 84% of their homosexual study group described their fathers as "indifferent and uninvolved at home during childhood". Dr Rekers, in his book *Growing up Straight* says many studies show that fathers of homosexual men have been found to be "less affectionate", and even "aloof, hostile and rejecting". In a majority of cases fathers had left the decision-making in the home to the mothers – a sign of absence. In one controlled study only 13% of homosexuals identified with their fathers in comparison to 66% of straight men in the same study. "In the many clinical studies of homosexuals the characteristics of the father that would foster normal psychosexual adjustment – nurturance, affection and active leadership in the family – are all notably lacking," says Rekers. Quoting from numerous studies by Rekers, Comiskey puts paternal "warmth and affection" at the top of the list for "secure masculine identity" (rather than encouragement of masculine behaviours); quality of time spent between father and son, rather than quantity; and "evident leadership in the household", particularly of the kind that "sets limits with a nurturing hand".

Eliot said his Christian father was not physically absent but always immersed in his latest project "for the Lord". He also modelled "a heterosexual stereotype that was clinical, emotionally cold and frigid. Men were not supposed to throw their arms around other males and give them hugs."

Studies of solo mother families are contradictory in showing whether there is any contribution to homosexuality in sons. If the breakup doesn't cause a breach with his father, or if a son finds a replacement male hero the risks are minimized. If he rejects his father and sides with his mother, there are risks.

THE ABUSIVE FATHER

Abusive fathers figure prominently in the lives of homosexual men. Pillard found alcoholic fathers figure three times more prominently than other kinds of "distant" fathers in studies of gay men.

John-Christopher's earliest memory is of hiding under a bed at the age of three, "trying to escape my father's large hands and fists during one of his drunken rages". As he grew older and his father's drinking increased, he "lived in absolute terror and fear of him".

He never held me, he never taught me to throw a baseball, and to this very day he has never said, "I love you, son."

What he taught me was violence and "secrets" and inferiority. I was never good enough. I did everything wrong. And it was from my father that I first heard those words, those awful words: sissy, queer and faggot.

Like many homosexuals I grew up without that essential good "male image". I didn't want to be like my father. I didn't like my father. I didn't like myself either. There weren't any Christian men – uncles or neighbours – who could intervene, and my father would never have allowed that anyway. Besides, there wasn't any problem. We kept our secrets inside the family.

The only people in my life who seemed to like me were my mother, my grandmother, my sisters, cousins, aunts and teachers, most of whom were women. I soon learned to be uncomfortable around other boys and men. I started to feel apart at a very early age. I longed for my father's approval and for male acceptance. All I found was rejection and more rejection. What was wrong with me? Why didn't I fit in? I wanted to be a baseball player, I wanted a girlfriend, I wanted to get married and have children. What made me feel so different, and why was I feeling this sexual attraction to other boys and men? At age fourteen I remember vividly the crush I had on my ninth grade maths teacher, a man. He was young and handsome – but beyond that he was gentle and treated me with respect – he even liked me.[1]

Former gay men can sometimes remember incidents in childhood where they believed they made some sort of decision never to be like their fathers, or to let him near them again. John says the day of his parent's divorce when he was five was "traumatic and unforgettable". "My Dad took my sister Vicky and me to a park, knelt down beside us and told us good-bye. For the rest of my childhood I lived with my mother. I felt terribly insecure and different from the other boys." Sometimes the memory is only of a final vow capping years of painful relationship:

Karl, a gay man, said he was twelve when he vowed he would never let his father near him again, "he had hurt me too much". Don was older, fifteen. Shuttled back and forth between his separated parents – his alcoholic father who abused him and told him he would never amount to anything, and his mother, who had remarried a man Don could not get on with – he finally vowed "never to let anyone get close to me again; it hurt too much". A model student to that point, his life deteriorated the following year into drugs, drink and homosexuality. "In the arms of another man, I felt a tremendous security."

One father mentioned the incident that he said he now knows "damaged" his very young son, Michael, who grew up homosexual. Trapped by pregnancy into a teenage marriage and unwanted son, and furious one night at his fractious offspring, he bawled at him: "I hate you, I wish you'd never been born." "Inside I was thinking he was too young to remember what I said. But I know now that he never forgot that moment."

HOMOSEXUAL CHILDREN CAN HAPPEN TO ANYONE

Sy

Sy Rogers, who lived for years as a woman, was once only a hairsbreadth away from a sex change operation. But he never had it and is now glad he didn't. His story shows the power of a defensive breach once it has occurred and the uphill struggle parents can have trying to repair it when the child is not aware enough to understand what has happened or why.

Sy says his alcoholic mother was killed in a car accident when he was five, and his father was advised by professional counsellors to send Sy away to a stable environment while he put his life back together again.

> Dad wanted to do whatever was good for me so he sent me, with regret, to live with relatives for a year. But when I moved back with Dad and he wanted to interact normally with me and develop a healthy relationship with me I didn't want anything to do with him. Though my father's motive towards me was pure in sending me away, I

perceived it as abandonment and betrayal at a time when I desperately needed him following my mother's death.

Sy had defensively detached:

> My little five-year-old mind could not understand that he had my best interests at heart. All I thought was, "You weren't there when I needed you and I'm not going to open up my heart to you again." And I began to look to other sources to meet the need my father should have met.

Sy said that search began at about the same time he closed his heart to his father. "I can remember very clearly at six years old at the movies seeing that it was always the heroine that the hero was after and I wanted to be the object of a man's love and affection like that." Sy had his first sexual experience at the age of seven – with peers – and soon discovered that that was also the way he could get intimacy and affection from a man. "So, later, as an adolescent I developed the formula that sex with a man equals love."

Sy's father remarried when Sy was eleven and he and his new wife did all they could to correct the developing effeminacy in Sy's life – but they had no understanding of its origins and by now Sy was totally resistant to his father. They tried to develop the man in him by getting him involved in masculine pursuits.

> I was in swim team, track team, football team, had two motorcycles and went dirt-bike riding and back-packing in the Western Rockies, I was an eagle scout and did a lot of manly things, but it didn't make a man out of me. I became increasingly effeminate because I felt that as a man I wouldn't find love and affection from a man; I had to be more like a girl.

After a hair-raising life on the street as a "recreational prostitute", in which he was chased by police, nearly strangled, shot and knifed, he settled on a sex-change operation as the answer to all his problems. It was then his parents asked him to leave home. He left with a defiant, "OK, I don't need you either." Sy's parents really tried, but it made no difference.

David

Andy Comiskey tells David's story. David grew up detached from his parents – "not really emotionally connected, even though they nurtured and cared for me throughout my childhood". During high school he "shut down to any kind of love from them and felt mostly misunderstood". To ease his emotional isolation he "embraced the homosexual lifestyle". Failing to find love and emotional security after several relationships he sought help from an ex-gay ministry and during prayer a significant "repressed" memory emerged. David believes it led to his sense of distance from his parents and detachment from his own gender. David's parents could never have known; their actions were only loving.

> I remembered myself at four years, my dad holding me up by the legs while my mom administered an enema. I cried out for them to stop, I screamed, "I hate you." Moments later, sitting on the toilet, I thought, "This is how little girls go to the bathroom." Somehow, in my child's mind I believed my parents were rejecting their little boy and wanted a little girl.

The child's inner shutdown can place him outside the best attempts at reconciliation by loving parents.

REINFORCING FACTORS IN MALE HOMOSEXUALITY

But about one fifth of male homosexuals don't have difficult relationships with their fathers. David told me that very early on in life he decided he didn't like the power games that small boys played. He preferred the co-operation he found in the way girls played so he withdrew from male groups, and all the more defensively when they began to call him a sissy. Peter was a gay man with AIDS. He told me that he witnessed on several occasions violent rape of his mother by his father. He grew up disowning his genitalia. John said being a man in his household was measured in terms of drunkenness and sexual exploits, and he rejected the model. Van den Ardweg in his 1986 review of the psychoanalytic data said poor relationships with peer groups were even more common in the backgrounds of male homosexuals than poor relationships with fathers. But rejection of our gender leaves us very vulnerable to the compensating drive to reconnect.

There are other factors in the formation of homosexuality – each case is unique in particulars but here are some common themes.

- The relationship with the opposite-sex parent. A mother's relationship with her son can be too close. Some homosexual men have found themselves their mother's confidants, and may have experienced their mothers as emotionally needy, smothering, bossy or manipulative, making intimate relationships with women appear a harrowing prospect. (See Myths, below.)
- Attitude to marriage: If the marriage of parents is bad, or sour, heterosexual union will not appeal as a source of happiness and love.
- Sexual abuse: For a male, it can combine longed-for male closeness and connection with eroticism – a very potent factor in the development of homosexuality.
- Labelling – linked to peer group rejection: If a child is labelled queer, faggot, homosexual, he will tend to believe it and finally act on it. If he is not attracted to the opposite sex he may take up the homosexual identity by default: If I'm not heterosexual then I must be homosexual.
- Physical inadequacy: too fat, thin, scrawny, under-developed.
- Poor performance at traditionally male sports and interests.
- Strong inferiority, or fear in relation to older brothers or sisters.
- Touch deprivation: Lack of same-sex touch in early life can feed into homosexual desires.
- Continual devaluation of the opposite sex, e.g. women only want to trap you.

- Adulation of the same sex: this can become sexualized at puberty, feeding homosexual fantasy.

Anything which adds to his idea that "masculinity" is too difficult or frightening for him to personally attain will tip the balance towards a homosexual orientation.

THE CHURCH AND HOMOSEXUAL SEX

The church's focus on the homosexual sex act is unhelpful.

The "same-sex love urge" should not be sexually expressed, says Moberly, but should be responded to non-sexually. The love urge is not in itself abnormal, it is merely the attempt to meet needs for love, dependency and gender identity left unmet in the process of growth. "What is abnormal," Moberly says, "is the continued existence in the adult of love needs that should have been met through the parent-child attachment, but weren't." To this I would add breakdown in peer group attachment. "It is the deficits that are against the will of God – not the attempt to meet them," she says.

To tell homosexuals to remain celibate, changes very little because they remain homosexual in their heads. A non-practising homosexual is still a homosexual. "No-one becomes a former homosexual unless and until unmet same-sex needs have been fulfilled," says Dr Moberly. "The mistake of the conservatives has been to ignore the homosexual's unmet needs, the mistake of the liberals to believe he should be able to eroticize them."

Preoccupation with the issue of homosexual sex is understandable but misses the point. Homosexuality is much more than a sex act. It also means that if a church counsels celibacy it's making an assumption that what continues to go on in a man's head doesn't matter or that the problem miraculously disappears. It doesn't.

SAME-SEX FRIENDSHIPS

It is precisely because the "same-sex love urge" is the instinctive search for missing male affirmation and gender identity, that one of the key antidotes is non-erotic friendship with peers of the same sex. "An attachment to the same sex is precisely the right thing for meeting same-sex deficits," says Dr Moberly.

> To block the homosexual urge, as distinct from its sexual expression, is to block the very process of healing... This reparative attempt is the solution and not the problem. God does not cure people of legitimate needs, legitimate needs are to be met in legitimate ways, that is to say, non sexually...

What a homosexual man needs is male friends who will relate consistently, warmly, and non-sexually with him. But that is what many straight men feel unable to do.

PROMISCUITY

As the love urge becomes confused with sex, and sexual addiction kicks in, homosexuality's fabled promiscuity is the result. In a 1978 study by Bell and Weinberg of 574 white homosexual males, 30% had had more than 1000 sexual partners, 75% more than 100. In eight out of ten cases most of the relationships were with strangers. The AIDS epidemic has pulled that figure down substantially but left to itself homosexuality is three to four times more promiscuous than heterosexuality. (*My Genes Made Me Do It!*)

Homosexual men fantasize about Mr Right – the man who will meet all their needs, but homosexuality is the slow discovery that Mr Right will never come. "We look for Mr Right, but Mr Rightaway will do," one gay man told me. One wit described promiscuity as "the search for monogamy, from bed to bed".

STABLE LONG-TERM RELATIONSHIPS
EXTREMELY RARE

The stable, long-term relationship of gay propaganda is a rare exception, and a stable, long-term, faithful relationship rarer still. Mattison and McWhirter (a gay couple, psychiatrist and psychologist) in their book, *The Male Couple*, could locate only seven sexually faithful couples among 156 male couples they could find who had been together up to 37 years, and of those none had been together more than five years. This does not appear to be because society forbids civil unions (though that is fast changing in the West) but because stable relationships are not intrinsic to homosexuality. Dr Moberly holds that the "defensive detachment" at the heart of homosexuality is in constant tension with the drive to connect, so that stability in a relationship is impossible for any length of time. A second reason is that two people intent on using the other to meet their own needs can overwhelm each other. A third reason is that an erotic relationship is not the means by which childhood and teenage emotional and gender needs are filled up, but an addictive substitute that fuels unfaithfulness. "The solution to homosexuality is to become a complete member of one's own sex," says Dr Moberly. In fact, long-lasting relationships – particularly in lesbianism – are often much less homosexual in nature.

DISCARDING A FEW MYTHS

- The homosexual is not a homosexual because of a mother-fixation. The father who is not there for his son, is often not there for his wife. Rejecting his father, the son becomes too enmeshed with his mother; neglected by her husband, the wife too enmeshed with her son. "To be attached to one's mother is, in itself entirely normal," says Dr Moberly. "But what is normal in the presence of a healthy 'father-attachment' is abnormal in isolation from it." When a boy had a good relationship with his father he never became a homosexual whatever the relationship with the mother was like, says Irving Bieber in *Homosexuality: a Psychoanalytic Study*.

- A man is not homosexual because he has an aversion to the opposite sex. He is homosexual because of difficulties relating to the same sex. The homosexual in fact, often likes women and gets on well with them, because he often feels closer to them than to men. But he can go no further. God gave woman to a man who was truly *heteros* – other/different from her. A man who is not yet fully heterosexual is not attracted to a woman to complement himself. An essential part of heterosexual gender identity development is a strong focus on the same sex until gender identity is sufficiently fully formed that women begin to appear different enough to be interesting.

- A homosexual is not cured by marriage, or by having a girl-friend. He is seeking affirmation, identity, and affection from males, not females. If marriage cured homosexuality, married men would not constitute such a high percentage (anything from 30% to 70%) of practising homosexual men. (*My Genes Made Me Do It!*) The need for same-sex love will continue even if he marries a sex symbol – it will only highlight his gender insecurity.

- The homosexual is not a homosexual because he wants to imitate women or be a woman. He may develop effeminate mannerisms but only by default, because he is failing to develop his masculine identity, not because he is deliberately cultivating a female one.

- You can't always identify a homosexual from the outside. The effeminate, limp-wristed, lisping homosexual is a 10–15% minority often avoided by the rest. Most homosexuals look as masculine as – even more masculine than – many heterosexual men; their gender insecurity is inward.

- Homosexuality can no more be exorcized than legitimate love needs. The underlying needs must be meet, non-erotically.

WHAT HOMOSEXUALITY IS NOT

Having defined what causes homosexuality, it is easy enough to say what homosexuality is not.

- It is not the one-time sexual encounter that happened a long time ago for a lark, or under the influence of drugs or alcohol. Nor is it even several of them. Sy Rogers says he can't count the number of heterosexual men he has counselled who were terrified they were homosexual or were going to become homosexual because they had had several "homosexual" experiences. Some men had carried their anxieties around for up to 20 years, becoming Christians in the meantime.

- It is not sudden homosexual thoughts or imagery, nor even thoughts that you make the mistake of turning into fantasy. "There's not a Christian man alive, who has never had a homosexual idea come to his mind, as repulsed as you may have been," says Jack Hayford, senior pastor at Church on the Way, Van Nuys, California. "Because of it, and because of all the talk that homosexuality is normal you can somehow deduce from that, 'I wonder if I'm homosexual?'"

- It is not your slender or small build, combined with your love of music, drama, the arts and humanities. It is not your sensitive nature and dislike of sports.

- It is not the orgasmic male behaviour that develops among straight men in prisons, where power, self-preservation and hostility lead to frequent homosexual rape – or in the military where women are not available. The true heterosexual reverts to heterosexual relationships once they are available.

- It is not innocent early childhood genital curiosity. "Kids playing doctor and experimenting; the effects are minimal," says John Smid, director of an ex-gay group, Love in Action.

- It is not the adolescent experience you had at boarding school.

- It is not an affectionate drawing to a person of your own sex.

- A homosexual is not the man who sells his body to males for quick money, then goes home to his girlfriend.

- He is not the man who is phobic about the opposite sex.

So why do straight men have homosexual sex?

Masters, Johnson and Kolodny in their publication, *Human Sexuality* found homosexual fantasy was the fourth most common fantasy of straight men – after replacement of their own partners, forced sex with women and watching sexual acts.

According to the Kinsey Institute's latest survey, *Sex and Morality in the US*, published in 1989, more than one man in ten is happy to have a sexual relationship with either a man or a woman.

What is going on with these men?

Remember gender researchers, Brad Sargent and Bob Hendrick (Chapter 3). Their concept of the "real man" is one capable of a self-sacrificial, open, intimate, faithful, life-long, sexual relationship with one mature member of the opposite sex. On their Threatened Sexuality Scale, Sargent and Hendrick place the bisexual (the man attracted sexually to both sexes), between the heterosexual, who is "strongly aligned" with his masculine gender, and the "weakly aligned" homosexual, as "a flip flop" between the two. Dr Moberly also suggests a spectrum running from minimal defensive detachment and unmet love needs through to the severe. "Where the same-sex deficit is less marked one would expect to find the bisexual; in the centre, the homosexual; where most extreme, the transsexual" (where defensive detachment has been so severe a person seeks a sex change).

But Sargent and Hendrick also comment that the more addicted to sex a heterosexual man is, the more the search for sexual novelty is likely to take him "over the boundary" into sex with men, or into heterosexual paraphilias: telephone and internet sex, fetishes, group sex, voyeurism.

Nor is there any shortage of enticements for straight men to try male sex. It's easy, says Frank.

> In the permissive society a greater range of sexual experience is on offer and the taboos have come off. There is no need to take time and trouble developing a relationship: no emotional commitment is required, no care or interest need be shown. No time need be involved: it can all be over in a matter of minutes, in the shopping centre, without the wife suspecting a thing. No financial commitment is required. No flowers, meals out, or gifts are needed to sweeten the atmosphere.

When Jesus addressed the Pharisees who brought a woman caught in adultery to him for stoning, he stooped in the dust to write some unknown words. There has been much speculation about what he wrote – but whatever it was it seems he wrote large on the conscience of every man there because each stole out, leaving Jesus alone with a woman he did not condemn, though he told her to leave her sin. Though the Mosaic law said she should be stoned, the Mosaic law also said those who cast the stones must not be guilty of the same sin.

A great many of us – men and women – struggle with compulsions and behaviours that, like the homosexual's, have their origins in unmet need, insecurity, loneliness, and attempts to fill our love tanks the wrong way. When we single homosexuals out for special condemnation we point at ourselves also.

But maybe you think this chapter places too much emphasis on environmental factors and makes a mistake in categorising heterosexuals with homosexuals. Perhaps there's some biological basis to homosexuality?

Note

1. From a testimony printed by Regeneration – an "ex-gay" group.

Chapter Eight

SOME MISCONCEPTIONS
Biology, psychiatry, incidence and change

Are homosexuals born that way?

For a comprehensive discussion of the contribution of genes, hormones, brain microstructure, intersex conditions and environment to homosexuality see *My Genes Made Me Do It! – a scientific look at sexual orientation* (Neil and Briar Whitehead, Huntington House, 1999, 233pp).

Researchers have tried for decades to identify a biomedical basis to homosexuality, but haven't yet succeeded.

Biology

Hormones

Numerous studies have shown that the blood levels of hormones are the same in heterosexuals and homosexuals. The only effect hormonal tests have had on gay or lesbian behaviour is to raise or lower sex drive towards the same sex. Prenatal exposure of girls to excess synthetic oestrogens and androgens has been shown not to determine female sexual orientation. Hormonal abnormalities have had no effect on sexual orientation: men who lose their testicular function and experience a dramatic fall in testosterone levels; women treated with androgens because of breast cancer, have not undergone a shift in sexual orientation. "It has never been reported that sexual orientation underwent a shift induced by the change of levels of androgens and oestrogens," says Louis Gooren in a 1989 paper critically examining biomedical theories of sexual orientation. One study has showed slightly raised testosterone levels in one third of a group of lesbians, but the study was ruled inconclusive, given that such levels could be consequent on homosexual behaviour, not causative.

Neurobiology

In 1991 LeVay, a gay researcher at the Salk Institute in California, found a part of the hypothalamus in the brain involved in controlling sexual behaviour was twice as large in heterosexual as in homosexual men, suggesting a neuroanatomic link. As LeVay himself said, the finding raised more questions than it answered, among them: is the difference a result of homosexual behaviour or a cause? The study is inconclusive. Another, since then, has been unable to replicate LeVay's findings.

The most recent studies suggesting neurobiological links are also tentative and raise more questions than they answer. In 1992 researchers apparently found that the anterior commissure – a bundle of nerve fibres connecting the right and left cerebral hemispheres of the brain – was bigger on average in homosexual men than heterosexual. But another study showed the opposite. Though attempts have been made to link male homosexual orientation to a "female"-sized corpus callosum (the largest cable of fibres linking both hemispheres of the brain) 23 studies attempting to find even male-female differences have yielded conflicting results. Tests looking for a correlation between homosexuality and left-handedness, lesbianism and "masculine" finger length ratios, are all inconclusive. Heterosexual women with "masculine" finger length ratios outnumber lesbians 60 to one, and only about 3.5% of left-handed people are homosexual and lesbian. Even sympathetic critics still concede things need a lot more sorting out before any correlations are solid – and that even then correlation does not necessarily imply causality.

Genetics

Because gays say they have "felt this way" for as long as they can remember, there has been some speculation that there may be a genetic content to homosexuality. The best indicator of genetic causality is studies of genetically identical twins in which one twin is gay. Several of these studies have been undertaken and in no case do they show the other twin is inevitably gay if one is.

The studies are contradictory and consistent with anything from a 10% to 50% genetic contribution. But if the genetic component were determinative all would have been gay. Nor do studies of family trees show homosexuality appearing in any identifiably genetic pattern through the family lineage.

The search for a biological link is often politically motivated. As LeVay said when he announced his results: "This is one more nail in the coffin of critics who argue that homosexuality is a choice and thus immoral." But the evidence is not mounting on the side of the "born-gay" theorists.

A biological link may yet be discovered but most researchers doubt it will be determinative. Anatomy is not destiny – it can have an indirect influence, but never determines.

Given the absence of any established links between biology and homosexuality we return to the psychologists. What do they say about homosexuality? Especially what do they say about the claim that homosexuals can change?

Psychiatry, Homosexuality and Change

In 1999 the Board of the American Psychiatric Association (APA) officially opposed reparative therapy for homosexuals, saying that there was no scientific evidence that reparative therapy was effective in changing a person's sexual orientation. The statement is a continuation of a line that started in 1973 when 34% of APA members voted to remove homosexuality from the *Diagnostic and Statistical Manual of Psychiatric Disorders* (DSM-II). It is no secret that the vote was taken after months of harassment by gay activists who disrupted scientific research and conferences, forged credentials and physically intimidated psychiatrists. It also gathered up a growing sentiment among psychiatrists that homosexual people did not deserve the stigma that came from being classified as mentally ill. But the effect of the vote was to put an end to professional discussion and on-going scientific research on homosexuality as a disorder, influence student training programmes and in an age of democratic freedoms and minority rights make reparative therapy a politically incorrect, discriminatory act, not the educated and popular thing to do. No medical judgment was ever made by the APA about homosexuality, but gradually pro-homosexual values were mandated for the profession by small but powerful lobby groups within the APA and other mental health groups, including the American Psychological Association – until the "no-change" policy prevailed.

The climate may be changing, however, with the May 2001 reversal of stance by Professor Robert Spitzer, who studied 200 individuals who claimed to have changed their sexual orientation. It left Dr Spitzer, a psychiatrist and prime mover in the 1973 APA decision, saying that he now believed some homosexuals could change their orientation, when he formerly believed none could. His report, predictably, met a hostile reception from gay activism.

Spitzer's study is not the only one giving evidence of substantial orientation change. In 1997 the California-based National Association for Research and Therapy of Homosexuality (NARTH) released the results of a study of 860 homosexual individuals seeking a heterosexual identity and more than 200 professionals treating them. It showed a large shift in sexual orientation. Before treatment 68% of respondents viewed themselves as exclusively or almost entirely homosexual but after treatment only 13% still put themselves in that category.

It will take some time for prevailing attitudes in the mental health professions to shift, but before the 1973 APA vote many psychiatrists were on record supporting change in sexual orientation.

Dr Reuben Fine, Director of the New York Centre for Psychoanalytic training wrote: "if patients are motivated to change, a considerable percentage of overt homosexuals (become) heterosexuals… The misinformation… that homosexuality is untreatable by psychotherapy does incalculable harm to thousands of men and women." Dr Edmund Bergler concluded after analysis and consultations with 600 homosexuals over 30 years: "homosexuality has an excellent prognosis in psychiatric-psychoanalytic treatment of one to two years duration, with a minimum of three appointments each week – provided the patient really wishes to change. Cure denotes not bisexuality but real and unfaked heterosexuality." Twenty years after a comparative study of homosexuals and heterosexuals Dr Irving Bieber wrote: "reversals (homosexual to heterosexual) estimates now range from 30% to an optimistic 50%." Pro-gay scientists, Masters and Johnson, after work with 67 homosexuals and fourteen lesbians who wanted to develop heterosexually, remarked, "No longer should the qualified psychotherapist avoid the responsibility of either accepting the homosexual client in treatment or... referring him or her to an acceptable treatment source."

Dr Robert Kronemeyer, clinical psychologist:

I firmly believe that homosexuality is a learned response to early painful experiences and that it can be unlearned... About 80% of homosexual men and women in syntonic therapy have been able to free themselves, and achieve a healthy and satisfying heterosexual adjustment.

Dr E. Mansell Pattison "eight of our eleven subjects amply demonstrated a 'cure'. The remaining three subjects had a major behavioural and intrapsychic shift to heterosexual behaviour... " Dr Gerard van den Aardweg, after 20 years research into treatment of homosexuality: "two thirds reached a stage where homosexual feelings were occasional impulses at most, or completely absent."[1]

"The homosexual's real enemy," says Dr Bergler, "is his ignorance of the possibility that he can be helped."

The influence of the landmark 1973 APA decision created a negative spiral: professionals backed away from treating homosexuality (it was no longer a disorder), so people seeking sexual re-orientation received no assistance, so no significant data stacked up showing sexual re-orientation was possible, so no-one knew it was possible, so no-one sought help.... But things appear to be changing.

WHY DO HOMOSEXUALS RESIST CHANGE?

- Because they don't know they can change and they don't know how. The homosexual orientation feels so deeply ingrained it is as if they were born that way. Earliest memories are of feeling "different" (gender non-conformity) and it seems it will always be that way. "But many gays would get out, if only they knew how," says Frank Worthen.

• Talk of change only throws up bitter memories of long, futile, guilt-plagued struggles to resist the relentless onset of homosexuality, and threatens another struggle equally as futile. Says Frank:

> There have been years of torment, they have fought a fierce battle against the identity of being homosexual, but for the sake of sanity and peace of mind, finally given up the battle and accepted what they thought they were. Then they are asked to dump the identity that came at such a high cost and since they don't believe they can change they think they are being asked to return to those hard years of indecision and struggle. There is no-one in the lifestyle who cannot make the change – but many will be too fearful to seek it.

• Once a "closet" homosexual "comes out" he trades the rejection of the straight community and the tension of the double life for the acceptance and understanding of the gay community. It's like a new beginning. He has found himself, is captivated with his new lover or searching for his dream man. He is fulfilling his fantasy. He can immerse himself in a completely gay world: do business with gay doctors, dentists, lawyers, business men, travel agents, find a gay-friendly church. The inevitable disillusionment is a long way down the track. He's having a great time. Why on earth would he want to change?

• The sexual high has become too addictive to give up. It's now inseparable from his needs for male love. The adrenaline rush associated with forbidden excitement is also addictive.

• Change is associated with judgmental Christianity. After all, homosexuality is sin. "Church!" exploded Sy Rogers

when he was first asked to come along after years as a practising homosexual, "Isn't that where God hates me!" The
conservative church is where homosexuals take a vow of
silence never to let any Christians know they are homosexual. God "hates" homosexuality and has ignored their
desperate prayers for help.

- Change is too much hard work. "A lot of people still in the
lifestyle say they would love to change if there was a pill
they could take that would transform them overnight," says
Dr Moberly. "They're not motivated to spend several years
in personal growth. It's easier to stay the way they are."

- Gay propaganda. Gay activists have constructed an elaborate justification of homosexuality, and are crusading for
recognized legal status as a legitimate minority group and
getting it. Activist gays have to fight the idea of change.
Change attacks a foundation of the gay rights agenda: a
"minority" that can change doesn't need special protec-
tions and rights. The gay lobby has to say that anyone who
claims he has changed is lying or was never homosexual in
the first place, though it can get ridiculous, as one woman
said who was told she had obviously never been gay in the
first place. "I broke up a woman's marriage, then lived with
her for seven years. How long do you have to live with a
woman and how many times do you have to make love to
her before they'll let you say you were gay?" Among those
thousands who are somewhere on the growth curve into
heterosexuality are a fair share of gays who were once
deeply erotically attracted to others of the same sex, and
often promiscuous, committed, long-term advocates of the
homosexual lifestyle.

But for all their resistance to change, gays are not happy. Most
surveys have shown that gays do not want their children to be
gay. Four independent surveys over the years 1998 to 2001 show
homosexuals and bisexuals are at least twice as likely to be alcohol dependent as heterosexuals. In spite of more gay rights,
homosexual men are still three times more likely to attempt suicide than heterosexual men – a figure confirmed by numerous

recent studies that has remained unchanged since 1978. Gays still characteristically blame these indicators of unhappiness on society's rejection. But compulsive gamblers are also six times more likely to commit suicide and societal rejection doesn't appear to be a major factor. It is true that some societies can be harsh towards homosexuality, but that is not the chief cause of gay unhappiness. The homosexual has gender needs that he is trying to meet erotically: that is the problem. Sy Rogers says nine of every ten homosexuals who write to him want to change, not because of public rejection, or even hostility, but because of an inner realisation that what they are doing is not yielding the promised satisfaction.

HOMOSEXUALITY IS NOT A CHOICE

In this age of freedom and rights some homosexuals parade with placards saying *Gay is My Choice*, but the homosexual is not homosexual by choice. He did not wake up one day and decide to be gay. He did not ask for the orientation; he certainly didn't want it. He went through misery as he slowly discovered he was not like the other guys and did not share their growing interest in women. He heard all the jokes and snide remarks about gays and knew that he had to hide what he was at all costs. He tried to date but it didn't work. He longed for male acceptance, and envied the guys who looked and acted the way he wanted to. He found himself eroticizing his longing to belong and his needs for closeness and connection and panicked. He tried to deny it, struggled hopelessly against it, but slowly came to accept the inevitable "truth".

If he had had the courage to open up to someone, he might have found help. But the chances are he wouldn't have. (I generalize to make the point.) Mental health professionals and social workers would have told him he couldn't change, and tried to help him accept his sexuality so he could resolve his conflict; the church would have looked at him sideways in distaste or confusion, or welcomed him with open arms and encouraged him to rejoice in his sexuality: God's beautiful gift. His parents would have erupted in hurt and anger and accusations, or avoided the issue, or languished in self-blame, or told him to get deliverance. His friends would have backed away. In his isolation and pain there would have been one voice he did hear: the warm, comforting, non-judgmental words of the Master Seducer: "Come to me all you that labour and are heavy-laden and I will show you other gays who will understand you and help you discover and accept who you really are." And the gay community really will accept him, and for the first time the young person with same-sex attraction will feel he belongs.

LIES, DAMNED LIES AND KINSEY

Just how many homosexuals are there?

It's because of Dr Alfred Kinsey that gay activism has argued for so long that one person in ten is homosexual – a high proportion that has lent considerable force to the campaign for gay rights.

In 1948 Dr Alfred Kinsey, the founder of the Kinsey Institute for Research in Sex, Gender and Reproduction, bowled the West over with his "scientific" study showing Americans were far more sexually permissive than anyone had believed. Among his "findings" this one: 13% of men are more or less homosexual for "at least three years between the ages of 16 and 55". Kinsey said his figures reflected homosexual orientation: "psychologic reactions and overt experience", that is, fantasy about male sex and homosexual acts. When his female study was released in 1953 the comparable figure for lesbianism was 7%. Gays averaged out the two figures at 10%.

Kinsey also drew a diagram that has become popularly known as the Kinsey continuum (Fig. 2)[2]

The appearance of the continuum is visually deceptive. It appears to place large numbers of the population in the homosexual and bisexual categories. The Kinsey continuum has found its way into full-page reproduction in educational materials for schools. What the continuum says to students and many who see it, is: if you find yourself in the bisexual or homosexal parts of the continuum that is your normal sexuality, rejoice and be glad in it, along with the many others who are like you. Which is exactly what Dr Kinsey wanted.

But the most recent data on homosexual incidence from

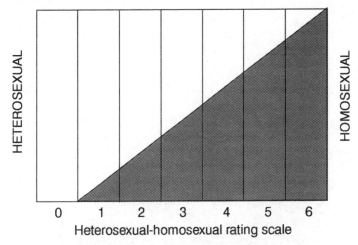

Heterosexual-homosexual rating scale

0. Exclusively heterosexual with no homosexual
1. Predominantly heterosexual, only incidentally homosexual
2. Predominantly heterosexual, but more than incidentally homosexual
3. Equally heterosexual and homosexual
4. Predominantly homosexual, but more than incidentally heterosexual
5. Predominantly homosexual, but incidentally heterosexual
6. Exclusively homosexual.

the Kinsey Institute for Research in Sex, Gender and Reproduction presents quite a different picture (Fig. 3). It shows there is a very clear clustering of the great majority of the population near the heterosexual end of the continuum.[3]

WHO WAS DR KINSEY?

Dr Alfred Kinsey was a professor of zoology who wanted to establish himself as the world's foremost sex researcher. But that was only his second objective. His first was to change society's view of what normal human sexuality was. His speciality before he turned to human sexuality was gall wasps, on which he became the world's leading expert. He was an avid and painstaking collector of statistics.

Kinsey's findings have been challenged before, but only piecemeal: the overwhelming, voluminous nature of his research, the plethora of figures, tables, graphs, defied analysis. It took 40 years for the first comprehensive critique of Kinsey's

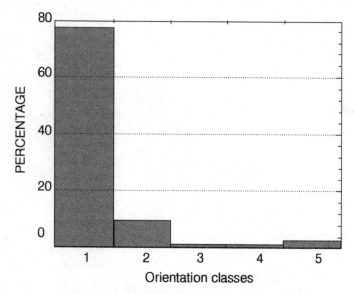

Orientation classes

1. Exclusively heterosexual with no homosexual
2. Predominantly heterosexual, only incidentally homosexual
2. Equally heterosexual and homosexual
4. Predominantly homosexual, only incidentally heterosexual
5. Exclusively homosexual with no heterosexual

1948 survey to appear: *Kinsey, Sex and Fraud*, by Reisman and Eichel in 1990. Forty years too long.

Quoting extensively from Kinsey himself, his co-author Wardell Pomeroy, and a biographer, the authors argue that Kinsey knew exactly what he wanted to say before he started his research. "His co-workers were chosen for their bias. Kinsey was a man on the way to a scientific conclusion regardless of the evidence," say Reisman and Eichel.

His aim was "to show that heterosexuality was not the norm", and to establish bisexuality as the "balanced, sexual orientation for normal uninhibited people, in effect ... (to) encourage heterosexuals to have homosexual experiences". Kinsey himself was bisexual. Kinsey advocated involvement in all types of sexual activity: incest, sex with children and animals not excluded. He wanted to create a society in which children would be instructed in early peer sex and sex with adults. He was indignant about cultural and religious restrictions on sexuality.

Kinsey's "normal" research sample of 5300 men was deliberately and heavily biased – which is why his homosexual figures were so high. Kinsey "clearly set out to obtain – or did not try to avoid – a high percentage of sexually promiscuous persons in his sample": several hundred male prostitutes, 1200 convicted sex offenders, 300 students from a high school renowned for its "aberrant" (homosexual) sexuality, inappropriately high numbers of paedophiles and exhibitionists, prison inmates, known to be highly disproportionately homosexual in activity, and calculated to be possibly a quarter of the total sample; and several hundred infants and children from two months to 15 years of age who were "criminally" manually and orally masturbated to "orgasm" by workers.

The authors say Kinsey's findings are "the most egregious example of scientific deception this century... If even some of the information we now have of Kinsey's research methods had come out 40 years ago, the Kinsey team would have been scientific pariahs instead of instant celebrities."

The Sex Research Institute Kinsey founded published another tome in 1989, *Sex and Morality in the US*, written around another comprehensive survey of sexuality undertaken in 1970. The Institute is at pains in this volume to put some distance between itself and its founder and clear this survey of impropriety. It has met with a hugely better reception from the scientific community. That and further studies in the nineties, on well randomized samples in the U.S., U.K. and some other European countries put the grand average of exclusive homosexuals and bisexuals for both sexes at 2.2%, a long way short of Kinsey's 10% (see *My Genes Made Me Do It!*). According to one recent study these figures have risen slightly to about 3.5% (see Chapter 13).

Even at 2.2% of the population the number of homosexuals in the western world is still huge – at least 35 million people – thousands of them in the church.

Notes

1. From a paper compiled by Sy Rogers and Alan Medinger.
2. Alfred C Kinsey, Wardell B Pomeroy and Clyde E Martin, *Sexual Behaviour in the Human Male* (WB Saunders Co: Philadelphia and London, 1948), p 638. Reproduced by permission of The Kinsey Institute for Research in Sex, Gender, and Reproduction, Inc.
3. Compiled from statistics drawn from *Sex and Morality in the US*, copyright 1989 by The Kinsey Institute for Research in Sex, Gender, and Reproduction.

Chapter Nine

LESBIANISM

In this chapter we will take a look at some of the causes of lesbianism and discuss women's relationships in terms of a continuum from good friendships through to lesbianism, within the context of the Christian community.

Defensive detachment

Lesbianism is an absorbing relationship between women that is eroticized, though sex is far more incidental to lesbian relationships, than to male gay relationships. They *can* be very sensual and very sexual, but their distinguishing feature is emotional intensity. A definition of lesbianism might be: a preferential adult *emotional and erotic* attraction to other women over a significant period of time.

It is common in lesbianism to find a similar breach with the parent of the same sex as we find in male homosexuality (see Chapter 7). The pattern is clear in the literature: Saghir and Robins' findings are typical in their comprehensive study *Male and Female Homosexuality*. They found only 23% of homosexual women reported positive relationships and identification with their mothers compared with 85% of heterosexual women. Drawing on her extensive counselling experience, Leanne Payne remarks in her book, *The Broken Image*: "the prime category in lesbian behaviour (is) that of the absence of mother love, or the inability to receive it when proffered". Children with reduced identification are more likely to develop "gender non-conformity", the strongest indicator of later homosexuality. Saghir and Robins also found 70% of homosexual women were tomboys in childhood compared with 16% of heterosexual women. They had no girl playmates (unlike pre-heterosexual girls), played mostly with boys and were active in team sports. Most rejected playing with dolls and showed no interest in domestic role modelling. These difficulties in feeling part of female peer groups, a default identification with males and male interests slowly widens the gap between the girl and what she needs. What Dr Moberly calls the "repressed love urge" begins to make itself felt, and the girl begins to experience strong drawings to women of the same sex to make up love and gender deficits.

None of this means that girls who are tomboys as children or have difficult relationships with their mothers will grow up lesbian. The vast majority don't. There are also other factors. But of those who do experience strong same-sex attraction, most did have negative relationships with their mothers and were tomboys as children.

Jeanette Howard, who lived for years as a lesbian, says most lesbians she deals with respond to Moberly's theory of detachment from the mother figure.

> Some say it's not true – that their relationship with their mother is perfect, but a lot of that is denial. When women say, "I had a fine relationship with my mother", I always question it, because, why are they looking for completeness in another woman?

EARLY ROOTS

Some women are aware of specific early roots of their lesbianism. As a teenager Dawn only knew that she was "forever fighting with her mother" and did not feel as loved by her parents as her brother and sisters, though she says her parents were decent and kind people. Dawn became a practising lesbian, drug abuser and "hopeless, chronic alcoholic", finally gaoled for arson. In prison she renewed an earlier Christian commitment and got a better glimpse of earlier shaping factors as she began praying through her family history: her adoption at six months, her birth to a teenage mother who did not want her. She says she had a vision. "I saw my mother beating her stomach and saying, 'I hate you, I hate you, I don't want you.'" Dawn was rejected by her birth mother and spent her first six months unnurtured by her. It didn't help that her adoptive mother was a strict, emotionally undemonstrative person: "she was shut down, she did not know how to love me".

Rebecca felt strong attraction to women for many years. It was only when she was an adult that her mother told her of an early incident consistent with defensive detachment. Rebecca had no memory of it, but when she was about three her mother was admitted to hospital for three operations. "After the last operation," she told Rebecca, "you refused to even look at me for six months."

Marion, once a construction welder and outwardly indistinguishable from a man, has clear memories of lying in bed night after night as a very young child waiting for her mother to come and say good-night, as she had promised, and never coming. "I decided I could not trust her to keep her promises." The other memory is of "screaming kids" and her mother "always working". Time for emotional nurture was obviously scarce.

Lorna's mother was simply never there. "My mother was totally engrossed in teaching. I missed out on her love; she was too busy. I spent all my life looking for the love she never gave me. My sister mothered me." Lorna grew up with so little in common with her mother that she used to wonder, "Am I really her daughter?"

Roberta and Robyn's earliest memories are of not being the boys their mothers had planned for.

TOO FAR-FETCHED?

Dr Penfield's experiments (see Chapter 4) showed that vivid detailed memories are locked into the unconscious, and felt and "relived" when they are brought to consciousness. In this context it is not hard to see that very early, forgotten, traumatic experiences, powerful enough to cause early defensive detachment, can continue repressed in the personality. But is it taking it too far to argue that forgotten pre-birth and infantile experiences can be traumatic enough to cause the defensive detachment that affects gender development – as in Dawn's case? It seems not. It is commonly acknowledged that the human foetus can experience trauma, and through the intimate umbilical connection even experience the full range of its mother's emotions. In a study of 1200 cases, Dr Frank Lake identified what he called the Maternal-Foetal Distress Syndrome. In *Tight Corners in Pastoral Counselling* he comments that a mother's joy over her pregnancy leads to foetal joy at being recognized, accepted, welcomed, but that her distress even in the first trimester "invades the foetus in the form of a bitter black flood". An unwanted pregnancy, an unwanted girl – it's recorded. Workers in the healing ministries deal at times with people clearly reliving foetal distress not accessible to the conscious mind. A 2001 British psychological study by the University of Leicester shows the foetus has full hearing by 20 weeks. Allan Schore's exhaustive examination of the neurobiology of infant emotional development in *Affect Regulation and the Origin of the Self* paints the extraordinary picture of the infant child scanning the mother's emotionally expressive face to engrave it into the neuronal networks of its developing brain in the first year. Mother

> is the major source of the environmental stimulation that facilitates (or inhibits) the experience-dependent maturation of the child's developing... neurological structures. Her essential role as the psycho-biological regulator of the child's immature psychophysiological systems directly influences the child's bio-chemical growth processes.

Same-sex defensive detachment is no light thing. Dr Moberly remarks that the same-sex love urge produced by detachment is only half the picture: the other half is hostility and anger – intrinsic to any powerful defensive reaction linked to loss of trust and love. Both can continue repressed in the personality until they emerge under pressure. Lorna (above) almost murdered her mother when she was in her early twenties. "At Christmas I nearly put a carving knife in my mother's back. I had the knife and everything. She was doing the dishes and I was about to lift it. The only reason I didn't go through with it was because I heard someone coming." Significantly, Lorna was unable to see at the time that she was angry or hostile, revealing the repressed nature of her hostility. She could only see that she was probably "disappointed".

REINFORCING FACTORS IN LESBIANISM: THE MALE FACTOR

Sexual abuse

You could say that if early defensive detachment from mother and a sense of distance and difference from other girls produces intense needs to belong to another woman then male abuse can reinforce it.

Clearly male sexual abuse does not cause lesbianism. Some clinical surveys show high levels of male sexual abuse in lesbianism: anything from twice that of heterosexual women to 75% to 85% of all lesbians compared to about 28% of heterosexuals. Taking the highest figure and given the best estimates of the percentage of lesbians in the population (about 1.7%) it works out that about nine in ten of those who have been sexually abused grow up heterosexual.

Other surveys – of non-clinical groups – appear to find no difference in male sexual abuse between lesbian and heterosexual women.

But where it has occurred – in conjunction with other factors – male sexual abuse tends to create an even stronger resistance to becoming a woman. To trust and to be a woman becomes equated with weakness and vulnerability *vis-à-vis* men. Alan Medinger, a former homosexual, puts it this way: *"While the average gay man longs for manhood, and generally gets on well with women, the lesbian does not want to be a woman, and hates or fears men."* I would add she does not always hate men. She can simply be indifferent.

But sexual abuse can feed the gender disengagement that fuels the same-sex love urge. A woman may even identify with the male aggressor in her determination to avoid vulnerability and weakness.

"Where there has been sexual abuse we find that has to be dealt with first," says Jeanette Howard. "But then, always, we get the mother–daughter issues coming up." Moberly agrees: "Opposite sex abuse issues may need more immediate therapeutic attention."

Dr Moberly is not surprised that some lesbians don't initially respond to the idea of a critical early breakdown in the mother–daughter relationship. "Much of it is repressed, forgotten, and not immediately accessible to conscious reflection. The hurt a lesbian experiences in relation to her mother may have happened at age two or three." Often "the difficulty with men happened later and was a continuing problem, so that it seemed uppermost as a cause".

Sexual abuse causing detachment

Male sexual abuse can be a factor in defensive detachment from a mother. A mother's refusal to protect her daughter from repeated sexual abuse, to even believe her, can cause defensive detachment. More so the mother who abuses her daughter upon discovery of sexual abuse. Jody Spinuzza (Desert Stream), says the maternal blind eye to abuse often presents itself as a key factor in "the kid detaching from her mother".

OTHER REINFORCING FACTORS IN LESBIANISM

Though male sexual abuse is a major reinforcing factor in lesbianism, there are others:

- The father who was "never there" to affirm his daughter's femininity (or who affirmed her as a boy).
- The father who constantly abused her mother. (Lesbians often talk about mothers victimized by their fathers.)
- The mother who defined femininity too narrowly for her boisterous young daughter, leading to a rejection of the"feminine" world.
- The mother who undervalues herself and women, making masculinity more attractive.
- The girl who simply finds Dad more attractive than Mum, and role models off him.
- The rejection of the female world because of perceived social inequalities and injustices.

Roberta

Roberta's story illustrates a string of reinforcing factors all very clear in Roberta's memory. Roberta was called Roberta because her mother had wanted a boy and only had one name ready when she was born: Robert. In her early years her mother was too ill with arthritis and a heart condition to "do as much with her as other mothers did with their daughters": Roberta felt abandoned by her mother. By eight years the fruit of early defensive detachment was obvious: Roberta was no longer modelling off her mother; her gender model was her brother: "I imitated everything he did from smoking cigarettes to dating girls." An often-repeated story of the death of her father's first wife in childbirth filled her with fear of ever having children. Filled with secret longings for a beautiful brunette in her class (the repressed love-urge surfacing) she tried to be "normal" by dating guys but her father wouldn't let her. Then her mother became a Christian and her father poured verbal abuse on her: "These times sent me into a rage. It was during this time that I decided no man would ever treat me like that." Her anger against her father increased when he "got Mom pregnant again" when she was so sick and didn't want another child. Then at 16, her "steady boyfriend" raped her.

Marion (the construction welder)

Marion put a lot of store on the unequal division of labour round home: She saw her mother slog on a poorly-paying farm with her father, then watched her father come in, "crack open a beer can, put his feet up and watch television, while my mother had to come in, cook the meal, tidy the house, tend to screaming kids, and work three nights a week". She realized that "men had it good and women didn't". But these appear to have been reinforcing factors. Well before a child becomes aware of male and female roles, Marion had already decided her mother couldn't be trusted. Her gender detachment was further strengthened by the lack of girlfriends her own age in her isolated rural town.

Lorna's dad, who should have encouraged her femininity, instead encouraged her "masculine pursuits". For Lorna (above) her father was "a blur – not there emotionally" and a "passive figure". He coloured her attitude to men. "I concluded men were incidental to my life, worthless creatures that just happened to hang round the planet: I had no respect for them." She believes her relationship with her father was only a reinforcing factor. "Really I was looking for the love my mother never gave me."

BLAME

As with fathers and sons, so much is unintentional in the development of a homosexual identity that no one thing or person is all to blame. In wilful abuse parents are more to blame than their children. Mothers are usually doing the best they can with the resources they have; when they are abusive or inadequate it is usually because of their own emotional problems.

MORE ABOUT LESBIANISM: EMOTION NOT SEX

Kaufman *et al* in the *American Journal of Psychiatry, Vol 14*, use a few words to describe lesbian relationships and sexual is not one of them. "Excessive closeness", "fusion", "too closely merged" and "symbiotic", are the words they say characterize lesbianism. This "oneness" was the "expected state they would strive to achieve and maintain through more and more closeness" – each ignoring her own needs for space as well as those of her partner. They describe a cluster of behaviours typical of "fused" lesbian couples:

> attempts to share all social, recreational and sometimes professional activities; the absence of individual friendships; little or no separate physical space for belongings, including clothing; regular telephone intrusions into the workday so that partners rarely spend even a few hours without being in contact with each other; and communication patterns that indicate assumptions of shared thoughts, values and ideas, e.g. sentences started by one woman may be completed by another.

Lesbianism is "a relationship in which two women's strongest emotions and affections are directed towards each other... Sexual contact... may be entirely absent," says Faderman in *Homosexuality/Heterosexuality*. "They will want to be together all the time," says Barbara, formerly house leader at Love in Action's live-in course for lesbian women seeking to leave lesbianism behind. "They puppy-dog one another; they're hooked at the thigh or something. You won't see one without the other."

Because sex is not necessarily a vital feature of lesbianism, lesbians often make the mistake of believing they are no longer lesbian simply because they have stopped having sex. Unless she is also sexually addicted, what the lesbian finds hardest to do is to give up the emotional addiction – because it seems to meet her unmet need for female love. Starla, a former lesbian, says the issue of sex in a lesbian relationship is irrelevant. "Emotional dependency and sex are as bad as each other... One is a sexual orgasm, the other is an emotional orgasm – what's the difference?"

THE CANNIBAL COMPULSION (ENVY, ADMIRATION)

As in male homosexuality so frequently in lesbianism: the lesbian connects intensely with the person who exemplifies the qualities she most wants for herself and at some level recognizes she lacks. In lesbianism this often shows itself to be related in some way with her mother. Says Barbara (above), herself a former lesbian:

> We get the girls to write a list of all their lovers and attributes they have in common. Once they find a thread we get them to compare that attribute or those attributes with their mothers, and over and over again they find they have been attracted to features in other women that reflect how they feel about their mothers. They either say, "This is everything my mom never was", or "My mom was like that!"

Women whose mothers were poor role models, or weak or abused, may reject that model and choose partners and lovers for themselves who are opposite: strong, domineering, aggressive, educated, competent. "They say: 'This is who I want for my image for my mom, I'll attach myself to that,'" says Barbara. "Or if their mother was aggressive or artsy or fun-loving, they might go for that. Sometimes it can be a build or a look but often it's a particular character."

Marion, the welder, was attracted to very feminine women. Femininity was something Marion conspicuously lacked, and, she admitted later, wanted to have. At the time she sought to gain it by taking a very feminine looking lover.

But what the cannibal compulsion means is that gay relationships – like all addictive relationships – are not essentially loving, they are essentially devouring, "Me-first" affairs. Though they may have the magic "click", that incredible "lock and key" quality that makes the heart feel it has come home, they are not comfortable, stable, giving affairs. Homosexuality and relationship addiction are attempts to cram a person into an emotional hole. When the needs are considerable as they often are, the relationship can collapse under its intensity because the other party is usually treating the relationship the same way.

MALE AND FEMALE ROLES?

It's popularly believed that lesbian couples have male and female roles: that one plays the part of the man, the other the woman. This is far from true. It is true that one may be "butch", the other "femme" as with Marion (above), but far more commonly lesbian relationships display the same sorts of features found in heterosexual dependency: codependency (need-meeting), and emotional dependency (meet my need). The configurations tend to be a needy one (apparently weaker) and a rescuer (apparently stronger); counsellor/counsellee, mother/daughter. Some of these could be reconstructions of the mother-daughter relationship in the attempt to find missing mother love this time around.

MANIPULATION AND CONTROL

This often characterizes lesbian relationships, as it does heterosexual relationship dependency. "Manipulation is the currency gays use to purchase relationships," says Frank Worthen. The lesbian seeks to be in control of anything that might remove the perceived source of love. Lesbians manipulate to bind others to them but also to protect themselves from being used. "Vulnerability is a hideous word to a lesbian," says Jeanette Howard.

> If I am vulnerable I am going to be abused. I have to be in control otherwise you will step all over me and use me. It's a general problem, but for lesbians, being in control is so highly developed that if I stop being in control, I don't know who I am any longer.

Jeanette has seen patterns in lesbian manipulation that resemble those found in heterosexual relationship addiction (Chapter 2). She identifies the aggressor, the victim, the server, and the cute ultra-femme, and admits to having used them all herself, often in the course of one evening. The aggressor keeps others on the defensive, withdraws favours (such as hugs or emotional support), doesn't discuss, only dictates; is unpredictable. Her demeanour, her attitudes and words show she is in charge of a relationship. The victim appeals to the protective instinct: coming across as rejected and negative, eliciting pity and rescuing behaviour. The server tries to buy love by putting people into a relationship of debt and obligation. The ultra femme exudes cuteness, loveableness and appeal, translating into, "Love me, meet my needs". "We play all the roles depending on who we are with and what will appeal," says Jeanette. "We do it because we have to be in control."

Jeanette would manipulate to inject fresh romantic interest into stale relationships by feigning disinterest and arousing jealousy. "I would stay out very late, coming home early in the morning and not saying anything. They would think I had another relationship cooking and I would have them!" Plenty of heterosexuals do the same. "In fact I hadn't been up to anything, I would just go somewhere and sit around." On that occasion she was playing the role of aggressor, putting her lover on the defensive "though I never raised my voice, and was always very controlled". But she also remembers sitting outside in the hallway all night on one occasion, too frightened to enter the room she shared with another woman. The aggressor had become the victim.

RELATIONSHIP ADDICTION BETWEEN CHRISTIAN WOMEN

Deborah Tannen in her book, *You just don't understand* (see Chapter 2), says that whereas men tend to see themselves as independent individuals in hierarchical social orders in which they are either one-up or one-down, women tend to see themselves in a world of connection, seeking closeness and intimacy, minimising differences, and seeking consensus. Key words she uses for men are status and independence and for women, intimacy and connection.

Women then, are more likely than men to look for intimacy and connection, men are more likely to turn to things that prove their mastery, prowess or status (sex, work, sport, toys). As Satinover said (Chapter 4), when we are in need of emotional painkillers we make symbolic substitutions that can become habits and finally life-dominating addictions. So whereas a man may turn to sex or work, or sport, when he is feeling inferior or inadequate, a woman can turn to relationships when she is needing comfort or tender loving care.

There is nothing wrong with close friendships with other women. They can be sustaining, warm, delightfully refreshing, hilarious, transparently honest and greatly encouraging and thoroughly mutual affairs. Women are meant to have and enjoy them.

But where emotional need enters the picture sufficiently that one person begins to look to another as an all-in-all, the relationship can become unhealthy. A woman with deep same-sex gender and love needs can attach herself to another woman who also needs to feel herself the object of another's loving focus, and the stage is set for intense mutual preoccupation that can become eroticized, that is, lesbian.

So there is a long continuum in women's friendships – with, at one end, a good, healthy mutuality, free of any attempt to lock into anybody, and at the other end emotional enmeshment that is exclusive, jealous, all-absorbing and erotic – hard-core lesbianism.

There are times when one woman needs to be, for a period, something of a mother replacement to another. But this is a managed mentoring that needs "clean" mentors. By that I mean women who are not seeking any self-gratification from the relationship in any way, and can freely let the other go at any time.

In the following cases bear in mind that lesbianism is a pattern of strong, preferential adult emotional and erotic attachment to other women. Strong emotional connection to another woman *per se* does not denote lesbianism, though may indicate some level of need-meeting you need to be aware of. It's OK to have needs, and God may be using your relationship with your friend to help meet them. If you both have strong connection, be aware that God may have given you to each other for a while, but that friendship with anyone is a gift from God that he is entitled to move you on from at any time.

GRACE AND JANET

Grace and Janet were two unmarried missionaries who lived and served together for many years, until Grace retired. It was only then that the extent of Janet's dependency on Grace emerged. When Grace retired, Janet, the younger of the two, still had some years left to serve, but she refused to stay on station without her companion. She wanted them both to retire and live together in her home country. But Grace wanted to return to her country of birth. Janet then tried to arrange a stay of indefinite duration in Grace's tiny living quarters in Grace's home country. But Grace wanted her own place and space after 40 years of busy missionary life. Janet went disconsolately to her own country and began writing long letters to Grace about her plight and struggles. Grace tried to respond sympathetically with scriptures giving comfort and strength, but soon found it made little difference what advice she offered her friend: Janet just kept on saying exactly the same things. Progressively Janet sank into a slough of despond from which Grace could not raise her. She would not return to the field, she showed no interest in working with any other mission group or using her foreign language skills in any way. She couldn't settle. She wrote that life had lost all purpose. It is risky to attribute all of Janet's depression to her dependency on Grace, but her relationship with Grace certainly bears some of the hallmarks of an absorbing relationship: her inability to make plans that did not include Grace, grief and depression at the separation, manipulation to keep the partnership together, and an inability to live without Grace or start a new life without her.

Janet's dependency hid itself well behind joint devotion to the missionary task, a close friendship, and a certain naiveté in Grace. It took separation to reveal its unhealthy side, and what we do not know is whether Janet also had sexually-tinged feelings for Grace. If she did have, she would never have dared own up to it in her denomination.

CHRISTIAN COUNSELLORS

Relationships between pastors' wives, women counsellors and counsellees can develop into strong dependency and even lesbianism. "We get quite a few people caught in the counsellor/struggler situation," says Jeanette Howard:

> The counsellor is offering the struggler love and attention she's never had before, and the counsellor herself often has unmet same-sex emotional needs that she is getting met by being needed. If the counsellor is not getting her same-sex needs met through small groups of women or if something's amiss in her marriage: if her husband is too busy, she can walk into a lesbian relationship.

Some men "not able to give emotionally to their wives are actually quite relieved their wives have an intimate friend and confidante outside the marriage," says Starla Allen, a former lesbian. Such a man has a part in the complex interplay of factors that lead to unhealthy relationships between women.

JODY

Jody was a committed Christian and missionary, working overseas with a well-known international organisation for years. She says her relationships with other girls were characterized by "emotional dependencies with a lesbian edge" from the age of nine. "I kept falling in love with my girlfriends." She knew lesbianism was wrong – "my cultural and moral values denounced it" – but the relationships continued: "intense, clinging, possessive". They always happened with women who were "more feminine" than she was, and "stronger", though on par with her "spiritually and experientially. I wasn't the codependent type – looking for someone to help, I was more emotionally dependent, wanting someone I could look up to. And I was pretty strong myself, mature and experienced, so the women I fell for were not a dime a dozen." She fantasized about the women she fell for:

> lying in bed holding one another, that sort of thing. But I tried to curtail them and I was mostly successful. My will was strongly developed. I was a strong leader. I knew a lot about bucking up, praise, warfare, intercession, arising and going forth – but emotionally I needed a mother.

On the field all her dependencies were one-way, and it was only back in the USA for a stretch that she fell into the most obsessive, intense relationship with a Christian woman on her team that she had ever experienced.

> As much as I prayed and tried in Jesus' name to contain my feelings I was overtaken by an intense power within that I could no longer subordinate. It was so heavy that had she come on sexually I couldn't have resisted it, though I was strong enough to resist initiating.

Jody didn't know what was happening. "I knew it was idolatrous, but I didn't know anything about emotional dependency. I would say to myself, 'Why can't I have a normal relationship?'"

The relationship blew up in her face. The other woman stormed at her one day, "I hate your guts. I feel smothered, get out." Jody spent hours on the beach, weeping, and months grieving. "I felt bruised, bloodied and powerless."

Then she heard about an ex-gay group, attended group sessions, and underwent counselling. "That's when the lid began to lift off my sexual suppression. What I had held down for so long by sheer will-power began to bubble to the surface and surge out towards my friends – including a pretty intense lesbian fantasy life."

It faced Jody with a new dilemma. On the advice of Christian counsellors she had suppressed her sexual struggle all her Christian life in the name of integrity and holiness, sublimating it in radical Christian service.

> *Now, in order to be truly healed I had to let surface what I had held down all of my life. How could I do this and still have Christian integrity? I had to begin to face the fact that healing was a process and we sometimes have to get worse before we get better. I decided that the most honorable thing for me to do was to be honest with myself, honest with God, and at least one other Christian. I had to lay aside my religious self in order to find real healing.*

THOU SHALT NOT KID THYSELF

Many of us have been shaped by emotional deprivations that have left us with deep longings for love and intimacy, longings that can almost overwhelm us, and that sometimes heave threateningly against the walls of our sexuality. If significant unmet emotional needs have been our lot, they will be affecting our adult relationships and behaviour. Needs need to be met, not sublimated, ignored, denied or left to hi-jack our friendships. A woman can justify an unhealthy relationship with another woman a number of ways: by arguing women are naturally more emotionally close or physically affectionate with each other than men are (true); that the real reason they are together so much is to pray, to minister together, to get or give counsel or do Bible study. She can tell herself that her friend has drawn her "closer to God". But none of these is really the heart of the matter.

Just because a relationship is not sexual does not mean it is healthy. Just because it is unhealthy does not mean it will ever become sexual. Rather, it just remains an unhealthy relationship which appears to be spiritual or necessary or justifiable – while the needs behind it remain unhealed. Needs for female love do not make a woman lesbian at all, but the more considerable they are the greater her vulnerability if the "right" person comes along.

Where defensive detachment was deep and early it can show up in hard-core lesbianism; where the unmet need is milder but still significant it can show up as it did in Sandra: in possessive, monopolising, trouble-making dependency (Chapter 2). The deeper the unmet need for female love the more likely it is to involve our sexuality – as it did with Jody.

Jody didn't run from what she discovered about herself. God took her hand and the task began, with others, of "sorting out the hurts, abuses and confusion that were at the core of my lesbianism".

OLDER WOMEN AND LESBIANISM

Vivienne Cass comments in *Homosexuality/Heterosexuality*, Kinsey Institute (1990)

It is not uncommon to see a woman who in mid-life "falls in love" with another woman for the first time in her life. This experience may not necessarily include sexual responses (but)... where a sexual component does become present this may occur after a period of time or after the emotional responses have been reciprocated.

These women may repeat the "in love" experience several times at various points in life, drifting into and out of relationships with other women. Sometimes it only happens once.

An older woman may have gone through marriage "aware that something was wrong and something was missing, that she was not able to commit to the marriage relationship fully, but not able to formulate it as a same-sex love deficit – until something happened," says Dr Moberly.

There is some evidence that lesbianism attracts a significant proportion of divorced, separated and widowed women, possibly reflected in the greater number of lesbians who have had children than gay men: two lesbians in five as against one gay man in five, according to Bell and Weinberg in *Homosexualities*.

These are women who are vulnerable. Some may feel cast-off, alone, unloved, unappreciated after years of (often sacrificial) child raising and home-keeping. Their husbands may have left them for other younger women. Hurt by men, they turn to women for comfort and strength and empowerment. Sometimes they find themselves in the company of other women who believe in the solidarity of the sisterhood.

LESBIANISM AND FEMINISM

Patty was a case in point. She drifted into a lesbian relationship after her marriage broke up:

> Feminism appealed to me very much at this point. It promised personal power to women and emotional support at a time when I felt that no one but another woman could understand me. With my damaged self-esteem, that power and emotional strength was very inviting. The step into lesbianism from there was very easy, as my determination to identify with women grew. I eventually became sexually involved with my best friend of ten years. We were fighting together for our rights as women. As she had always been the person in my life most able to understand my intimate thoughts and feelings, she seemed the perfect partner for me.

Reasonably enough, the women's movement, particularly in the seventies, drew women who wanted to reform traditional social structures to redress an unfair balance in favour of men. The women's movement has achieved many of its aims and is now a pale shadow of what it was in the seventies. But in the seventies and eighties apart from middle-class reformers the movement also attracted women who had large same-sex deficits (high levels of need for female intimacy and connection) and high levels of hostility or scorn towards men. They became the movement's radical fringe and their demands for the recognition of same-sex love initially created schisms in the women's movement. But it didn't take long for the movement to endorse a woman's right to do what she wanted with her own sexuality.

When a "straight" woman joins the women's movement, in which strong emotional ties with other women are accepted, she may come under pressure to try a sexual relationship.

Masters, Johnson and Kolodny quote such a woman in *Human Sexuality*:

> As I worked extensively with women's groups, I began to feel more and more pressure to "try" a sexual experience with another woman, the implication being that if I didn't I wasn't really into sisterhood and was enslaved by male cultural propaganda. I finally gave into that pressure and had an awful time. Shortly after that I began drifting away from the movement because it hit too raw a nerve in me.

HOSTILITY IN LESBIANISM

We have already mentioned the hostile side of the "same-sex ambivalence" in homosexuality. When an essential love source is perceived as such a source of pain that a child breaks away, then hostility is inevitably a part of the process. Hostility (lack of trust, fear, anger at loss of love) keeps the protective detachment in place. But the love-urge (the constantly re-emerging need to re-connect) is the other side of the ambivalence. When a person with a strong same-sex love urge finds her lock-and-key combination in another woman, one part of her is in heaven. She has found her heart's desire. But she also brings into the relationship her dread of loss, her inability to trust, her anger if she thinks she is about to be abandoned again. In other words, if the relationship begins to look shaky, she is never far from another defensive detachment with its load of associated hostility.

Dr Moberly argues that one side of the ambivalence will tend to be more prominent than the other and that hostility can be much more primal in a girl than a boy. A boy's relationship with his father does not really begin until *after* the essential early nurturing relationship with his mother, but a girl's detachment from her mother can occur much earlier than between a boy and his father, so that the lesbian can miss out on a lot more developmental growth, she says. "Very often there is a more extensive developmental deficit in women and aggression can be more primitive."

Charlotte Wolff in *Love between Women* finds a significantly higher incidence of "abuse", "violence", and "paroxysms of aggression" in lesbian women than in straight women, and relates it to "rejection, insecurity and frustration", but particularly to jealousy. Wolff links lesbian hostility and violence to separation between mother and infant.

Jeanette, a former lesbian, says she has watched a number of "the most horrendous lesbian fights – far worse than men fighting".

She also believes lesbian hostility goes back to "unresolved mother issues" which she describes thus:

> I want her (mother) to love me, I want to love her; she didn't. I'm angry at that. I've got this substitute here, and I'm angry that I have to have it, but I love it at the same time. I want the love, I hate her. I love you (my lover) and hate you with the same intensity because you bring up all these needs in me.

Willa Medinger, who counsels lesbians and wives of gay men, sees lesbian hostility as "just a powerful defence mechanism":

> They're people who have been terribly hurt and who are protecting themselves in order not to be killed. They're scared to death – like cornered animals. There's nothing there to be afraid of. Nothing. I just look at all their kicking and screaming and yelling and it breaks my heart, because I know that what is alive underneath all their attempts to look fierce and scare me is beautiful and terribly afraid and terribly weak.

LESBIAN RELATIONSHIPS MORE ENDURING?

It has been commonly believed that lesbian relationships are more satisfying and last longer than male gay relationships, but recent statistics do not seem to bear that out. In a study of a large sample of lesbian, gay male and co-habiting heterosexual couples over an eighteen-month period, Peplau and Cochran (*Heterosexuality/Homosexuality*), found that of all couples who had been together for less than ten years, breakups were highest among lesbians.

Why? Margaret Nichols (*Homosexuality/Heterosexuality*), suggests that lesbians move very fast from "attraction" to "commitment" (as in heterosexual relationship addiction), allowing little opportunity for partners to explore the practical feasibility of the relationship and the "inappropriateness of partner choice". Barbara (page 139) agrees: "You'll find they'll get absolutely enamoured with the *image* they have of one another though they've hardly had time to get to know each other."

When lesbian relationships break up it tends to be over an outside affair, unlike male gay couplings which usually allow either occasional or a great deal of sex with persons other than one's partner.

SUMMARY

We have defined lesbianism as a preferential adult *emotional and erotic* attraction to other women over a period of time. We have also said that lesbianism is far more emotional than sexual. According to the statistics at least one woman in every 50 or so (Christian or not) has strong same-sex attraction. Others might find they tend to get into relationships with other women that are too absorbing of the time of both, a little exclusive maybe, a little jealous if someone else appears to be as special as you want to be. The reasons women can lock together will be as varied as the locks and keys in the doors of our houses, but they will have to do with needs for love and the hope that this person or this relationship can provide it.

Friendships do meet needs. They can enrich us with good things. But friendships cannot fill up emotional black holes, and it is destructive of friendship when we expect them to. God can fill up emotional black holes, and (outside the therapeutic situation) he will sometimes use a special relationship to do it – but that situation is most advisably triangular, the mentors must be past the point of using relationships to meet their own needs, and big enough to let any hostility run off their backs.

Relationship addiction between women is little different in nature from the way women can get hooked into men, or the way men can get hooked into things, sex or status. We are still talking about attempts to meet our own needs. Unmet needs are legitimate things to have, but when we try to meet them the wrong way our relief is transitory only. A good thing is misused, and our pain comes back.

Homosexuality arises out of pain and creates more of it – not only in the homosexual but also in others. Let's look now at other people hurt by it – wives, children and parents.

Chapter Ten

FOR WIVES AND CHILDREN: PAIN

Homosexuality *causes* a lot of pain: in wives and children. But, like most people locked into the addictive panacea the homosexual is often too preoccupied with meeting his own needs to really see it.

Wives are hurt, not just because they don't understand homosexuality, but because of infidelity, lies, and – the hardest blow of all: the realization that they have never really had their husbands' hearts. Smith and Allred in a study of women divorced from homosexual men found they were different in one respect from women divorced from heterosexual spouses – they were angrier.

WHY DO HOMOSEXUAL MEN MARRY?

Just because a man is homosexual does not mean he does not have sex with women. Most homosexuals (somewhere between 30% and 70% according to several studies) are married or have been married. Homosexual men have an erotic preference for other men but they marry for a variety of reasons.

- Most want what everyone else has: social acceptance, home life and children.
- They (16%) may genuinely hope sex with a woman will cure their orientation. It won't.
- They may marry early, before the full realization that they are homosexual (30% to 60%), and then practise secretly and stay married for reasons of convenience, cover, and because they don't want to hurt wives and families.
- They marry to escape their homosexuality.

Most homosexual men (two thirds of those who marry, according to Bell and Weinberg) never tell their wives about their homosexuality. A 2001 Family Research Institute report quotes a recent study of over 200 HIV-infected men in Los Angeles, 76% of whom were practising homosexuals. Half the homosexual men did not tell their partners they were HIV+.

INSIDE A FAMILY

Carrie's husband was a secretly practising homosexual man. He decided to have another affair on the night of their eighteenth wedding anniversary. It wasn't the first time. Nine years before he had left her for a live-in homosexual affair of nine months, but was contrite afterwards. Her pastor had advised Carrie to take Tait back. But he didn't understand homosexuality and neither did Carrie. While Carrie trusted Tait, Tait took his homosexuality underground. Nine years of secret affairs and regular lavatory encounters followed, until Carrie discovered another affair. She "railroaded" him to an ex-gay group, but he wasn't interested and only continued to deceive her. After six months Carrie had had enough. She was willing to stick with him if he wanted to do something about his homosexuality but not live with his adultery and deceit. She gave him a week's ultimatum – homosexuality or your marriage – and he chose another lover.

Tait never believed Carrie when she gave him the ultimatum; he thought she would take him back as she had before. He wanted to come back. He told her he loved her. But after the statutory two years of separation were up, Carrie divorced him, against his wishes. He made no serious effort to change over those two years, so he certainly wouldn't have changed if she had taken him back, Carrie said. Ten years after the divorce Tait is still in a homosexual relationship. The lover who caused the ultimatum was a professing Christian, so was Carrie, so was Tait.

Carrie and Tait's three bright, dark-eyed children learned about their father's homosexuality over the six months Tait attended an ex-gay group. The night Tait left home and the kids had been told, Carrie asked them to write brief private notes to their father. But they were so graphic they were never delivered. Here they are, grammar and spelling unchanged:

Dear Dad, Well I've been told to tell you what I think of you and what your've done. I thought you were a really neat father in spite what you did. It wasn't a very clever idea with X you had. I'm really discusted in what you did with X. But it's your choise. If you want to go back to being gay that's all right with us because its your life your ruining, not ours. I still think about you all the time and wish so much (my heart breaks) you would go straight but is your choise. I hope you relise your've hert mum she is so badly hert I surpose you don't relise so you better think about how much mums herts. Your loving daughter Sara xxxxxx (Aged eleven)

To the thing that calls himself My *Father*. Thanks for nothing, 14 years of nothing. You couldn't wait until you were married before you had to go out and find some nice GAY man to have sex in a toilet with!!!! Oh I forgot… last year, while mum was away you left ME in charge, instead of mum while you went of and had a jolly good time with M★★★ honey!! You were such a WIMP coming to me with all your "poor me", "poor me" problems. I believed all the bullshit you told me. As far as I'm concerned your a total losing, lying, using, abusing bastard. With all the deceit you've lived behind here I was, innocent little Trixie, the *sensible reliable* little girl who didn't suspect a *thing*. I thought the sun shone out of your arse. Well F★★★ OFF. Your ex-daughter… Trixie (Aged fourteen, Trixie changed her surname in this note to her mother's maiden name.)

PS, I hope you feel good about yourself. I have enclosed a few things I don't want (from you of course) and don't try that "I still love you", "you'll always be my daughter" crapp I don't believe it. Please don't expect me to nurse you when you have AIDS! You never could keep a promise could you. When I was only 4 you promised you would never leave me, you bullshitting lier. Give my best wishes to X, but if you don't ever see him again (which I doubt) I hope you find another faggot to spend the rest of your life with. I hope you realise that your life is ruined, because if you haven't, it is. Trixie.

Dear Dad, I love you Dad. Darren. (Aged nine)

Another mother of three children whose homosexual husband left her for an openly gay lifestyle also encouraged her children to write out what they wanted to say to their father. These also were never delivered.

To Dad, I think what you are doing to us is bloody awful. We trusted you. But then to find out you run of with other men. And to think you would rather have other men than Mum. That's mean. You cover it up well because I didn't suspect a thing. When I found out I was very upset. I hate what you are doing to us. From Lisa. (Aged eleven)

To dad. (There were a number of false starts to this letter. It finally read:) How are you? you are so disusting DIS-USTING. From Karin (Aged seven)

To Dad. I think you'r inbetwen I sort of like and sort hate you. You'r just like a completly different person to me. From Kirby (Aged nine)

INSIDE A DIARY

Carrie began her diary nine months after Tait left. Some of the pages are streaked with tears, some entries are at lam, some 3am, some at 4am. Here are some of them:

... You have been my greatest love and therefore separating from you is bringing me the greatest pain I have ever known. You have been my greatest friend and companion... I have been completely loyal and faithful to you. I feel I have been betrayed by my closest friend. When I married you I was serious about committing myself to you for life and I know I have loved, honoured and cherished you to the best of my ability.

... I really really hate what homosexuality has done to our marriage. It has robbed and destroyed our marriage. It has left me bereft, unhappy, alone, bewildered, afraid and unloved. It has been like a giant octopus slowly but surely entangling us with its ugly tentacles, and then it sucked and squeezed everything that was precious and lovely and good and beautiful. How I would love to get a great big machete and slaughter that octopus and chop it into millions of pieces. How I would love to watch it die a hideous, cruel death like the death our marriage has died.

... This is the biggest, greatest saddest death I will ever die. It is saying goodbye to a world where I was a wife and we had a shared family. Saying goodbye to the person who has meant the most to me in the world, goodbye to the father of my children, goodbye to my security and support. Death is all about losses — a loss of love, of a large part of myself, of status — I am now a solo parent. I have lost a friend, a lover, a companion.

... Your relationships with R... and G, T, M, M and now R. Oh the grief and pain of each of these situations, especially M and the realisation that you were not free of your gayness. Tait, the reality of that was AGONISING, and my world came crashing down with it and I could virtually share it with no-one.

... Remember how I said, "I, Carrie, take you Tait... till death parts us according to God's holy ordinance." Well, it's a different kind of death than the death I was imagining. I thought I would be much older when I grieved for you. But it is death, all the same. I have really loved you and without you something inside me has died.

... the children got those big fabric mice that (Tait's lover) gave them and slit them open and pulled out all the stuffing and chopped them up into tiny pieces.

… I have cried and cried and cried and sometimes it feels like it will never stop… I have a great big pain… A broken leg is visible, but a broken heart is not. No matter how the disclosure is made it is the most mind-blowing, devastating information a woman can hear about her spouse. It alters the course of your life. . . It almost feels like my heart is bleeding – it's a weird feeling.

… Darren rushed in last night and said, "I love you Mum" and I know why. Because he saw his Dad again today.

… I hate what he's done. I am angry with his dishonesty, disgusted with his disloyalty, pained for the children and his lack of contact, jealous of his new love. I feel usurped, I'm unattractive, unfeminine, unloveable, not a proper woman, useless, worthless, ashamed, foolish, unhappy, sorrowful, mournful, trapped, alone. His lies, his deceit, his frustration and depression and manipulation – all directed at me.

… It really screws me up seeing him. It nearly kills me emotionally. I feel so torn. I am trying desperately hard to let go, get myself together, sort myself out. I cannot face seeing him, it's a living hell. The grief is intense. I am trying really hard to put him out of my mind when I'm at work.

… Yes, I can give myself half an hour a day to mourn him and then I'll stop. Then I'll get on with living – and not this half-cocked living. I want real living, life in all its fullness. I am sick of having an obsession called Tait like a millstone around my neck. How could one individual be the cause of so much disruption and pain and hurt. He has chosen his lifestyle, has his darling R. I am so easily replaced. God help me make speedy progress out of all this. I want to be free. I want to enjoy you. I want to bring you joy. I love you Lord. You are everything to me. I want someone's support, and I have the support of the God of the Universe. I want someone to love me and I have the love of the God of the Universe.

… I suppose the thing that hurts me most is when you said to me, "You don't turn me on, no female turns me on." That comment really undermined my femininity.

… Dear Tait… I do not put you down in the children's eyes. I encourage the children to love you, but they don't have to love what you have done or the lifestyle you have chosen. However it is your responsibility to keep the bond between yourself and the children intact − not mine. You break your word to the children and do not consider their feelings.

… I feel humiliated, abused, betrayed. The wives and children of gay men are the ones whose rights have been violated: the right to an open, honest, trusting relationship; the right not to get AIDS. I have tested negative fortunately.

… he has often said he would never have coped if I had treated him the way he has treated me.

… I will to forgive Tait and R. Lord, I really face all the hard, hard work. I see the children's pain and I see my own, and I feel Tait gets off scot-free. Free to frolic around in his new-found relationship. Where is the justice Lord?

Chris said that when she learned after years of marriage that her husband was homosexual, the "rage and sense of betrayal" was "beyond anything (she) had ever experienced". Her husband was also HIV+ and had exposed her to the AIDS virus for seven years. She tested negative.

"The impact of learning someone close to you is gay can be as great as if that person had died," says ex-gay leader, Sy Rogers. He describes the flood of emotion common to the grieving process: shock, denial, disbelief, and in its wake, a rush of shame, anger and tears, depression, even physical symptoms of distress, and "tremendous feelings of guilt": "Where did I go wrong?", to which parents and spouses in particular are so vulnerable. Then anger and resentment leading to bitterness: "How could you do this to me?", the shipwreck of expectations and hopes for the future.

Pain? There is an ocean of it. Hurt people hurt people. Pain causes homosexuality and homosexuality causes pain. Those who think it's cool to have a relative in the lifestyle are rarely spouses or children – or parents. When this view is held by close relatives it is either an attempt to preserve the relationship, or genuine (or wilful) ignorance of the causes of homosexuality. Others are remote enough from the pain to be able to be either blasé or merely fashionable in their thinking.

WHAT SORT OF WOMAN MARRIES A GAY MAN?

A woman who marries a gay man often has low self-esteem. She may marry him for any of the three following reasons.

She is insecure in her own gender identity

To varying degrees she may be ashamed or unsure of herself as a woman, undemanding and undiscriminating about the masculinity of her partner, easily pleased with the man who shows interest. She is ideally suited then to the homosexual man who is not wanting a sexually-exciting woman. Nor will she ask much of him in any way.

She may simply be emotionally dependent – clinging to a source of love

Jeff, a former gay man, was married to Daphne. "She wanted my love and approval so much that she would do anything to keep me," he says. "She was a doormat, I could cheat on her with her blessing." "I just wanted to please him," says Daphne. "Our social circle was gay and I accepted it because I felt that he loved me enough."

She is attracted to men insecure in their masculinity

In reaction to harsh fathering, a woman may be attracted to the gentleness and sensitivity of gay men without realizing that gentleness and sensitivity in gay men is often a symptom of insecure masculinity, passivity, and an over-developed feminine side. She will often be quite unaware he is homosexual.

She is codependent

She has to be needed to believe she is loved. She may marry a homosexual man knowing he is gay believing she can help him; that her love and sex with a woman will change him. One ex-gay leader says she has lost count of the number of "300 pound wonders married to great looking gay guys". He's thinking, *She won't be expecting much of me.* She's thinking, *If I just fix this little area I've got myself a real hunk.* The need-meeter who *unknowingly* marries a homosexual man may have responded to the neediness of the secret homosexual: maybe his passivity, insecurity, emotional immaturity, self-preoccupation, shyness, moodiness, isolation. Homosexual men often respond to rescuers: the strong, capable types who won't need them to lead, but will mother them.

"When you boil it all down," says Willa, former codependent wife of a gay man:

> she marries a gay man because he will hurt her, *because* he cannot possibly fulfil her. To her, conditional love is love; it's how she's learned to survive all her life. If she's codependent she goes into marriage thinking, "Somehow, if I just love him enough, he will love me"; that everything that's wrong is in her. It's the same sort of message she picked up in her home.

It's easy for the partner of a gay man to believe him when he tells her that it's her weight or her looks that are responsible for his lack of sexual interest.

According to Annette Comiskey, wife of former gay man, Andy Comiskey, many wives of gay men come from alcoholic homes and have backgrounds of sexual abuse or trauma. Often they have physical impairment. Their unconscious unmet needs are so great that, aside from relationships, many are also addicted to drugs, food, spending, work. They come to believe they are in "terrible" marriages because they are "terrible". If they aren't codependent when they get involved they can become so. "Becoming a 'saviour' is the antidote to low self-esteem," says Annette. "It's only a short step from believing you don't deserve any better, to trying to redeem yourself by taking responsibility for everything, and single-handedly trying to save the marriage and the man."

Chapter Eleven
FOR PARENTS

Wives and children are not the only ones to feel the wrench of admitted or discovered homosexuality in a loved one: parents do too.

In this chapter we will look at ways some parents have handled the discovery that a son or daughter is homosexual and offer a few guidelines.

As if I was bleeding to death...

Barbara Johnson wrote a book, *Where Does a Mother Go to Resign?* – a sort of diary of her struggle to stay alive and functioning after the discovery that her son – her *Christian!* son – was homosexual. She knew nothing about homosexuality, except that it was sin, and like a good evangelical found it repugnant. Her husband minimized it, said it was "just a phase". They said and did "all the wrong things". Her son left home and cut all contact. She was given a lot of wrong advice. She wanted to drive the car off the road; wondered if she would ever be able to think of anything but homosexuality and death; she confined herself to bed, couldn't eat, or sleep; was too proud, too scared, too exhausted from crying to tell anyone. She wondered if she was going insane, struggled with waves of nausea and choking sensations, wondered if any other mother had ever experienced what she was going through; couldn't find any other mother of a homosexual son to find out (she wondered if they had all died an early death or committed suicide), she pounded pillows and turned her parked car into a "scream chamber". She was alone and she couldn't even pray. She felt "amputated", as if her legs had been sawn off and she was slowly bleeding to death. Yet Barb Johnson was a veteran: her husband had almost been reduced to a zombie in a devastating car accident (he made a slow, but remarkable recovery); one son had been killed in Vietnam, and another in a car accident. Why, she wondered, was a homosexual son so much harder than the others? "Why does the word homosexual go round and round in my head like a needle stuck on a record?" There's not much that mothers of homosexual children go through that Barb Johnson hasn't. Barb began running a support group for mothers of gay children.

Mary Lebsock says "something died" when she found her son was homosexual, though she managed to tell her son she loved him. The "bombshell" came when her marriage was at a low point. She "became a robot", only aware she was still alive because of intermittent grief. "I would sit at the typewriter at work hoping no-one would see the tears squeezing out the corner of my eyes. I felt if I ever let go and really wept, I'd never be able to stop." She was convinced she was a total failure as a parent. She didn't want anyone else to know what had happened to her son. She had "monumental pity parties where no one came but me". She was guilty and ashamed. She bargained with God, "If you will get my son back on track, I'll go to Africa, I'll never sin again." Baking a batch of biscuits was beyond her. She totally lost her appetite – and 25lbs. "If it hadn't been for Lipton's Tomato Cup O'Soup I think I would have starved to death." One day she was afraid she was going to die, "the next day I'd pray that I would". She blamed herself, then everyone else around her; was mad at her husband. She "had personal sexual dysfunction: I could only think of what my son was doing". She was finally hospitalized, but the doctors could find nothing medically wrong. She says God found her – a Sunday Christian – at the bottom of a pit of depression with nowhere to look but up. Mary is now there for other parents of gay children.

Lydia went into "total shock" when her son owned up about the phone numbers in his wallet. "I had always believed, 'I'm a Christian, my son is a Christian. God protects our children from these horrible, worldly sins.'" She felt as though she was going to throw up. "This was my little boy. I'd never thought of him doing anything like that – not even with a woman." She went to a counsellor, but "all he could do was read me scriptures on homosexuality. Inside I felt like I was dying. I'd go to church and see normal young men sitting in front of me and I would burst into tears and have to leave. When I saw homosexuals on the street I wanted to strangle them. And there was nobody to tell me things could ever be any different."

Men process the pain less emotionally, but it is still wrenching. Pete says the news that his son was gay was a "shattering experience, like a big hole inside him was getting larger and larger". He said he reeled inwardly. "I hate that word gay. It's a lie. Powell is not really that way. Our son is too well liked, too good-looking, too loving. We're Christians." These were his first inner responses. Pete said his "inner turmoil" never really showed: outwardly he was calm, though it felt as if he would never recover. He felt intense pain and longed to be numb. And self-condemnation and guilt: "we had tried to raise our children according to the best guidance available through books, articles, and of course religious views. Where had we gone wrong?"

THE MOMENT OF TRUTH

No parent sets out to have a gay son or daughter. The question is, what are you supposed to do when you find out?

"Making this disclosure to you is probably one of the major decisions of his (her) life," says Barb Johnson.

> Your reaction will long be remembered. Get across to him that you love him no matter what. If he is caught in deep sin, willing to change, unwilling to change, or even if he is too uptight to talk about it with you, make him aware that your love does not depend on his behaviour.

"He's hoping against hope that you won't react badly," says Frank Worthen.

> He's taking a real risk. He is fearful and insecure. At this point you can lose him or win him. Now more than any other time in his life he needs your understanding and love. Thoughts will probably flash through your mind of sexual

scenes. Don't lose his love for you in a moment of revulsion. He's still the same person you've always known. It's just that now you know even more about him. Don't allow him to become a label. He's still Mike. If he were standing there with a broken leg you wouldn't call him a cripple, you would still think of him as Mike with a broken leg.

"That lovable person you thought you knew so intimately hasn't suddenly become a monster," says an ex-gay recovery group pamphlet. The best advice is: Stay calm, the world is not falling apart. Try to put yourself out of the picture for just a moment and tell yourself: my reaction right now is crucial. It's not, what am *I* needing, but what is *he* needing from me.

This is all a tall order when you're numb and dumb with disbelief and the emotions rushing through your mind cover the spectrum.

"Sons usually tell mothers because they fear their fathers' reactions, and many times they are right," says Frank.

Fathers have a lot of identity wrapped up in sons and when they hear the news they often drag up all the hurts and disappointments they have felt about their sons through the years and make broad condemning statements. It is a rare father who embraces his son on hearing the news and offers to stand with him helping him to face his problem.

Some parents kick their kids out and tell them to come back when they're straight, but rejection, hostility and angry lectures only widen the gulf.

After disclosure you need to go somewhere to fall apart – somewhere where he can't hear you. Call a close friend, beat the walls, howl in despair. Let it out. Then prepare yourself to work through the grief process.

GRIEF

The grief process is well understood now. Don't be upset when you experience all or some of the following: shock, denial and disbelief; overwhelming emotions; self-pity, depression and isolation; physical symptoms (you won't die, you only feel as if you will); panic; guilt; anger and resentment. You're well through when you're realizing life goes on and so must you, and when you wake up some days feeling better. You're almost there when life is basically back to normal and memories only sweep painfully over you from time to time.

If homosexuality disgusts or frightens you, that's OK, but as we will see in Chapter 12, homosexuality is no worse than many other non-sexual sins, some of which most of us have committed and maybe still do. In many ways our reaction to homosexuality is God showing us something about ourselves. Don't be afraid of it.

GUILT

This is a biggie for most parents. You may hang back from seeking help and understanding because you think that somewhere in the process everything is going to be hung on you. But no parent directly *causes* homosexuality (Chapters 7 and 9).

"I needed to recognize and accept that I did the best I could with what I had – right or wrong, good or bad," says one mother who battled drugs, alcohol and divorce during her daughter's upbringing. "I did not cause Sheryl's lesbianism any more than my parents caused my problems."

You *will* probably have *some* things to face about yourself in relation to your child's homosexuality, some parents a lot more than others. Each parent should honestly seek to identify and confess his/her failures *where they occurred*, but watch out for the bogey of false guilt and self-condemnation. Where you did get things wrong, God is right by your side to help. "God is bigger than our mistakes," says Mary. "He forgives."

"It may be necessary for a father to seek the forgiveness of his son for being unavailable in the son's critical times of need," says Frank. "A mother may need to seek forgiveness for being jealous and possessive of her son." If the disclosure was handled badly things will need to be put right. Where parents back away from honest self-evaluation, reconciliation and healing will be more difficult. Remember, owning up to your involvement is *not* accepting all the blame.

SUPPORT GROUPS

You need supportive, understanding and informed people around you. Join a support group for parents of gays if possible, or start one! Your church may or may not be understanding or supportive. You may have to be a pioneer. Get tapes and literature that will help you understand homosexuality – from groups that believe in change. Don't let homosexuality become an ogre you run away from. God wants you to be a parent who understands homosexuality, so you can build better bridges with your son or daughter, and help other parents.

"Support groups," says Mary, "are places where we can go and have nervous breakdowns, where we can take our masks off." They are places where you find you aren't the only person in the world with your problem – though it may feel like it. "Support groups are places where you can vent your fear, anger, frustration, learn and get healing," says Sy.

Don't let fear and pride keep you away from the people and places that can give you most help. "I was a parent in the closet with the door nailed shut," says Mary. "I did not want anyone to know about this, absolutely not!" Then Mary discovered that "Satan couldn't blackmail me any more" if she owned up. She decided to throw away her reputation and "go public".

Informed wives and parents who set up support groups to help others will be able to help their churches towards a better understanding of homosexuality. And in the process something interesting may start to happen: other people may slowly begin to feel that the church is a safe place to talk about *their* problems and addictions too.

CONTINUING COMMUNICATION

How do you continue relating with a gay son if he has left home and is homosexually active or living with his lover?

Many Christian parents tie themselves in knots trying to be both principled and loving, not knowing where to draw the line. Here are some guidelines, drawn from parents of gay children and leaders in the ex-gay movement. *The best guideline is to treat your gay son or daughter exactly as you would treat a heterosexual son or daughter living in a de facto relationship.*

- It's OK to accept a dinner invitation at his house and eat with him and his lover. (Jesus dined with "sinners".) It's OK to have them both over at your house for a meal or an evening as often as you or they wish. It's OK to drop in on each other as the whim takes you.
- It's OK if they come together to celebrate family occasions – birthdays, Christmases.

The condition for both is that there are no overt physical displays. Most will respect that. The point is your son's lover is a person worth getting to know in his own right – and a rejected one at that. Sex aside, he is also a person who matters to your son.

- Don't give them gifts as a couple: for the household. But there's no reason why his lover shouldn't receive an individual small gift from you at Christmas time – particularly if you get to know and like him. Lana, living with her lesbian lover, cried as she told me that her brother's current live-in girlfriend was welcome at all family birthdays and was given a Christmas gift, but not her lover. Her parents are Christians. "He's in the wrong as much as I am; there should be no difference. She is a person; they are not treating her as a person."
- It's OK to go out with them to a social event or concert – if it's the kind you'd go to anyway.
- Should they spend the night in your house? Opinions differ. Some say it's OK as long as they sleep in different rooms. Others won't let them pass the night in the same house. It's sense not to sleep overnight in their house while they're lovers, better if one is away.

"It's no more sinful for your son to sleep with a guy than with a girl," says Sy. "What guidelines would you have for your heterosexually immoral child? Apply the same guidelines."

"I just take the homosexuality out of it," says Anita. "Say my son is sleeping with some girl. I wouldn't like it, but I wouldn't hate her for it. She's not the problem, or the reason;

I'm not going to turn my back on him for it – or her. But they won't do it in my house."

Gay sons and daughters who see the same standard being applied across the board know they aren't being picked on just because they are gay. Generally, parents said, they don't break the rules or compromise their parents.

Don't make rules that turn your *adult* children into dependents. If they don't want to change and you tell them they can only remain at home on condition they stop all sex, go to a counsellor, and you control the purse-strings, you're playing God and the relationship will lead to deceit, recrimination and breakdown.

"As much as you can, establish communication and keep developing it, treating him/her as you would a straight son or daughter," says Sy.

How should parents relate to sons and daughters after the disclosure?

Father: You will probably feel helpless confronted with the news of a lesbian daughter and tempted to offload responsibility for support and counsel onto your wife. Don't. Your daughter needs your support, care, interest and conversation. Don't condemn her. Be her friend, reinforce her female traits and gently encourage a heterosexual lifestyle.

Try to come to grips with your role in the breach between yourself and your son. Maybe your son was incidental in a life dominated by work or other interests, maybe you favoured another son, maybe you were critical and undemonstrative, or passive and uninvolved. God may be wanting to use your son's homosexuality to reconstruct some of your attitudes and behaviour and one of the first things to benefit from that could be your relationship with your son. Remember the characteristics found to be most notably lacking in fathers of gay sons (Chapter 7).

Mother: Try to encourage the father-son relationship, though if your husband denies your son's homosexuality, or is rejecting or indifferent, that will be difficult. Try to back off from possessive, over-protective, over-involvement in your son's life.

If lack of affection and intimacy has been the nature of your relationship with your daughter, try to develop these traits.

If you have been living through your daughter or trying to make sure she reflects well on you, ease off. Try now to convey love and concern. Don't criticize her male traits, or rehearse your disappointment. Reinforce her female traits. Be patient, healing takes time.

Sometimes a gay son or daughter needs to leave home – but not because of homosexuality. "Sometimes there has to be expulsion because of the immaturity and rebellion which is often associated with homosexuality," says Sy. "My homosexuality wasn't such a big problem for my parents – it was my lying, my flouting the rules, my determination to do what they did not want me to do, my unwillingness to co-operate and contribute round the home, my lack of responsibility and my laziness. My parents had to put their foot down firmly and say, 'Cross this line and out you go.' I crossed it and out I went, and I learned the consequences."

YOU CANNOT CHANGE HIM

"Tell me what to do to change my son." This is one of the most common questions ex-gay groups are asked by parents who have just found out their child is homosexual. It's an understandable but futile one. You can't change him. He's been a long time becoming homosexual, and there are no instant cures. What is more, he has to be the one motivated to change. One of the reasons parents want a quick solution is that fixing him is the quickest way out of their pain and embarrassment. Obviously if a child is a struggling teenager who confides wanting help, or even an adult who owns up after years of painful struggle wanting help, he has everything going for him. But if the disclosure takes place when he believes the answers to his needs lie in homosexual relationships, he won't welcome your help to change. He has now given himself to the fulfilment of a fantasy. If he has also committed himself to the lifestyle and gay activism, you'll be banging your head against a brick wall talking about change. He's probably gone for some time; give him to God.

"Parents have been responsible for their children all their lives; it's hard to let go and not try to manipulate somehow," says

Sy. "But you cannot change their sexuality, make them surrender to God, or go to counselling if they do not want to."

"You can't ensure an emotionally and psychologically happy and fulfilling life for your grown child and you are not responsible for it," says Harvest, an ex-gay group, in a letter to parents. "All attempts to rescue, however sincere and from the most loving motives, can leave you emotionally drained and in despair."

But don't fall for the line that unless you support homosexuality as an alternative life-style you do not love or accept your child. That's politics and emotional blackmail and sometimes parents capitulate just to get their child back.

Nor does your unconditional love of him imply agreement that Gay is Good.

DON'T BADGER

"It's important not to preach," says Sy. "Letting them know just once that you don't approve of their homosexuality is all that it takes. They aren't going to forget your attitude. You don't have to make every visit a sermon on sin. Being nice to your child is not condoning homosexuality, it's being nice to your child. Don't focus on their sex life so much. It's only a symptom."

Children who have grown up secretly homosexual in Christian homes have been silent for good reason: they know what many Christians, and probably their own parents, think about homosexuality. They have probably prayed, struggled and sweated over their homosexual orientation for years. When they finally give the church away it's often in defeat and bitterness. In the Christian home, preaching is the very last thing that's going to work.

But certainly let your gay son or daughter know that change is possible: most of them don't know it. Without overdoing it, give them literature and ex-gay testimonies.

RELINQUISHMENT

"I was determined to get my son back on track," says Mary Lebsock.

I thought it was my Christian duty. I sent him all sorts of tracts, scriptures, Christian books and tapes – most of which, I know now, wound up in the wastebasket. I came to realize I was interfering in God's work. I was in between God and my son; this is what God showed me. He finally said, "Shut up Mom and put your son on the altar." So that's what I did, and when I did my son started to look back over his shoulder, and it was like. "Gee, she's not there any more," so he slowed down, turned around and came back towards us. That's when he realized how much his parents loved him and how much God loved him.

Sometimes you just have to wait it out, like the father of the prodigal son. Personal experience and natural consequences are sometimes the best teachers. Let God work without your intervention. God loves him more than you do.

Relinquishment is not abandonment. But, as John White says, in his book, *Parents in Pain*, it does mean yielding up the hopes and dreams you had for him, being willing to forgo any repayment for all your investment in his life, giving up your right to respectability, and hardest of all, allowing him to bear the consequences of his actions: pain, tragedy and even death.

The prayer of relinquishment is not an easy one. "I put my son on the altar and took him off so many times he got altarburn," said Mary. She sometimes worries she is not praying for him enough, but then realizes she simply has "a peace about what God is doing".

Relinquishment means you don't bail him out financially if he keeps on throwing gay parties. It does not mean that loving communication stops.

Jack said it was his parents' "unconditional love" towards him and his homosexual partner in spite of his "nasty attitude and constant manipulation" that "touched him deeply", pulled him out of homosexuality and kept him "from the final break with God". Particularly it was a letter from his father after he had told his parents he was homosexual and taken off:

"Son, I do not know what caused this situation with you but I want you to know that I love you because you are my flesh and your mother's and we want to help you. Come and talk to us any time. We love you."

Even so, it took ten years and a break-up with his lover to do it.

CONFRONTATION

This word has taken on unnecessarily combative tones. Confrontation can be gentle and in the case of homosexuality in your offspring, must be. If you suspect your child is gay approach him, but only when you are quite sure that his admission will not affect your love for him. Expect denial.

PRAYER

Sometimes in deep relinquishment even prayer stops, but generally if you can do nothing else you can pray. Mary says that in prayer God has shown her "very painful things" that happened to her son in early years. She prays for "Jesus to touch the bruises in his soul". Some parents pray for the protection of their children from AIDS; others have found their children have found their way back to a Christian commitment through AIDS. Others pray God will prevent their children having any satisfying gay relationships – but the pursuit of that elusive relationship is exactly what keeps most gays in the lifestyle. Better perhaps to pray that disillusionment sets in fast. Frank encourages parents with Job 22:30: He will even deliver the one for whom you intercede who is not innocent, yes, he will be delivered through the cleanness of your hands.

But don't impose time limits on God. Some things take time.

FORGIVENESS

Be realistic. Don't say, I forgive, before you can mean it. See Chapter 15. Forgiveness is a process, not an event. It will be easier as you begin to understand the causes of homosexuality.

GOOD ADVICE

No parents stand over the crib and say, "Let's see how badly we can mess this kid up," says Mary. But it happens anyway. These tips may help minimize the chances.

About daughters:

Mothers: Try to make sure your daughter is conceived inside a framework of love and long-term commitment. Want your child from the beginning; even if it is hard, work at it. Don't insist on a boy or treat her like one. Give her plenty of affectionate and physical nurture. Don't spend long periods separated from her, or if you have to – protect her with prayer. Don't dominate or live through your daughter, or make her feel that everything she does must reflect well on you; try not to meet your emotional needs through her. Work to make the marital relationship mutually loving and considerate. It might be better to leave an abusive marriage than remain in it if there is no improvement. If your daughter reports sexual abuse by her father or a relative don't deny it, ignore it, or abuse her for it. Investigate it, get help, confront the abuser (don't make a issue of it before the child), and make sure she gets counselling. If your daughter has been adopted, and was an unwanted or abused child beforehand, pray often for her healing and investigate tell-tale signs of rejection when you see them. Don't fill your daughter's head with anti-male one-liners, e.g. men only want one thing. Don't create in her a fear of men and male sexuality. Keep the communication lines wide open. Be available.

Fathers: If you detect clearly emerging masculine interests, behaviour and appearance in your daughter don't encourage it. If you have sexually abused her, don't deny it, get help. Sexual abuse is a strong reinforcing factor in lesbianism. Another major factor is the way you treat her mother. Be affectionate and considerate with both, don't dominate or abuse; lead lovingly, share the domestic burden, don't put women down.

About sons

Fathers, early in his life avoid long absences if at all possible. Don't be indifferent, workaholic, absentee – either physically or psychologically. Be affectionate, communicate. Don't forget, the most common complaint of gays is, "My father? I never knew him!" Set boundaries with a nurturing hand. If you've been abusive, get yourself straightened out and put things right. Be faithful to your wife. Ideally, love his mother as your life's companion and equal; that way she won't turn to your son for emotional support and intimacy, strengthening his existing estrangement from you.

Mothers: Don't want a girl, don't treat your young son like a girl, don't tell him his sex was a mistake. When he is older try to avoid an emotionally tight relationship with your son, especially if his relationship with his father is not close. Try not to be in league with him against his father.

Although the Western world has been flooded with the misinformation that change is impossible or unnecessary, parents of homosexual children can hope and pray for change. It's already happening and will continue to. Here's to some wonderful reconciliations and home-comings!

CHAPTER TWELVE

THE CHURCH AND HOMOSEXUALITY

The Anglican Synod of New Westminster, Canada, and its Bishop have authorized a liturgy of blessing of same-sex unions. (June 15, 2002 [www.anglican.ca/])

"God loves you," the preacher called to the angry gay man in the balcony. "Yes," the man replied, "but you don't."

The liberal church wants to bless same-sex unions and ordain practising homosexuals – radical conservatives want to hang them. In between, a lot of good people are very confused. Most people don't know that homosexuality has identifiable causes and that homosexuals can become heterosexual.

THE LIBERAL CHURCH

The liberals speak the language of love. Their favourite scriptures – what they know of them – are "Judge not that ye be not judged" and "God is love". Within limits, it's a bit irrelevant who loves whom, or how, as long as there is love. To love means not to condemn but to foster tolerance and acceptance. The liberal church gets indignant about words like oppression, discrimination, injustice and intolerance – words that gays say describe the way they are treated by Christians who do *not* know the way of love. The liberal church understands words like self-esteem, dignity, human rights, self-realisation, empowerment. The liberal church is educated, intelligent, and modern. It easily understands that gays are misunderstood, discriminated against and should be able to express in loving relationships the sexuality that is natural to them. In the liberal church the gay sob-story finds receptive hearts and open minds.

Hear the liberal church on homosexuality:

> "There should be no automatic condemnation of 'any sexual relations in which there is *genuine equality and mutual respect*'." (My italics.) (Instead) "we should be asking *whether the relationship is responsible, the dynamics genuinely mutual, and the loving full, joyful, caring…* "

says a Presbyterian special committee report typical of many of its kind.

The accepting sympathy that the liberal church extends the homosexual offers him only acceptance (and acceptance certainly has its merits) but it does nothing to help him out of homosexuality. Leanne Payne calls it "a false compassion that is as cruel as death". Liberal theology on homosexuality is frequently gay-aligned, and naturally enough argues that the scriptural prohibitions on homosexual acts aren't what they say they are at all. Or, if it is accepted "that the Bible clearly considers homosexuality a sin" – then "the issue is whether we do or do not accept the biblical judgment," says a Methodist discussion paper.

The church infiltrated by the gay movement is one of the movement's greatest allies, not only validating its ideological claims but promoting them as well. After all, why does a homosexual have to change when all he has to do is change the church? This is no doubt one reason why there are strenuous efforts in the established churches to highest levels to block and thoroughly discredit any evidence that homosexuals can become heterosexual.

THE CONSERVATIVE CHURCH

Conservatives, on the other hand, can be rigidly rejecting of homosexuals. Homosexual people can be told:

> The Bible says homosexuality is a perversion and the Bible is inspired by God. You can't be one of us or acceptable to God if you're a homosexual, so stop your perversion.

But conservative Christians protective of the authority of Scripture often don't realize that they are not always interpreting the Bible soundly but expressing a deep-seated attitude with roots in fear, ignorance and moral self-righteousness – conscious or unconscious.

"Whether we fear the militant nature of this (gay) subculture or their evangelistic zeal in making converts, or the threat of losing our children to them I don't really know," says Dr Don Baker in his book *Beyond Rejection*. "Many of us are downright scared by the spread of diseases related to the practice. Some fear God's judgment may fall on a nation that tolerates such behaviour. Others of us may have an indefinable fear that we ourselves are possibly latent homosexuals… "

The end effect is that conservatives ostracize homosexuals as if they were an enemy rather than people caught in a trap.

But, as they try to acquaint the church with the causes of homosexuality and wake it up to its redemptive power in the lives of people attracted to the same sex, the Christian ex-gay movement nevertheless finds the conservative church easier to bring onside than the liberal church. The conservative church at least believes in a personal God who wants to help us, a personal devil who wants to destroy us and keep us separated from God, a sin-divide that has been bridged by Jesus Christ – the sinner's friend – and power to change. And these are the realities to which homosexuality reduces in the end. But the liberal isn't sure about these. The idea that the homosexual should need to change is offensive: it implies there is something wrong with homosexuality, itself implying judgmentalism and lack of love (the two cardinal sins in the liberal church). The liberal cannot heal the homosexual. Talk to him about God's desire to meet the homosexual's underlying gender and emotional needs so that his latent heterosexuality begins to develop, and you can find yourself meeting a wall of indignation. But for all that, liberal church people are relating a lot more to homosexuals than most conservatives. The conservative church can afford to take a leaf out of the liberal church's book: the one with the words on it: interest, friendship, non-judgmentalism.

But it is only in the last 40 years – with the era's growing

endorsement of sexual freedoms, self-actualisation, anti-discrimination, human rights, inclusiveness – that the church has
embraced homosexuality with high-sounding appeals to imper-
atives about love, acceptance and a higher morality. Until then
its history was one of rejection towards homosexuals.

CHURCH HISTORY OF HOSTILITY

When "gay pride" marchers used to take to the streets in San
Francisco, one placard was always on display: *First they burned us,
then they imprisoned us, then they said we were diseased, then they said
we were demonized.* It is directed at the church and to a large
measure it is true. It was Augustine in the fourth century who
helped set the tone: homosexuality was a "shameful", "foul" and
illicit" act, he wrote, "to be understood as more damnable than
if (men or women) sinned through the natural use by adultery
or fornication" (*Corpus juris canonici*, 1144). Augustine was
quoted in the *Decretum* of Gratian of 1140 – a vast, fundamen-
tal work of church law that not only summarized a millennium
of doctrine and discipline, but set the tone for the next 800
years. The Roman Emperor, Constantine, a convert to
Christianity, prescribed the death penalty for homosexuality, and
the Roman Emperor Justinian incorporated Constantine's edicts
in the sixth century *Corpus juris civilis*, which became a basis for
European and American secular and Canon law. Homosexual
activity in the West was much rarer then than now but for those
who were discovered over the next thousand years the punish-
ments included mutilation, torture, drowning, public parades,
execution, hanging, and burning. In the 20th century homosexuals were castrated, given shock treatment, and confined to
mental institutions, often with the approval of the church. In the
seventies and eighties the big anti-gay lobby in the US church
spent millions and millions of dollars on crusades to stamp out
homosexuals.

Laws in the West against homosexuality today are benign
in comparison and societal tolerance is much more the norm,
but hostility and rejection are still abroad – not least in the conservative church. The rejection many gays feel from the conservative church convinces them that God feels the same way about

them – which is a natural enough conclusion. "Many homosexuals come to the conclusion that I came to when I was finally forced to accept the label homosexual on my life," says Frank Worthen. "I thought I had been created to be lost. Can you imagine what it feels like to think God created you to be lost?"

MANY HOMOSEXUALS IN THE CHURCH

Many homosexuals have been members of churches. About 70% of the 2000 or so gays who made their way over twelve years to Love in Action's casual Friday evening drop-in meeting in San Francisco, the gay capital, to test what might be involved in change, say that they did at one time seriously try the church but that it failed them. The meeting typically drew between 30 and 40 people each week. "These are people whose commitments to Christ were genuine and who were serious about change but who felt so rejected by the churches they joined that they drifted out," says Frank. Almost everyone spoken to on the streets of San Francisco's gay districts when Love in Action's street teams first started, had made "some kind of commitment to Jesus Christ at some time or another," he says. "But they have lost respect for the church, many are bitter and contemptuous and some outrightly hostile. Though it is generally only militant homosexuals who hate the church, many homosexuals have been bruised by it, and intensely distrust it."

But homosexuals who once were involved with the church weren't just church members. "The gay husbands of most women who call Love in Action for help are pastors, ministry leaders and pillars of strength in the church," says Anita Worthen. "The wife doesn't want anyone to know."

DENIAL

Many churches deny any of their members struggle with homosexual attraction. "But we're a Bible-believing, evangelical church – the people here don't do those kind of things," pastors say. Ah, but they do! Sy Rogers says about such pastors and officers, "I could say to them, 'Do you want me to show you my mail?'" Many people with a homosexual conflict have sat in misery through sermons against homosexuality, and become all the more determined that no one shall ever know, becoming more and more isolated, until they drop out. Christians will probably never know just how many Christians struggling with same-sex attraction they pushed a little further into despair while they made their opinions about homosexuals known in snide remarks, or jokes about "faggots", "queers" and "fairies". One ex-gay group leader told me of a man in his church who was openly disgusted by gays, but oblivious that his own son was homosexual – and obviously in no doubt what his father really thought of him.

In the ex-gay movement's experience, congregations of 200 have at least five to ten men struggling with homosexual attraction, and two to five women; another fifteen of both sexes have had some homosexual experience. Some would argue the figures are even higher in the church than in the general community, given that people often turn to religion when they're looking for answers. Certainly churches have their share of absentee fathers. Among professional people, pastors and counsellors are some of those with highest percentages of sons in the lifestyle, one Exodus official told me. Others are doctors and lawyers.

Not only are these fathers busy tending to everybody else – so that there is a high level of absenteeism – they are more judgmental and have a lot of expectations of their children, and are more often "always right", leaving a lot less room for negotiation.

Those in the ex-gay movement who speak at churches are invariably quietly approached afterwards by people with homosexual attraction who have never opened their mouths in their own churches. Chad (Chapter 6) says leaders in many respected, international Christian ministries have confided that they are HIV+ but haven't dared tell their organisations or churches. Eighty per cent of those who contact the Exodus-linked ex-gay ministries in America and Europe for help, go to church every Sunday. One third of them are married. Certainly most of those now committing themselves to ex-gay programmes for help are Christians who have had homosexual attraction for years.

"If you think you don't know a homosexual you're probably wrong," says Sy Rogers. "Someone you know or love is gay. You just don't know it." One in four families in the United States is estimated to have a family member who is sexually attracted to the same sex.

PREJUDICE

It is not uncommon in the USA that men who have left employment, and travelled across half a continent to undergo a year of ex-gay counselling in another city are not wanted back in conservative home churches, or are not permitted to serve, once the nature of their difficulty has become known. People with a homosexual struggle have been put out of churches once pastors have learned they have signed up for help for a homosexual problem; or employers have been informed. Some churches don't want association with people finding their way out of homosexuality in case people think they are doctrinally pro-gay. Many don't want the size of their congregations to shrink as indignant churchgoers leave in protest as homosexual strugglers start putting in an appearance at church services and Bible studies. Many ex-gays have memories of mothers snatching young children out of harm's way as they approach, and of men responding awkwardly. When he first began going to church, says Sy, "the women grabbed their children and said, 'My God, what is it?', and the men said, 'Well, brother, I'd hug you but I don't want you to get excited'."

Here is the general tone of several random letters on homosexuality that appeared in one middle-of-the-road Christian newspaper: "Sodomy intolerable to the Lord", "Perversions pervert character", the letters are headed. Here are key words and phrases, "Sodomy is not tolerated by God, and Sodom was destroyed... God wants purity not perversion... any orientation other than normal didn't come from God but from the devil... these people have no part in the Kingdom ... sick, diseased... nothing ambiguous about the scriptures." Decent Christian people, but their letters display the lack of compassion that comes from ignorance and fear. No homosexual looking for help would ever approach the writers. A street evangelist rails against perverts, a woman in the congregation physically recoils at the thought that an ex-gay might come and speak at a service; a young stud says he'd kill any gay who touched him.

Says Frank:

> How do you reach wounded people? If you see someone with a cane, do you shout out, "Hey, cripple! Come here, I want to talk to you about Jesus." If a person is in a wheelchair, do you shout, "Hey, freak! Jesus loves you."

There are no homosexuals, says Frank, only men and women who struggle homosexually. Why should we define a man or woman by his addiction? Have you ever read an obituary, Chain Smoker Dies in Whitehall?

ONLY ONE CHURCH IN TEN

One common estimate is that nine churches in ten don't know, or don't believe homosexuality can be changed. Here are some samples of responses people received from church staff when they sought help to deal with same-sex attraction:

"You will learn to live with your sexuality."

"God will understand."

"I'm sorry, you will have to leave my church."

"You're damaged goods."

"I don't know what to tell you."

"How would you like me to counsel you? If you want to stay in the lifestyle, fine. If you want to repent, fine."

James was told, "You can worship here but just don't let anyone know about it." Jeremy was advised: keep your feelings under control and live a celibate life. John spent two years looking for help.

> I went to a Roman Catholic priest, a psychiatrist and two psychologists, and participated in group therapy. They were unanimous: homosexuality was just another lifestyle, it was OK to practise it, and when I freed myself from my guilt, my religious beliefs and my own fear of it, then I could live a normal and happy life.

With a few exceptions, the one church in ten that does believe change is possible doesn't know how, and at the same time often forbids disclosure to the church. A lot of pastors advise, "Find a nice girl and get married!" Or they single out one particular doctrine as the answer. Then there are the "zappers". "You're a Christian now, the devil is defeated, old things have passed away, all things are new. You have power over sin, so stop it. Jesus lives inside you now and he wouldn't do that." All true in themselves but quite inadequate by themselves. "The church often wants 'zap' to work, because it is uncomfortable with the homosexual issue and 'zap' gets the person and the problem out of their hair instantly," says Dr Moberly. Sy Rogers says:

> We want them all to get fixed at the altar so we won't be inconvenienced, so we won't have to sacrifice our precious personal agendas to nurture them. But these people are emotionally crippled and unless they get nurture they will never mature – they will just go back to the gay commu- nity where they felt more accepted.

"In all cases I know of, God has never zapped anyone out of homosexuality by a simple prayer," says Frank. "Though they didn't want the orientation and desperately sought God, it still persisted." Homosexuals are not changed by "zap", though many of them would also like it that way. Working your way out of homosexuality is a process – an up and down one that takes years rather than months but slowly produces enormous changes.

Pastors and churches can be fooled by the not uncommon reprieve from homosexual urges following conversion – some- times six months or so. It seems like a miracle healing, but heal- ing hasn't even started. When temptation suddenly returns, as it inevitably does, it's just the start of classes: time for the serious work that will identify the roots of the homosexual condition. This is when the struggler needs all the help he can get, but when no one knows how to help him and when he is left most alone. Too scared to share his struggles and failures, he will tend to act healed when he isn't. If men in the church are still avoiding him – as they probably will be – he will be getting no male support. He will characteristically think he is sinning when he is only being tempted. Sure of God's disapproval, he will gradually turn again to the acceptance of the gay scene and the way things were. Or he may lead a double life; acting straight, maybe leading the church youth group during the week, but secretly living as a homosexual, for as long as he can stand the hypocrisy.

Unanswered prayer

Many homosexuals have agonized, wept and prayed and begged God to take away their homosexuality. Frank remembers at the age of 16 begging God to take his life to save him from living as a homosexual. It was almost 30 years before Frank found any answers.

Eliot, a son of missionaries, but no longer a church-goer, says he first became aware of wanting to be "really close to boys" when he was four. As a high-profile Christian teenager, and worship leader, fighting attraction to men, he spent hours on his knees, praying till he broke out in sweats, plagued with guilt. "I can't tell you the number of times I was on my knees in prayer about wanting to be different and wanting to change. I can't describe – it was agony at some stages – emotional agony." He begged God for help. It made no difference. After "a hell of a year" at age seventeen in which he finally concluded he was gay he came home to tell his mother, and his father, who was an elder. "My mother cried for it seemed like six years and said, 'How could you? How could you?' My father just pulled back, became his usual distant, clinical self – as if he wasn't really there – and analyzed everything." His pastor visited and gave him an ultimatum: Go and get prayer and deliverance and stop what you're doing, or you'll have to resign your membership. "I got a lot of judgment, I was told to pray about this and pray about that, go for runs and have cold showers and get deliverance." His former friends in the church avoided him:

> I couldn't believe how these people who had been my close friends all of a sudden wouldn't speak to me on the street; people walking straight past me, or disappearing into

shops so they wouldn't have to talk to me. There wasn't a shred of warmth or support. It would have been really nice if someone had just said, "It's OK, you're going through this and it's OK." But no, they had a public meeting about my membership and decided that I wasn't to be involved in the church any more. I was only 18. Even if people had said to me, "Look maybe we don't understand… " that's actually a lot better than people saying, "We understand." In fact for people to have said to me that they understood would have been totally patronising and too late, because I'd heard all the negative messages right from when I was a child about homosexuality. They didn't understand at all. All I got was judgment and fear and ignorance, and I don't know how people who supposedly have been loving and warm and open just… click… just like that…. When I said I lost all my friends, I lost *all* my friends, because when my parents came back from missionary service I didn't know a soul and I made my friends in the church because they were open and warm and friendly.

When he left home, Eliot said, "I got letters from my parents laying it on, 'We pray for you constantly that God will deliver you from this.'"

Not surprisingly perhaps, Eliot went into the gay scene, and became a convert to gay theology – finding no conflict between the Bible and his lifestyle. But it's clear as he talks that the Christianity he knew as a teenager was getting nowhere near the deep needs that underlay his homosexuality.

The joyous Christian life was very rarely joyous for me, and I can't say how much energy I put into trying to get this thing – this joyous Christian life. There were just all these rules and you had to do them or die and go to hell. The Holy Spirit came to give you the power to do the rules – so that your whole life was going to be a struggle of trying to get the Holy Spirit so you could do the rules. And God sat up there and if you tried hard enough to be close to him, then he would sometimes reach down and give a little stroke and that would be a spiritual buzz that would happen about once every couple of years to keep you going.

Eliot had been craving male love for a long time, love from his father, love from God. His concept of God mirrored that of his father – distant, aloof, unaffirming. He remembers doing many things to try to get his father's approval but never succeeding, just as he tried to win God's approval but felt he never succeeded there either. When he finally concluded he was gay, and his support system crashed around him, his relationship with God – built as it was upon rules and earning God's love – was too fragile to hold him. Thousands of other genuine Christian men and women who are homosexually attracted will talk just as Eliot has, of striving as hard as any Christian could reasonably be expected to, against something they didn't understand and didn't want, trying to follow Christ and live a holy life, while they felt the church was their foe rather than their friend. Eliot's church is just like so many churches – full of good and genuine people – who don't know how else to respond.

HOMOSEXUALITY – ONE OF THE WORST SINS?

Those who believe that homosexuality is worse than most other sins will at some point appeal to the Bible. They will say that the Bible talks of homosexuality as a "perversion" or as an abomination with no equal in scripture except perhaps in bestiality. They will quote the destruction of Sodom and Gomorrah for homosexuality, and note that sodomy got its name from Sodom. They will quote Romans 1, concluding from it that homosexuality is some sort of ultimate defilement and that a man who is homosexual is a man God has "given over", that is, forsaken.

A PERVERSION?

Let's have a look at these words and passages. There are four New Testament references to homosexuality, and in three of these the New International Version calls homosexuality "perversion", and homosexuals "perverts". The fourth reference is translated: homosexual offenders.

In the first, in Romans 1:27 the word "perversion" is the translation given to a Greek word *plane* which otherwise means only "to stray". Mainly the word is translated "to err". Other renditions are only "to turn away from, or into its opposite", to "turn inside out", "to deceive", "to delude". Why should *plane* suddenly come to mean "perversion" when applied to homosexuality? If *plane* were to be consistently translated perversion, then the words of Jesus, "You are in error (*plane*) because you do not know the scriptures" (Matthew 22:19), would turn us all into perverts.

In the second, 1 Timothy 1:10 the word translated "perverts" is a word *arsenokoitai*, strictly meaning, male and coitus (from its original meaning, bed), in other words simply "male intercourse". It does not mean perversion; that is the word the translators chose. In the third, Jude, the word translated "perversion" literally means "going after other/different flesh" (*sarkos heteras*). The translations "perversion" and "perverts" from these three Greek words, as applying to homosexuality, cannot be adequately defended.

AN ABOMINATION?

Nowhere in the Old Testament does a Hebrew word meaning "perversion" apply to homosexuality. Instead the word abomination is used. Ahah! So what's the difference then? More than you might think. Because the word for abomination *toebah* – a word that means abhorrent, loathsome, disgusting, detestable – is applied to many other things besides homosexuality. Homosexuality is certainly not in a class all by itself. What are some of the other things the Bible calls *toebah*? (I exclude the more obvious, such as idol-making and idol worship, temple prostitution, child sacrifice, bestiality.) Here they are: partiality, unjust gain, pride and haughtiness, deceit and lying, creating division and discord, letting the guilty go free and condemning the innocent, meaningless and hypocritical prayers, greed for gain and love of money, taking sin lightly, superficial spiritual healing, adultery, incest, spiritism and divination, oppression of the poor and needy, robbery, failure to honour agreements and keep promises, lending at excessive interest, the death of the innocent, thoughts of harm to another, readiness to do harm or create trouble. Homosexuality is in good company!

The pattern continues into the New Testament: Romans 1 lumps homosexuality in with all sexual impurity (fornication and adultery), and a catalogue of other sins including envy, strife, deceit, malice, gossip, slander, insolence, arrogance, boasting, disobedience to parents, faithlessness, heartlessness, ruthlessness. If the Romans 1 passage is to be considered a progression into depravity that culminates in homosexuality, the argument doesn't stand up: homosexuality is well towards the beginning of the slide. To be "given over" by God to homosexuality does not mean to be eternally forsaken; it simply means to be given free rein to do what you insist on doing. It is as if God says, "OK, if that's what you're bent on doing, go ahead." It does not mean damnation, perdition or eternal hopelessness. It should be noted that God does not "give over" (*paradidomi*) people only to homosexuality. The identical word is used in v24 of any sexual immorality. If we are intent on doing it, God will let us do it. In 1 Timothy 1:10 homosexuality appears alongside adultery as one of a number of things that "wholesome, healthful" teaching opposes. In 1 Corinthians 6:9-11, homosexuality is again in good company: it is only one of a number of things that prevent possession of the Kingdom of God in the here and now – meaning that if we are totally given to a pattern of gratification it has a way of absorbing our energy and diverting us from Kingdom living and building. In this passage homosexuality weighs in alongside the sexually immoral (*porneia*, a general word for any sexual intercourse outside the marriage bed), idolatry, adulterers, thieves, the greedy, drunkards, slanderers, and swindlers. In Jude 7 homosexuality is found alongside *porneia* again.

It is clear that homosexuality is not a sin apart. It is one of many that God considers alike. The homosexual is not irredeemably damned to hell any more than are adulterers, fornicators, the greedy, cheats or the malicious. Homosexuality is not a sign that God has forsaken anybody – unless he has also forsaken those who are engaging in other kinds of sexual immorality (a large percentage of the Western world). God came in Jesus Christ to save sinners – and each of us is a sinner turned to our own way. Homosexuality is reversible – as evidenced by the hope that shines out of 1 Corinthians 6:11 "that is what some of you *were*". If homosexuals cannot be saved, why are they in Paul's list of those able to be "washed, sanctified, and justified in the name of the Lord Jesus Christ"... and, evidently, *changed*?

WHAT ABOUT SODOM?

But what about Sodom? God destroyed Sodom because of its homosexuality! Did he? In Genesis 19:13 we read that God came to destroy Sodom, and the statement juxtaposed as it is with the account of the men of Sodom's attempts to have sex with Lot's "male" guests, gives rise to the widely held belief that God destroyed Sodom for homosexuality. But Jude 7 goes a little further: it mentions *sexual immorality* (generally) and "going after strange flesh" – commonly held to be homosexuality, as reasons for Sodom's destruction. But the Book of Ezekiel is clearest about the reasons – even categoric: "Now this was the sin of your sister Sodom: She and her daughters were arrogant, overfed, and unconcerned; they did not help the poor and needy. They were haughty and did detestable things before me. Therefore I did away with them as you have seen" (Ezekiel 16:49,50). It is interesting to note that the list of Sodom's sins echoes the things God called abomination. Sodom was destroyed because it practised abominations – not because of homosexuality alone. And let's not forget, God razed his Holy City to the ground as well and it wasn't for homosexuality.

If you still think that homosexuality is worse than anything else, why might that be?

- It may simply be that you think I have argued selectively from scripture. After all anyone can make a case for anything if they just pick the right verses. OK – have a good look yourself.
- It may be that you have a well-established view of homosexuality that goes back to your earliest years, absorbed from your family, your friends, your church, your community. None of these sorts of opinions changes fast.

- You may have kept your virginity and lived a clean and moral life. You have obeyed the rules and done things the right way. Homosexuality shocks you. Perhaps you have slowly forgotten or never really known, that God's love is not dependent on how good you are.
- It may be that you are one of those who is frightened – without grounds – that you have homosexual tendencies, and just don't want to get too close to the subject. Talk of homosexuality at all, or of opening the church doors to people from that lifestyle is threatening. (Check *What homosexuality is not* in Chapter 7.) You may have some simple misconceptions about yourself.
- Maybe you had sex with another guy when you were fooling around one night. Now you have sudden flashbacks and wonder if you're a secret homosexual – even though you're married or have a girlfriend. A heterosexual man may have male sex once or twice in his life for all sorts of reasons (because he's drunk, for a dare, etc.) but it doesn't make him homosexual in orientation. You need to get hold of that fact, talk to someone about that sexual incident, ask God for forgiveness, and let it go.
- Maybe you are heterosexually immoral but object to the idea that your kind of immorality is as objectionable to God as homosexuality. "I might have my weaknesses but at least I'm not homosexual!" The scriptures disagree with you.

HYPOCRISY ABOUNDING

Before the current "Don't ask, Don't tell" policy came into force in the US military it used to have a bar against conscription of homosexuals; those discovered were discharged: from 1943 to 1990 between 80,000 and 100,000 gays and lesbians. But during Operation Desert Storm the Pentagon suspended most investigations because all hands were needed at the front lines. Hundreds of admitted gay soldiers and reservists went off to the Gulf. In some cases they were told that once the fighting was over they would face discharge when they made it back home.

Naturally enough, gays shouted hypocrisy. But gay servicemen are no better – they lie about their sexual preferences when they sign up, pretend they have female lovers, or marry women they do not love to conceal their orientation. Many homosexuals are married and going to great lengths to conceal their orientation and their sexual encounters from their wives. Is that any less hypocritical?

Society's hypocrisy is one it doesn't even acknowledge. Men visit prostitutes and commit adultery and sodomize women every day yet believe their lust is holier. I quote from an article in a 1990 edition of *San Francisco Bay Guardian* by an angry columnist. The writer is very frustrated with a man named Hamill and writes:

> Hamill writes, "Homosexuals were constantly on the prowl, looking for kids who were drunk, lonesome, naive or broken-hearted..." Hamill and his friends responded like Real Men and as a result, "There was often violence, some gay men smashed and battered into the mud outside a tough joint after midnight!"

Says the columnist:

> As Real Men they probably also prowled for young *women* who were drunk, lonesome, naive or broken-hearted. But that's different I guess. Sleazy gays are worse than sleazy straights because they're, well *gay*. And it must be more OK for men to take advantage of women than of other men, because otherwise you'd surely find huge piles of *straight* men smashed and battered into the mud outside tough joints at midnight.

Twenty-five years ago, Los Angeles plain-clothes police in unmarked cars used to hunt down homosexuals, literally from doorway to doorway. Or police would converge on a gay bar, arrest patrons, throw them into paddy wagons and lock them up for several days. But while all this was happening city authorities were actively involved in prostitution rackets.

COVER-UPS IN THE CHURCH

Somehow you'd expect things to be a little better in the church, but it's not. While the church promotes chastity and celibacy on one hand, it has tried to conceal sexual indiscretion, homosexuality and sexual abuse on the other. It is easy to understand the church's persecution of homosexuals and its cover-up. It persecutes out of ignorance and self-righteousness. It conceals because it hasn't wanted to be found out and it hasn't wanted scandal: one sexually active man covers for another, then another, in case they're all exposed. It conceals because it wants to hang on to otherwise good and gifted men and because there is a need for compassion, correction and another chance for those who err. *The Kansas City Star* in February 2000 reported the story of a popular Jesuit college president who was also a highly respected community leader. He was also a closet homosexual. His death certificate said his death was linked to AIDS. But the college said only that he died of severe respiratory problems.

The rash of revelations in 2002 of homosexual activity in the Roman Catholic priesthood in the USA is no surprise really, yet, typically, there have still been attempts to disguise it. The media have used the words child sexual abuse, sexual abuse and paedophilia; they have carefully avoided the word homosexuality. Yet only 0.3% of the Roman Catholic priestly "sexual abuse" cases that have received publicity have been with children, according to Philip Jenkins (a long time researcher in the field) who merely echoes all who have studied the cases together. All the rest (99.7%) have been with post-pubertal young men. In other words this particular crisis in the Roman Catholic church in the West is about homosexuality in the clergy. The rate of paedophilia (sex with pre-pubertal children) is no higher than in the rest of the population.

In the main the church doesn't know how to handle homosexuality in its clergy because it doesn't understand its causes or know the extent of change that is possible. Particularly in the Roman Catholic Church, people think change stops at celibacy. But, increasingly, in some quarters, the church doesn't want to hear either. It's easier to invoke a liberal theology that accepts homosexuality than talk about redemption of mis-directed sex drives. It's easier for heterosexuals who are inappropriately sexually active to give their blessing to same-sex unions than agree they might both need some help. But without belief in change, all that remains is continuing unresolved homosexual struggles in the priesthood – at high rank and low – the loss of trust of millions of adherents, millions of dollars more in civil damages pay-outs, good priests condemned by association, and conversion to a liberal theology that weakens the church's power and opens to the doors to more homosexual candidates.

But the knife cuts two ways: why criticize the church for persecution of gays and concealment of homosexual clergy when gays are just as persecuting and hypocritical? What is gay hostility towards the church if it is not a kind of persecution? What is the homosexual double life if it is not a cover-up? *The Voice of Integrity*, a magazine for gay Episcopalians, tells the story of X, a Methodist Bishop who died of AIDS. According to *Integrity*, X was a frequent and homosexually active patron of gay bars, who managed to deceive his wife and family for 46 years. But X was also "an outspoken conservative" who always voted in favour of the church's repudiation of homosexuality and against ordination of "practising homosexuals" to the ministry. Is that not hypocritical?

Nor is it just straights versus gays and vice versa. Those of different sexuality look down their noses at each other. One ex-gay group leader told me about a male transvestite (a cross-dresser) who called for help and was mightily offended at the idea that he might like to sort through the roots of his sexual inclination with a group of homosexuals.

NUMBERS IN THE CLERGY

In March 2000 *The Times*, London, reported AIDS deaths within Church of England clergy were ten times higher than in the general population, and estimated that in some parts of the country as many of 20% of the clergy were actively gay. A similar confidential survey of 3000 US Roman Catholic priests undertaken by the *Kansas City Star* in 2000 found priests were more than three times more likely to have HIV or AIDS than the general population. If these reports are to be believed, then something between 10% and 30% of Church of England and Roman Catholic clergy are homosexually active in Britain and the USA. Anecdotal reports from students studying in two of England's foremost institutions of higher learning in the last 20 years say a large minority of men training for the Church of England and Roman Catholic priesthood and living at the university Halls of Residence were homosexual. Joseph Kramer, a homosexual man who attended an all-boys Jesuit school and later trained to be a Jesuit priest says in his 1992 book *Gay Soul*, "certainly the vast majority of Jesuits are homosexual". At the Jesuit seminary he attended, he remarked, twelve of the fifteen students were homosexual, and at least half of the students there had sexual encounters with one another. Heckler Feltz, in the February edition of *Ecumenical News*, 2000 quoted a survey in which 15% of respondents – all clergy – said they were homosexual, and 5% bisexual – much higher than percentages in the general population. Tom Roberts, managing editor of a leading Catholic newspaper *The National Catholic Reporter* remarked in 2001, "The church knows there is a significant gay population among the clergy… (It) also knows some are sexually active. (But) it refuses to engage in any significant discussion about sexuality."

Numbers of homosexuals in the clergy could be expected to at least reflect the incidence in the general population (about 3%), but the evidence is mounting that numbers are much higher than that, particularly in the Roman Catholic Church, where men can live in an all-male environment and never have to answer awkward questions about why they aren't married. There is no question gay activism is deeply engaged in trying to change the church's theology on homosexuality and a vocation in the church is one way to bring that about. Some homosexual clergy will be celibate, some will be trying to be celibate, some will be actively involved in the lifestyle whether they are single or married.

SUPERIORITY IN THE CHURCH

Probably the worst feature of the hypocrisy of which all parties are guilty is the way clerics and laity can roundly condemn homosexuality while they are privately heterosexually immoral.

The New Zealand Government has been passing gay rights legislation for years now, and, of course, it has had its opponents. Early in the debate one of the most well-argued, succinct and meaty submissions from the conservative church against homosexuality and gay rights came from two pastors. It was also one of the most uncompromising and hard-line. It was only afterwards that it became known that the writers – both married men – were having affairs at the time they made the submission. One stepped down from the ministry voluntarily – when the woman talked – the other had to be pushed.

But perhaps this one carries the prize: a young Christian homosexual man – the son of a pastor in the conservative US Bible Belt – getting help with an ex-gay group said he found some porn in his father's closet. He tackled his father: "Why are you reading this stuff?" His father's response, "Well, as long as I don't lust after it, it's not sin."

People with homosexual attraction often believe they can't change, and by and large the church hasn't helped them see it any differently. According to the Kinsey Institute in *Sex and Morality in the US*, "devoutness" is the single "most powerful predictor" of attitudes towards homosexuality. "Our finding is that the more religiously devout people are, the more likely they are to hold *highly negative* attitudes towards homosexuality" (my italics). It's OK to have negative attitudes towards homosexuality (it's not God's design for human sexuality), but it mustn't stop there, because Christians are the one group of people who have the greatest hope in the world to offer.

Those church-goers who see nothing wrong with ecclesiastical liturgies blessing same-sex unions are simply making the equal but opposite mistake. Having a highly positive attitude towards homosexuality is like throwing smiles, kisses and handfuls of candies to someone caught in a tar pit, then walking away and leaving him there.

Chapter Thirteen

GAY ACTIVISM AND A BETTER RESPONSE

People can become anxious when gays press for gay marriages, adoption rights, promotion of pro-gay values in schools and acceptance of homosexuality as a normal alternative sexuality. Conservative Christians can start to use words like abomination, perversion and hell – alienating liberals and gays. The lines are drawn and battle commences.

Aversion to the gay agenda is understandable, gay activism *does* intend to progressively transform the nature of society. But moral indignation doesn't work. There is a better way.

WHAT IS GAY ACTIVISM?

Gay activism is the attempt in the West to create a society in favour of homosexuality as a normal alternative sexuality and to gain as many heterosexually equivalent rights and privileges for gay couples as possible. This is achieved by bringing powerful people and institutions on side: celebrities, politicians, community leaders, the media, government departments, local authorities, the legal and healing professions, the educational establishment at all levels and the church. Here are some of the stated objectives of the gay activist agenda:

- acceptance of homosexuality as a "normal" alternative sexuality.
- status for homosexuals as a legitimate minority and legal protection from all discrimination.
- homosexual marriage (gay holy union) and rights to the same legal benefits, pensions and tax advantages as married couples – or the next closest – "domestic partnership"

legislation. Many countries in the West are opting for domestic partnerships in which gay couples ostensibly live lives indistinguishable from heterosexual couples, except they lack a civil marriage licence, religious blessing (though many churches now give their blessing) and the ability to naturally procreate.

- passage of "anti-vilification" or "hate crimes" legislation. Though on the surface this is intended to curb malicious activity directed at any minority group, gay activism intends to exploit it to prevent any negative comments against homosexuality. Anything which a gay activist could consider "threatening" or "insulting" causing "humiliation" or "hurt feelings" could be ruled an offence. It's already on the way: in 2001 the Human Rights Commission in Canada established a precedent by ruling in a case before it that scriptures used against homosexuality were inherently anti-gay.
- the redefinition of the family and facilitation of divorce to prepare the way for gay couple and family groups.
- rights for gays to adopt and foster children and removal of bars to child custody and visitation rights based on sexual orientation.
- incorporation of pro-homosexual ideology in school curricula.
- sex education to portray homosexuality as a valid, healthy lifestyle and viable sexual option, with encouragement for students to explore "alternative lifestyles". (Sex education has unanimous gay endorsement.) In the USA teenage students have been taught how to insert fists up rectums, urged to try a good gay experience or tell others about their gay fantasies, sixth graders are being asked to understand their sexual orientation – all with state funding.
- sexual freedom for all.
- repeal of all laws governing the age of sexual consent.
- repeal of all laws prohibiting sexual soliciting and prostitution.
- military recruitment of homosexuals.
- elimination of data files on individual's sexual preferences.

- state funding of gay organisations helping "oppressed" gays.
- an end to differential treatment of homosexuals by insurance companies.
- continuing exposure of the media and theatre to gay themes and use of the media to present a positive image of gays.
- equal media time and column-inches as all critics.
- promotion of moral relativism (it might be wrong for you but not for me), liberal humanism and blurring of sex roles.
- promotion of pornography as a means of satisfying human need.
- careful use of language for most appeal to the right power blocs, e.g. minority, love, alternative lifestyle, discrimination.
- the passage of pro-homosexual legislation.
- pro-gay measures passed by executive decree rather than democratic process.
- appointment of homosexuals to all government bodies.
- denial of state funds to discriminating groups, e.g. religious schools.
- support of gay or pro-gay candidates for political office.
- the ordination of homosexual clerics and wide spread acceptance of gay theology within the church.
- educating the public to believe AIDS is a discrimination issue.[1]

THE NATURE OF GAY ACTIVISM

Hostility towards any attempt to show there is a way out of homosexuality

Audiences at public meetings will often give gays a hearing, but gay activism rarely returns the courtesy. Gentle Dr Moberly, speaking at a learned medical society in London on the subject of her research, needed police protection, and gays constantly harassed her through the lecture. "All I was bringing them was good news," says Moberly. Scientists and psychiatrists have been on the other end of terrorist threats and hate campaigns. If anti-gay campaigners use the same tactics, gays will accuse them of discrimination.

Jim Johnson, a Roman Catholic lay minister and former homosexual who gave up a successful real estate career and sank all his livelihood into several hospices to care for dying homosexuals with AIDS at a cost of only $16 a day (compared with hospital charges of $800 a day and up), said gays fire-bombed his hospice, threatened his life and tried to run him out of business because he claimed he was a reformed homosexual. "If I had to make a choice between dying in the street and dying in his hospice, I'd choose dying in the street," said the incumbent executive director of the National Gay and Lesbian Task Force, Jeffrey Levi.

An ex-gay ministry in New Zealand which inoffensively advertised itself in the personal columns of the local evening newspaper, "Can gays change? For confidential counselling, telephone xxx", was literally deluged with nuisance and obscene phone calls running at 60-70 a day for seven months – until the police took action that ended in a court appearance for one offender. Many – logged on the answer-phone – were explicitly vile.

A few posters pasted up at the University of Kentucky showing a co-ed group of cheering ex-gays under the heading, "Can gays change? We did!" were torn down and called the most "homophobic" discrimination that gays on campus had ever experienced. They were immediately replaced by pro-gay posters while angry protests were made to the University Chancellor (who apologized to the campus' gay movement). A great threat is implied by the word "change".

Dishonest argument and dirty tricks in the campaign for acceptance

Noel, a leading gay activist in New Zealand in the seventies, remembers inventing cases of discrimination against gays to help the gay case for legislative reform forward. He wouldn't be the only activist to believe the end justified the means. I know firsthand the efforts that have been made to discredit our own work by using fabricated names, credentials, and letterheads and book reviews. What gay activists have done with AIDS is one of the 20th century's con jobs. Gays argue that discrimination against gays produces more AIDS casualties, on grounds that where homosexuality is not legal gays will not present for AIDS prevention education and will be too depressed to have safe sex. But in the new millennium, in spite of enormous leaps toward acceptance of homosexuality in the West, millions of dollars spent on AIDS education and high levels of knowledge of AIDS transmission routes among gays, HIV and AIDS is climbing again in the gay community. The Department of Public Health in San Francisco – one of the most gay-aware and gay-tolerant cities in the world – is now reporting a sharp rise in HIV infections and a doubling in rates of unsafe sex from 23% in 1994 to 43% in 1999. A 2000 review and discussion by Kalichman of numerous studies showed one in three HIV infected men and women is having unprotected sex. In May 2001 the US Centers for Disease Control reported a substantial increase in new HIV infection among young gay and bisexual men.

Something is driving the hunger for connection through sex that gay men and women seek that is stronger than the deterrent of suffering and (at this stage) inevitable death that await anyone who contracts the HIV virus.

Rejection in response to rejection

A report in 1981 in the *Wanderer*, a Roman Catholic publication of St Paul, Minnesota, described a gay parade that focused on a New York City cathedral and finished by leaving it "ablaze with signs and banners" – among them "God is Gay". The gay flag, decorated with fifty sex symbols, hung from its portals. Gay men have started mock religious orders: the sisters of Perpetual Indulgence, Sisters of the Guiltless Procession: among them Sister Sleaze, Sister Missionary Position, Mother Inferior.

DENIAL AND JUSTIFICATION AND NEEDS TO BE LOVED

What we see in the gay activist agenda is highly refined denial and justification of the kind that attends any well-established life-dominating behaviour – as we discussed in Chapter 4. Where we are unable to re-visit the influences that have fashioned us, we prefer to hang on to our survival kits. With the flood of media reports *purporting* to show that the survival kit is in fact biologically hard-wired, there is loss of hope. (See

My Genes Made Me Do It! for a thorough discussion of biological contributors to homosexuality.) About one third of gays now believe they were born that way – a 400% increase in 50 years.

The person attracted to the same sex comes to believe he *is* "homosexual". What do people do who cannot understand why they are the way they are and haven't been able to change – though they tried for many years? Some finally become activist and fight for the right to be accepted, to love and be loved and treated as any other member of society. The problem becomes society's attitude, and the object to change it.

Now, remember the contributors to homosexuality – often a "defensive detachment" from the parent who is the natural gender role model, rejection by peer groups who would otherwise be reinforcing gender identity, often sexual abuse (and broken trust), loss or absence of love, feelings of being different or unacceptable, insecurity, isolation, fear, defensive behaviours, anger, anti-authority attitudes. Condescending moral censure from any quarter on top of years of guilt and futile struggle against a developing homosexual orientation, can understandably finally stir all this up to produce violent antagonism. Having felt something is wrong with them all their lives, they refuse now to believe it any longer. They will begin to fight furiously for acceptance – sometimes with lack of principles.

Gay attitudes towards the conservative church in many ways just reflect what they feel they have experienced. Frank Worthen spent years mad at the church because of its "total rejection" of him. "Like an animal that has been wounded, but not killed, there is a rage inside you that wants to lash out at everything and everyone indiscriminately," he says. How do you gain the trust of a wounded and snarling animal? Not by kicking it. The moral crusades against homosexuality incited Christians against homosexuals to the point where compassion was blocked. Jerry Falwell, leader of the Moral Majority at the time is on record, urging, "Stop gays dead." Naturally enough gays countered with banners that read, "Stop the church before it stops you." The Moral Majority had a three-point programme to combat homosexuality: evicting, firing and jailing homosexuals. But it was the Pharisees who hounded the immoral – not

Jesus. "Can you imagine Jesus mounting a moral crusade to drive the prostitutes out of Israel?" says Chad.

Here's another illustration of what happens when Christians get morally outraged: Dr Virginia Uribe at a special dinner supporting "Project Ten" – a project launched in the eighties to introduce gay-sensitive curricula and counselling into schools. Dr Uribe, a lesbian, is urging her audience to take courage and get behind the project.

> Where will we get this courage? THEY will give it to you. The Lou Sheldons, and the Jessie Helms and the Bill Dannemeyers will make you fold or they will make you strong. THEIR vicious attacks will sharpen you. The hate-mongers will make you more resolute. THEY will do it to you. THEY'LL get you so mad you'll see blood. And just in case you weaken, groups like the Concerned Women of America, the Coalition of Traditional Values, Focus on the Family, the American Freedom Coalition, and the Eagle Forum, or the Heritage Foundation will surface, and they will do it for you. THEY will give you COURAGE because they will tap your rage.

Sy Rogers dissolves into helpless laughter as he tells this story from the American mid-west. "Some churches would stand outside the gay bars burning a cross, throwing stones, verbal and literal, their megaphones screaming, 'You're sinners, you're going to burn, you're going to burn.'" The gay response was to start "Holy Roller Madness Night" with costumes and contests, "Look like your favourite evangelist", and "Most famous Evangelist Hairdo". It became a camp party. Every time Christian teams turned up to picket the gay bars, free drinks would be turned on for the gay who would go and get a tract against homosexuality. "The Christians were totally ineffective," says Sy. "All they did was throw up the gay defence mechanism, that barrier that will shut you out no matter how much good you have to say."

SO WHAT DO WE DO?

One of the best things the church can do – across the board – is to begin to understand the causes of homosexuality. It produces compassion and identification rather than aversion and rejection in conservatives, and – if liberals can bring themselves to do it – can help them see that the desire to help homosexuals change does not necessarily have its origins in rejection and lack of love. It does not mean conservatives have to agree with or accept homosexuality as a lifestyle.

Workers with Sy's group – mainly straight college students – didn't picket gay bars, they went into them. Often they spent weeks just talking. They said, "We just want to talk and get to know you and understand you because God loves you." Slowly gays opened up. "Thousands weren't being saved," says Sy, but gradually gay bar managers and activist leaders made referrals from their bars and gay churches to Sy's ex-gay groups and made its materials available. "I've had many people who are pro-gay theologically and politically call me up and say, 'Make no mistake, I am politically pro-gay'," says Sy. "But I want you to know that I understand you want to help people and I want to make your materials available because I know there are a lot of unhappy gay people."

"Christians need to present the good news of reconciliation, not the code of ethics," says Sy.

> The code of ethics is "Homosexuality is sin – If you don't stop it, you'll pay" – which is true. But you can go into any gay bar and whether gays are bitter and militant or whether they're honest and crying in their beer, they will tell you that they know what they're doing is wrong from a biblical perspective. They just don't know what they can do about it.

Sy says he remembers very little of what Christians told him as a transsexual, "and I had people preach to me every ounce of knowledge that they knew against homosexuality from the Bible". What he does remember is the way they treated him. "People thought they could say all manner of ugly things to me

– as if it didn't matter, because I was only a queer." Those who "ministered" most to him were "people who treated me like I was anyone else, who weren't afraid to be seen with me in a public place. I felt like I had a little value." The revolution in Sy's life came when he realized he "was the object of God's love and affection. All my life I wanted to be the object of love and affection from a man. All the time I was trying to meet that need in the wrong way. Then I found God was jealous over me. I kinda liked that."

GOD WANTS TO REDEEM MORE THAN SOMEONE'S SEX-LIFE

"Christians look at homosexual sex as if it is the only obstacle between a homosexual and God," says Sy, "But God wants to redeem more than somebody's sex life. You don't bring gays to Christ by attacking their sex lives. If they got their sex lives all cleaned up and that was it, they'd still be in trouble. I tell them, 'Your sex life isn't my business, but you can be free from your anger and your hurt and your fear.'

"The important thing is that they're seeking God with all of their hearts. If they find that God is approachable and interested in them and wants a relationship with them, they'll give up their sex life, when the Holy Spirit convicts them.

"I assume some heterosexuals were sexually immoral before they became Christians and they would have found it ludicrous if a Christian had approached them and said, 'The only barrier between you and God is your sex life.'"

"Gays are very sensitive to being singled out just because they are gay," says Frank.

They think Christians are glad homosexuals have AIDS, and many of them are. They believe they are going to be condemned, shouted at, told to "stop it" or that "zap" will change everything. They expect to be told to be celibate – a very threatening prospect when sex has met their needs for closeness for so long. They often believe Christians are earning their salvation, or working for some wealthy evangelist. It's wise to put aside the gay issue and allow them to bring it up – which they most certainly will if you talk for any length of time. Don't immediately focus on their gay orientation or argue the point of whether a gay person can be saved, but see them simply as you would any other person who needs Jesus. Offer hope of change – because most gays don't believe it's possible; they've only read and heard the stories of gays who failed to make it out and returned to the lifestyle – never the success stories. But, be honest – let them know that it's not instant and it will not make life easier. Stay away from politics. Remember that gays are angry with fundamentalists. Use non-specific tracts.

POLITICAL ACTION?

Should Christians write to MPs, local authorities and school boards, organize delegations and write letters to editors against implementation of the gay agenda? Of course! But keep it low-key and courteous and stick to the facts and to the point – which is the issue of change. It lets a lot of decent, confused people know that the campaign for gay rights is often falsely premised.

But make sure you're seeing things clearly. Anti-discrimination legislation is not all bad. It's perfectly reasonable that people should not be thrown out of their accommodation or their jobs because someone discovers they have a homosexual orientation. Homosexuals are no worse or better tenants or workers than heterosexuals. You can argue a distinction: that there should not be discrimination against homosexuals in housing, employment, education, or public places, but that there should be exemptions for religious or ethical belief that is sincerely held and is not malicious or arbitrary, e.g. a private landlord should not be forced to rent his accommodation to a gay couple if it is against his ethical principles. You can argue special anti-discrimination privileges are normally granted on the basis of an immutable characteristic (like skin colour) and that homosexual orientation does not come into that category. You can argue that currrent statistics do not support gay disadvantage in housing, education, employment, or wealth, but rather advantage. Ex-gay groups themselves generally shy away from political action. "If we take a lot of 'stands' we create such hatred that when gays need us they will not come to us," says Frank. "You can't reach people you're fighting against." But there is need for deftly-targeted, political initiative from groups who know homosexual orientation can change. Gays target the political establishment; so should those with the counter-message: change. A series of advertisements introducing the concept of change of sexual orientation to the US public in 1998-1999 through TV and major daily newspapers was highly effective in this regard. They created a lot of interest in a society that was hearing only the opposite. They also, predictably, stirred up a lot of antagonism in the gay activist community.

POLITICAL ACTION IS WORTH TRYING, BUT OFTEN FRUITLESS

Enrique Rueda in *The Homosexual Network* argues that political and community leaders are frequently considerably more liberal than a typical cross-section of the country they represent. The thing is – they are in power and the constituency isn't, regardless of the democratic ideal. When most members of the ruling caucus have decided it's time for a change, they have a way of ignoring whatever reaction runs counter to their own agenda so long as it is not powerful enough to remove them from office. The gay agenda is riding in on the human rights bandwagon and no Western government wants to pass legislation that might be perceived as anti-minority, anti-individual freedoms and non-tolerant. When it comes to the gay agenda, society is now tolerant enough that Western governments can afford to ignore the political initiatives of small groups who try to say, for example, that children raised by gay parents do not emerge as well adjusted as children from heterosexual relationships. Usually, when legislators are ready to introduce pro-gay legislation, it's already too late to stop it. Western governments might listen to a majority voice that says gays should not be permitted civil marriage licences, but they will find another way of doing much the same thing through domestic partnership legislation.

Unless you have powerful friends in high places, or a chance to tip the balance on a close thing, you'll have more success working at grassroots levels and slowly altering attitudes there. It's a long, slow job but once a value becomes majority popular opinion, democratically elected governments rarely risk antagonizing it.

Don't count on a fair hearing before social issues committees in moderate to liberal churches. Stories of heavily biased pro-gay theological investigations of homosexuality are legion. But try anyway and stick to the issue of change. With the church hierarchy it's often best on a one-to-one basis. Two spokesmen for the ex-gay movement asked for a chat with an Anglican Archbishop after Archbishop X had put his signature to a circular supporting a Christian Gay Conference. Highly sceptical at the outset of reports that homosexuals could change, he told them afterwards that he was now open to being convinced.

PETITIONS, PROTESTS?

If you do plan to join demonstrations or protests against the gay agenda – be positive and stick to the subject: change. During the first Gay Freedom Day celebrations in Marin County, California, the Church of the Open Door held a silent prayer protest, but their 30 to 40 placards were not of the usual variety. They read: "Can homosexuals change? We did!", "You don't have to be gay", "Gay? you have a choice", "You can change", "Yes, the way out of gay: Jesus". Later, they took their banners to Main Street during a gay parade. "Our object was not to condemn or be judgmental," said Pastor Mike Riley. The church's "counter-statement" made the front pages of the local newspaper. "The church has to be politically involved at some level," Mike maintains, "but it's true – if you go too far you only polarize the parties."

THE MEDIA

The electronic media often sets out to exploit adversarial positions between pro-gay and anti-gay factions and in that context even compassionate advocates of change can still come across looking like homophobes. That said, exponents of change and articulate ex-gays speaking from personal experience can come over strongly in popular television shows exploring controversial issues, and in radio talkback shows. It's also educational viewing and listening for those millions of people who have never heard that gays can change. I remember clearly the stunned silence on air when an ex-gay group member called up a radio talkback show featuring a lesbian guest and said, "Hello, I used to be gay." The host spluttered, the guest spluttered and a lot of listeners would have said, "Did you hear that? *Used* to be gay?" Humour can help the case along: Sy Rogers, still showing vestiges of earlier effeminate transsexualism was ribbed about it by the popular former US talk-show host, Phil Donahue, and immediately retorted: "Listen Buster, I'm light-years away from pink panty-hose." Invite your local newspaper to interview someone who used to be gay. Offer a feature article on change. Use it to advertise your support meetings.

THE EX-GAY

If anything is undermining the idea that gays are entitled to all the rights and privileges of heterosexuals because they are born that way, it is the existence and slowly increasing visibility of support and recovery groups for people with a homosexual orientation and the simple stories of people who once were gay.

HOMOSEXUALITY ON THE RISE?

There is some evidence now of a rise in homosexual incidence in the West. Numerous surveys in the years 1988 to 1990 put the incidence of exclusive homosexuality and bisexuality at something round 2.2% of the adult population. But a recent study in the *Journal of Sex Research* (2001) argues sex between women has gone up fifteen times between 1988 and 1998 and doubled among men over the same period. In absolute terms the increase is not great: among women a rise from 0.2% to 3%, and among men from 2% to 4%. The author, Butler, cites positive media images of gay people as a factor and increased earning power by women – giving them freedom to opt for family structures that exclude men.

Another major factor is unprecedented sexual permissiveness in the West, and a vastly increased tolerance towards homosexuality along with a loss of moral bearings. This has several implications.

- Young people are more prepared to experiment sexually.
- In this climate common phases of heterosexual development, e.g. same-sex crushes or envy and admiration, are more likely to be confused with homosexuality. Young people may give themselves that label or be encouraged to wear it by gay-positive mentors thus fostering a gay identity and homosexual encounters.
- Adults in emotionally barren heterosexual relationships might be more easily persuaded than before to try a same-sex relationship.

The factors that cause homosexuality are probably also more prevalent in Western society now than they used to be. Marriages are breaking up at higher rates, there are fewer first-time marriages and more cohabiting couples and there are more serial partnerships. In other words there are more children separated from parents or in insecure family environments. In big cities and stressed work places, father absenteeism could be on the rise.

But the indignation of Christians does nothing to lower the incidence of homosexuality – it only makes the gay community – and often the general community – more rejecting of Christians.

It may help concerned Christians to know:

- The vast majority of homosexuals are not gay activists. They are, as Frank says, "still in the closet, going about their daily lives unnoticed, often deeply wounded and discouraged, and causing no one any trouble".
- The proliferation of pro-gay groups is far more apparent than real. They are often the same very active but limited group of people. The same names keep coming up.
- The media comprises a disproportionate number of pro-gay and gay producers, actors and journalists whose focus on the subject can make homosexuality appear much more

pervasive and accepted than it is. That said, media images certainly alter public perceptions.

- Gays can gain all the rights they want but it will make them no happier. An alcoholic can drink all the alcohol he wants but it doesn't help him in the long run. Chronic same-sex needs for love will not be healed by domestic partnership legislation and artificial insemination. Gay relationships will continue to be short-term and unstable and (particularly for men) unfaithful, whether gays are entitled to civil marriage licences or not. If they become stable, they will also have changed in nature and become less "gay" or "lesbian". Homosexuality is symptomatic, not innate.

JACQUES

Chad (Chapter 6) tells the story of Jacques. Jacques was a hospital chaplain and gay activist – a board member of a Gay and Lesbian group in Maryland. He had heard of Chad's ministry to hospitalized people with AIDS and wanted to see Chad, who expected the worst. "I thought he was coming to investigate us to get us out of Johns Hopkins hospital."

Jacques arrived, sat on the sofa in Chad's home-cum-office-cum-drop-in centre and looked squarely at Chad. "Why are you doing what you're doing?" was all he said. Chad told him the story of his struggle with homosexuality, his dread he had AIDS.

> I told him what God had done in my life. Then suddenly without my saying anything Jacques fell on his knees by the sofa and began sobbing. All he could say was, "God help me, please help me." I just put my arms around him and I hugged him and began praying for him. I prayed God would give him wisdom and direction to deal with his homosexuality. I didn't tell him what to do one way or another. He told me he was sexually involved with a Catholic priest and had been for several years.

Chad heard from Jacques the next morning at 11am.

He called me, he was so excited. He said, "The most amazing thing happened last night. I was standing by my bed and I saw Jesus on the cross. He was looking down at me and saying, 'Jacques, I do love you very much and I am going to help you.'" He told me he had resigned from the leadership of the Gay and Lesbian group and that he had phoned the Catholic priest and told him he could no longer see him on the same basis.

Two months later Jacques phoned again. This time it was a dinner invitation.

Over dinner he shared with me that he had been in touch with his wife whom he had divorced four years previously, and that his wife had agreed to see him again and that they would be dating. He was very excited about that. He'd also got involved in a professional counselling programme to help him with the issue of his orientation. Only a few months ago he phoned me again and said, "Chad, congratulations are in order. My former wife and I are engaged to be married."

Anti-gay attitudes from Christians give homosexuals one clear message: God does not want you. There is a better way. Christians can get better acquainted with homosexual people on an individual basis and start to gain an understanding of why people become homosexual. Genuine same-sex friendship and acceptance is one of the best things Christian heterosexuals can ever offer a gay person.

The level of heterosexual immorality and dysfunction within the church leaves Christians in no position to be condescending towards any other groups – let alone gays in particular. The church that reserves only fire and brimstone for homosexuals misses God's agenda by miles. And the church that celebrates homosexual love as one of God's good gifts is about as ineffectual.

Note

1. From *The Homosexual Network* by Enrique Rueda, and the Chicago Convention of the National Coalition of Gay Organisations (1972). It is a testimony to the power of the gay lobby that most of this agenda is already in place in many states and countries.

PART THREE:
HEALING

Chapter Fourteen

HEALING AND THE UNCONSCIOUS

Can I really hope to be any different? Me? A relationship addict? A food-addict? A Don Juan? An over-achiever? A compulsive masturbator? A workaholic? A homosexual?

Yes.

Don't lie to me!

I'm not lying.

Listen, I know myself and how long this thing's been around and how much I tried to stop it before. It didn't work. Don't hand me your pious promises. You Christians are just a lot of religious, condescending humbugs.

Yes, I know. I'm sorry. We're working on it. We haven't been able to help you because we haven't known how to heal ourselves. We haven't even known how sick we are.

God hates homosexuals anyway.

Wrong.

He hates homosexuality.

God hates anything that enslaves and masters us.

I'm not enslaved! I do it because I want to!

Wrong, you do it because you have to, not because you want to. That's the nature of all addiction. And we remain addicts if we aren't mastered and healed at our core by the love of Christ.

In this chapter we will discuss the loss to the church of the cure of souls, and look at ways to access the unconscious mind with its memories of the incidents that keep us caught in behaviours we can't understand. We will look at ways to bring healing to these places.

Respectable Christianity

People who were formerly gay have had to come to terms with the idea that something deeper has been driving them, that they have been meeting these needs the wrong way and need to set about meeting them the right way.

Those who are working their way out of homosexuality often show many of the rest of us up in a rather superficial light. We're not too good at recognising and doing much about our own deep-seated and often secret drives and stubborn addictions, so we're not equipped to help people with same-sex attraction do much about theirs. Usually, it's not that we don't want to; it's just that we don't know how.

The mental health profession – psychiatrists, psychologists and counsellors – have become the new practitioners of healing arts that were really bequeathed to the church.

The loss of the Great Physician

The Great Physician walked the earth 2000 years ago with good news for the poor – us. He had a mission to fulfil: the Isaiah mandate. Jesus said it of himself: to heal and bind up the broken-hearted, to make the blind see, to free the prisoners, deliver the captives: those who are oppressed, downtrodden, bruised, crushed and broken down by calamity; to comfort all who mourn and grieve, to give beauty for ashes, gladness for mourning, praise for despair (Isaiah 61:1-3). Wide-eyed with wonder the disciples saw, heard, touched, and tasted it all. They were right there with Jesus. "That which was from the beginning, which we have heard, which we have seen with our eyes, which we have looked at and our hands have touched," said the Apostle John. They lived with a Miracle for three years and watched him perform them every day. The experience engraved itself in their hearts, minds and lives forever.

But then Jesus returned to his Father who sent him. The man they had touched and seen and heard and talked to wasn't there any more and one by one the disciples who had been with Jesus died.

But in Jesus' last days on earth he uttered a paradox. I am going, but I am staying, he said in effect. I am going back to the

Father but I will still be with you – forever. You will still be able to touch me and see me and hear me. I will still appear to you. But this time I will be *in* you, not just with you (John 14:20, Amplified Bible). Jesus was speaking of the Holy Spirit whom the Father could not send until Jesus left. "… in that day… you will *see* me" (John 14:19), Jesus said.

Today's believer has more than the early disciples ever had. Today the Spirit of the Father and of Jesus lives *in* us, and, if we will allow it, we will – in another dimension, certainly, and sometimes vividly – also see, hear, and touch him. And in our lives and through us he will continue to fulfil Jesus' Isaiah mandate: heal our broken hearts, and set us free.

To encounter Jesus in this way through the Holy Spirit, in the deep places of our souls is to begin to remove the roots of our addictions, our mental, moral and emotional infirmities, and our psychosomatic disorders, which many psychologists believe constitute something between 30% to 90% of all health disorders.

Those of us with many life-dominating and compulsive behaviours that have not budged despite years of Christian belief, and the thousand things we have tried, are often crying out for the kind of intervention that Jesus Christ can bring. But we usually don't experience Jesus in this way in the evangelical church. Why not?

The very short answer is that evangelical spirituality is a "practical, rational, non-mystical, intellectually-based, theological spirituality", says David Benner in his book *Psychotherapy and the Spiritual Quest*. "Its activism and rationalism have tended to make it mistrustful of deep inner experience with God, and may be the reason for its frequent shallowness." A full answer would take books. The barely adequate answer is something like the following.

THE SCHISM BETWEEN "HEAD" AND "HEART"

Leanne Payne, in her book *The Healing Presence*, talks of the schism between head and heart: that "dreadful twentieth-century disease" that afflicts everyone "from the college professor to the ditch-digger". "Head" and "heart" belong together as the Christian mind but – generally speaking – the modern

Christian, as a child of his age, has divided heart from head, made much of the head and little of the heart – the intuitive way of knowing. Without even realizing it, many conservative Christians read their Bibles, understand God and communicate with him through their senses and their reason: they know by rational, conscious, logical, analytical, objective means. The unconscious, intuitive, feeling way of knowing – the heart – has been relegated to fuzzy thinkers, women, the intellectually inferior, mystics, followers of New Age and Eastern religions and funny people.

This mindset began to take hold of the church in the thirteenth century during a revival of Aristotelian thought, in which experience gained through the five senses and reason – not spiritual perception – was increasingly perceived as the only way man received knowledge. But that wasn't the only problem. From the fourth century the church had been slowly exchanging the experience of a comforting, loving, indwelling God for holy *things*: God had slowly become a remote and punishing figure, the inspiration behind the frightening hells of medieval painters, to be approached in guilt through mediators and priests. The Age of Reason came upon the world in the 17th and 18th centuries, sucked into the vacuum left by the loss of the heart's way of knowing an immanent God. Man's mind became master, and the new tools were science and secular philosophy, scepticism and empiricism. When astronomy found the heavens empty of God, he became more remote and irrelevant. After Darwin, man appeared the outcome of blind chance. The church, struggling to remain relevant in a rational world, kept redefining its teachings in the light of science and discovery. Or it retreated into a defensive religious and moral dogmatism that still denied the heart's way of knowing. "The Judeo-Christian understanding of the deep heart (the unconscious mind and its ways of knowing) simply dropped from sight," says Payne.

Protestantism today walks on one leg. Most evangelicals invite Jesus into their heads, not their hearts, no matter what they say and sing. In most Protestant Bible and theology dictionaries there are no entries on spirituality. Protestant spirituality has actually been *defined* by its mistrust of mysticism. Mysticism is merely the habit or tendency of religious *thought* and *feeling*, the use of *both* the heart and the head, of *both* ways of knowing God. When the conscious, analytical, rational "head" turns in on the more unconscious, intuitive, symbolic, feeling "heart", analysing and paralyzing it, we struggle to survive in a sterile theological and religious system.

THE RISE OF THE OCCULT

Masses today flock to the false spirituality of occult and Eastern religions because they appeal to heart-starved people in a technological and head-centred age. Freemasonry, the occult, Eastern, pagan, pantheistic, Jungian and New Age systems: it is these that now "inform the minds and hearts of many church-goers", says Payne. Psychology has flourished in the void left by the church's failure to understand the unconscious mind and allow it to speak. "The psychotherapist has replaced the cleric as the healer of the soul," says Benner. Psychiatry and psychology understand the language of the heart better than the church does, but still on a quest to understand man outside a Christian framework they often prescribe the wrong remedies. "Fallen man is not simply an imperfect creature who needs improvement; he is a rebel who must lay down his arms," said C.S. Lewis.

THE BIBLICAL HEART

The Bible knows nothing of the schism between "head" and "heart", "heart knowledge" and "head knowledge", conscious and unconscious. It lumps them all together and simply calls them: the heart. The biblical heart is conscious, emotional and rational: it thinks, muses, reasons and doubts, plans and schemes, it rejoices, is merry, and can be grieved, pained and sorrowful. But it is also unconscious: the seat of our deepest motivations, so deep that the Bible says no man can know it, not even ourselves. All the various psychologies are only attempts to know the heart, says Leanne Payne. In the many psychological models of the personality most (90%) is unconscious. But God knows our unconscious, and everything it contains. The Bible says he knows our heart (Luke 16:15), searches it (Romans 8:27), and can heal it (Jeremiah 30:17). The Greek words *sozo* (to save), and *soteria* (salvation), are often translated "healing", and this is always of the *whole* man: which must mean wounds that are conscious and those many that are unconscious.

IMAGINATION – THE HEART'S LANGUAGE

So the heart – being conscious and rational – learns about God through experience gained through the five senses, and reason. But it doesn't stop there: the heart is also unconscious and non-rational. It speaks another language as well: one that is vital to "walking in the spirit", Christian growth and particularly to healing of unconscious unmet need. It speaks in pictures, metaphors, symbols, dreams, images, concepts and words: not too far removed from the dictionary definition of *imagination*: "the faculty of forming images in the mind".

Evangelical Christians are often frightened of the word imagination because of the false schism between head and heart. "Somehow the same people who believe that God can enter the mind with his ideas and perspectives, the will with his strength and desires… balk at the thought that God can stimulate the imagination… " says John Powell, in *He Touched Me*. "To ignore or fear the imaginative faculty is dangerous, and is a kind of evil, just as misusing it is evil," says Leanne Payne.

People say Jesus never taught the use of the imagination. But he appealed to it constantly by speaking in pictures. Every time he told a parable, people had to use their imaginations: consider the parables of the sower, the prodigal son, the lost coin, the lost sheep. "The tendency of modern people to be cut off from the imaginative in metaphor, symbol, story and parable, and from the capacity either to visualize or intuit is abnormal," says Payne. The fact is we use our imaginations constantly, why should we stop when we relate to God, who made both "heart" and "head"? Even language is only a series of symbols; it is our imagination that turns them into pictures or concepts that yield meaning.

What does the scripture itself say about imagination? The word itself is very little help in any such study. But the poetic and prophetic books of the Bible were written using imagination: the Old Testament Hebrew makes it clear that the "visions" of the prophets were exercises in imagination rather than special divine visitations (which is not to say they were not qualitatively different from what most of us experience in the use of imagination). It only shows how deeply Christians have lost the biblical concept of the heart when we insist upon scriptural validation for its natural language.

Because man has separated himself from God, his imagination has become defiled. It is used in degraded and grotesque ways in art, literature, music and on the screen, and corrupted in the practice of the occult.

But Christians have over-reacted and thrown the baby out with the bath water. Imagery, symbol and picture are still a valid way the unconscious biblical heart communicates and still one way God gets in contact with it. The imagination, surrendered to Christ, will start saying revealing things about forgotten incidents and unmet need, if it is permitted. It will state the problem in some way – in a picture, a word, a symbol, a sudden memory – that brings the person in touch with the realities beyond the reach of the rational mind. Leanne Payne often leads counsellees to "look up and see with their hearts Christ on the cross dying to take into Himself whatever is amiss in their hearts" and says "it is amazing what they see".

Visualization

When Payne asks her counsellees to "see with the eyes of their heart Christ on the cross", she is asking them to visualize, that is, to picture history's most pivotal event with the eyes of their heart. There is nothing wrong with doing this; the Bible itself just uses other images – words – to describe exactly the same thing. Visualization is a word that makes many Christians nervous, but visualization only serves the imagination in the same way that a gentle push gets a car rolling downhill.

Diseased imagery

Because there is so much disease, disorder and pain in memories and incidents buried in the unhealed unconscious, what can come up in symbols, thoughts and images can be alarming. But the Christian should not be alarmed. The heart separated from the love of God is full of ugliness and distorted concepts of God, of love, truth, masculinity and femininity, of family, says Leanne Payne. Payne says she regularly encounters obscene imagery surfacing in people (often those who have been molested or illegitimately sexually active) when she asks them to look up and see with their hearts Christ on the cross. Diseased imagery is often something "welling up from an unhealed psyche, providing the clue to what needs healing", she says. It is the heart trying to say something in its native language in response to the picture of Christ on the cross that has been created before it. "The imagery is to be discerned... I will not (as some do) stop asking people to look up to God, thinking it to be a dangerous practice." The interaction between the diseased imagery and the visualized Christ on the cross becomes the means by which "all the saving power of God streams to the deepest reaches of the unconscious (the deep heart)".

All this is quite different from trying to use the imagination to induce some sort of psychological (merely wishful) mindset upon ourselves. People or groups who try to force the imagination to perform in this way will cause harm.

IMAGINATION IN PRACTICE

I was frightened and dismissive of the imagination in the Christian context, partly because I had tangled with the occult for many years and was anxious about possible psychic inroads; partly because my husband had a "head-centred" approach to his faith that I mistakenly thought, as his companion, I must also have; partly because I had heard so many warnings against visualization (in which people apparently invented an image and made it do certain things in a healing-prayer context), and partly because, in my shallow understanding of imagination in the biblical context, it always seemed to be associated with evil scheming. But I finally took the plunge at a conference called Listening to God, led by Joyce Huggett, and my heart was literally thudding with fear. The imaginative exercise was on Jesus' appearance behind closed doors to his disciples after his resurrection (John 20:19), and I was hanging for dear life onto Joyce Huggett's words, which I had written down:

> Don't be frightened, you're contemplating Christ and lis-
> tening to God with the whole of you. Ask for C.S. Lewis'
> baptized imagination and step into the scene. It's safe,
> though what may come up may be uncomfortable. But
> that's because, like the disciples, you're locked into it at the
> moment.

I started out visualizing: I put myself in the scriptural scene (it
helped that I had been to Jerusalem), and began walking along
its stone streets, looking about me. I was taken by surprise when
a grey donkey with a hairy, white muzzle, passed me from
behind on my right, led by an old man with a limp, a young
child in brightly coloured clothes skipping alongside. Soon, on
my right I found the door leading up to the room where the
disciples were gathered, and though the text mentions nothing
of stairs, I found stairs led up to a heavy locked door at the top.
I knocked, the door opened a crack and I found myself in an
upstairs room. At this point, my unconscious began to speak. I
was acutely aware of the atmosphere in the room: heavy with
disillusionment, grief, despair, and an overwhelming sense of
abandonment. I looked for John: he was silent, lost in his own
thoughts, leaning against a wall; Peter was seated, his head in his
hands. Then suddenly Jesus appeared. I found he flooded in as
light, and simply stood there. The disciples were first of all
incredulous, then wild with joy. The effect on me was amazing.
To my horror, emotions of despair, grief, and abandonment had
erupted with a will of their own from down where I had shoved
them and I was in a paroxysm of silent sobbing. When Jesus
showed the disciples his wounds I fell apart. They seemed to
shout into my despair and desolation in a way that I could at last
begin to believe: "I have experienced every bit of your despair
and desolation with you. You thought I didn't understand, but I
do. Did you really think I would leave you?" The rest of the
meditation trailed off; I remember none of it. The experience
was as real as if Jesus had personally appeared to me, as if I had
been with Jesus and touched, seen and heard him, as the disciples did. God had used the picture-making faculty of my heart,
my heart's way of knowing, to begin to break through to me at

last: the very faculty that I had considered so inferior to intellectual ways of knowing, and as a child of my age and limited religious perspective, had rejected.

It was my first experience with the language of the heart, but not nearly the last. After years of trying everything I knew to help myself – except the language of the unconscious – God began to use it to bring love to the unloved child, and healing to the unconscious emotional pain that had fuelled my years of relationship addictions.

IMAGINATION AND ADDICTION

Relationship addiction and anger

When Vaughan (Chapter 3) first came for prayer, his marriage of two years was at risk through anger and clinging, manipulative emotional dependency on his wife. He described his father as "emotionally dead, cold, distant, angry, impossible to please, critical". The youngest son in a family of five, he and his mother, emotionally starved in her relationship with Vaughan's father, had formed a manipulative and close bond, his mother keeping him at home as long as possible to avoid the emotional desert of the marital relationship. Their relationship was punctuated by outbursts of Vaughan's anger. Until he married at the age of 32, Vaughan had had no girlfriends, and when he did leave home it was for another woman to whom he clung, and upon whom he also discharged his pent-up anger and frustration.

When he came for help, Vaughan could remember nothing about his life before the age of twelve. Secretly he feared and hated his father, though always tried to behave affectionately and reasonably towards him. Now he couldn't keep up the act. He couldn't understand the Bible – though he often tried to read it; God was a void, remote and punishing. Only one memory surfaced as prayer began: of trips into town with his father as an eight-year-old boy every Friday night for months to buy him a promised pencil case. Vaughan never did get his pencil case; his father never got round to it. We asked Jesus into the scene, and Vaughan saw him immediately. Only it was God the Father who appeared to Vaughan's inner eye, not Jesus, and he was wearing the blue gown Jesus wore in a wall-picture in his childhood home. God took Vaughan into a large department store with wide aisles and let him choose his pencil case: a cylindrical red-tartan one with a circular zip at one end. Then they walked out together and Vaughan saw his father where he had left him, talking to a local farmer across the street. Then God told him that if he had no pencils for his case they would go shopping together next Friday for some. Throughout the episode Vaughan, a strong grown man of 34, was doubled up, crying like a child. He talked about it for days after, saying how much it had altered his concept of God who he conceptualized as like his father. (In his reading of the Bible, images of judgment, punishment and wrath always overwhelmed the merciful, gentle and loving images.) His imaginative experience helped correct inner imagery, helping him receive the right biblical pictures of a gentle, loving and kind Father. For Vaughan it was just the start of work on his deep inner insecurity and anger.

In his book *My Weakness His Strength*, Robert Girard, outwardly successful as a busy pastor of a growing church, talks about the uncontrollable, irrational anger that was destroying his marriage and his career. He was thinking of resigning his ministry. "All my public 'goodness' and 'Christlikeness' is so much rubbish," he wrote. "The secret reality of my life is laced with passion, hatred, bitterness, violence and murder." Nothing greatly changed for Girard in all his attempts over years to beat his anger and deep sense of rejection, until one day, with a prayer counsellor, he walked in his heart down a long corridor with many doors leading to single rooms. In one room which he knew represented his life before the age of twelve, he found a small terrified "grotesque, ugly, repulsive" little boy – "a worm, a reptile, a nearly lifeless, hardened, crumpled looking mass cowering in the darkest corner of the room", whom Jesus picked up and loved. As he did, the child took on "an increasingly human form", "bathed through with light", becoming more peaceful and secure. (This over-condenses the depth and extent of the healing encounter.) In his diary several days later he recorded: "I am his child. He holds me. He loves me. Imagination is bringing me in touch with reality, but it is not imaginary. It is a more intimate experience of everything the Bible says Jesus is to me."

Obsessive cleanliness

Merrell's life has been transformed as Jesus has entered through the picture language of her unconscious into traumatic memories of frequent sexual abuse by her father that occurred when she was between four and nine. Merrell had repressed all recollection of it, and along with it, it seems, her ability to feel anything. She was never angry, or jealous, or sad, or happy. The only emotion she ever experienced that she could identify was fear, though she never really *felt* that either; she just preferred to stay at home. She said she was "emotionally dead" when she became a Christian around 40. Even her bodily responses were numb. She only knew she was hungry or tired when her legs gave out on her. Merrell's addiction was compulsive house-cleaning and personal hygiene. "Every spare minute I had was spent cleaning the house." She never went away anywhere if she couldn't shower daily. By the time someone able to help her turned up, Merrell had found Christianity so irrelevant she was about to drop out.

Things began to change for Merrell when she watched a late-night two-hour television documentary on sexual abuse of very young children and found herself a horrified, frightened but compulsive viewer. "I hated it but I couldn't stop watching." In the morning she had absolutely no recollection of what the show was about, and had to consult the programme guide to find out. She had repressed all memory of it.

Time passed. She read a Christian book, and decided she should forgive her mother – who had tried to abort her – and her father for her lonely and actively atheistic upbringing. It was as she tried to forgive him she experienced spasms of horror and fear, similar to those she had had as she watched the film. Then an image flashed into her mind: of herself and her father in the bathroom at bath-time when she was about four. Over three days the image of her father's face became stronger. She called a friend and counsellor who came to pray with her and as he did the image became very clear. In prayer Jesus was invited into the bathroom scene that Merrell remembered and for Merrell, he came in through the bathroom window. She was only aware of his face, radiant with compassion and love. Her father vanished.

Then immediately she was in the lounge and Jesus was sitting in her father's armchair. He took her upon his knee and cuddled and comforted her, and as he did Merrell was aware how much she had yearned as a child simply to sit on her father's knee. The chair was transformed: it was no longer her father's chair, remote and frightening, but Jesus' chair.

But Merrell told herself she had invented everything; that her father, a respected professional man, would never have done that to her. Eighteen months passed while she continued to compulsively clean her house. Then, one night, her daughter brought home a video on child sexual abuse. Merrell watched it with no reaction, then went to bed. She had been asleep one hour when she awoke shaking with fear, her mind alive with images of her father and exactly what used to go on in the bathroom. For the rest of the night she got no sleep at all; every time she closed her eyes the "revolting" look on her father's face appeared against her closed eyelids. She called her counsellor friend first thing in the morning, and "cleaned the house like crazy" until he arrived. There was more prayer. The bathroom scene repeated, but this time disgust showed on Jesus' face, and guilt on her father's. Her father left as he had before, but Jesus continued the bathroom routine "putting me in the bath and washing me totally clean". But the child was terrified Jesus would go and her father would return. "Let's go away into the bedroom," suggested the counsellor, and that's when Merrell realized there had been bedroom abuse as well. "I saw the bedroom door handle slowly turning and my father coming in."

As adults Merrell and her sister had been puzzled by something that Merrell had frequently done as a child. Both remembered her running across the roof of the glasshouse, and scaling the wall to the family next door. It always left her with cuts on her bare feet. Merrell had never known why. Now she did: after her father had gone she would jump out of the window, onto the glasshouse roof and run to her best friend and protector, the boy next door. She also remembered crying at nights and writing notes to herself: I will tell my mother in the morning. But as an adult she could never remember what the notes were about, and concluded it was probably because she was unhappy at school. She never did tell her mother. This time, in prayer, as she saw her father "looming over the bed" she fled to the window, and as she jumped, it was into Jesus' arms. The sequence stopped right there. "I was totally safe." Though she could not see what Jesus did to her father, he left immediately.

As the inner trauma was being resolved Merrell slowly began to physically relax. As she did she became aware, by contrast, of continuous tension in her jaw muscles that became so severe that her jaw ached continuously. Her jaws were clenched shut. When she tried to eat, her throat would constrict so she was unable to swallow. "That's when I realized I had been forced to have oral sex with my father and I used to clench my jaws to try to stop him." Again the scenario came up in prayer, and again Jesus appeared – this time with a hose that he inserted in her mouth. The water that poured into her mouth and down her throat, and right through her, cleansed away the filth and the guilt. Her jaw unlocked and the problem has never recurred.

Wary and coiled as a spring when I first knew her, Merrell slowly and steadily became more spontaneous, open, and animated. Her commitment to the faith she had almost jettisoned for its irrelevance deepened. But Merrell still had one more step to take. Although she had seen horrible images of her father's face and revisited bedroom and bathroom, she had not *felt* the emotion of those events. It took her days to recover from the force of what hit her when she did. It happened over the course of a week, and Merrell needed someone with her much of the time. The buried pain erupted in "convulsions of fear, dread, terror, abandonment, and betrayal" that surged through her whole body leaving her shaking and nauseous. (Merrell had never felt nauseous.) "I could only hang onto my chest; I thought it was going to explode." Throughout she sensed and sometimes "saw" Jesus standing there. Not one to cry, she cried all week. It left her so exhausted she could barely walk, but grinning triumphantly nevertheless. The powerful re-experience of emotions so long suppressed not only yanked a deep, cancerous root of sexual abuse out of her personality, but also brought her emotionally to life as an adult. Though it is early days yet, she is beginning to talk excitedly of things she is "feeling" – a new experience for

Merrell. Incidentally, Merrell no longer compulsively cleans her house and hasn't for two years. That addiction of a lifetime is now behind her.

Merrell's addictions sprang from early sexual abuse. If she had reacted only slightly differently, and defensively detached from her mother because of her mother's indifference to her abuse, Merrell may not have been a cleanliness fanatic; she could easily have been lesbian.

Homosexuality

Imagination helped James – a homosexual struggler – during a communion service when his mind vividly replayed violent sexual abuse that occurred when he was three. The memory would sometimes come up when James was in a quiet or reflective mood. Usually he would "push it back down again" but he knew this time he had "to allow God to move in deeper". As he did he found he was hurt, bitter and angry at God that he had let the abuse happen, then alarmed and frightened to find that in his "heart" (not his "head") he really believed God would rape him if he let his anger at God show (diseased imagery).

> I felt so broken, and I pleaded for God to help. Gently he wrapped his huge arms around and held me to his comforting heart. I asked him to forgive me for believing that and heard him say that he understood. He also asked me to express the anger that I felt for being abandoned. As I let the thoughts and feelings out, I sensed the pain decrease. Looking onto the memory with him he showed me he had always been there. I saw that he had protected me from almost being killed, and that he had breathed life into my lungs. I saw him also fill the gaping wound inside me with his blood. The Lord was not changing what had happened, but was healing the destruction and lies that kept me from knowing him (and myself) more intimately. When he had finished this deep healing, he called forth a new inner man inside of me. He told me to move out in new strength and freedom, and not to walk back into the empty cage of the past.

I felt like I was able to, but deep inside me I still felt the craving to be fulfilled by another man. I still sought the intimacy and identity of another man for a sense of being. Once again the past could not be changed, nor the legitimate love that the little child within needed from the beginning.

A thought suddenly caught my attention. "Whoever eats my flesh and drinks my blood has eternal life… for my flesh is real food and my blood is real drink… " Jesus now stood in front of me. In my heart he said, "Do you still seek to devour another male's identity? Eat of me. Devour my flesh and know my true masculinity. I am the only man you will ever be satisfied with, and I will make you the man I want you to be."

When I opened my eyes, the bread and juice were still in my hands. I stared at them crying quietly. As I took in both of them, felt the warmth of God's healing presence well up within me.[1]

The experience did not heal James' homosexuality, but it was an important step forward – Christ speaking in the language of the heart, entering the childhood abuse, and comforting him, appearing as the true masculinity that James was searching for in other men.

Andy Comiskey, a former homosexual, whose ex-gay group used an inner healing approach, describes an experience in his own healing that happened as his heart was able to release some of its diseased imagery – "an image of a dark shrouded figure distinguishable only by a large phallus … the composite of cancerous, pornographic images that had become my standard of physical self-acceptance". Into the diseased imagery came a loving, affirming God. "The dark figure was lifted off me by the arms of a strong masculine presence, which I learned was God. He then anointed my body through laying his hands upon my head, shoulders, arms, torso and legs. He revealed his affirmation of my body in this manner, which graciously enabled me, in turn, to accept my physical self."

Marilyn Hardin says she often uses "creative prayer", to

restore correct images of God to lesbians who had abusive fathers or unresponsive, or demanding and smothering mothers, images they transfer to God, making it impossible for them to trust him. Such prayer identified the start of one ex-lesbian's defensive detachment from her mother. "The woman saw herself as a small child separated emotionally from her mother, longing for her love and approval. Jesus came in and picked up the hurting child. The woman cried saying again and again that she was receiving Jesus' love like a mother's love." The image ministered powerfully through the rest of her healing: she realized she could receive Jesus' love like a mother's love any time she needed it, that God could love her in a "rich, maternal" way.

IMAGINATION: VITAL TO HEALING

Bringing Jesus into the deep heart to minister to painful buried memory is often a vital part of the healing of early trauma that can give a compulsive edge to the way we live and relate in the present. *There is more to the healing of addiction than reaching into inner trauma and healing it, but without it there frequently will not be healing.* In this way Jesus can enter into the unmet need that lies beyond the reach of the Christian rational mind, and at the basis of homosexuality, relationship addiction and other ways we try to compensate for our inner pain. He comes to pick up, and hold the abandoned, or bereaved or unloved or abused or terrified child – or comfort the lonely, humiliated adolescent. Usually all he has to do is come and be there: his mere presence in those wounded places of the heart is often all the miracle that is needed. There his presence lays the axe to the root of the tree and its branches begin to wither.

This healing of unconscious pain does not blot out the past or try to reconstruct or deny what happened. Jesus simply fills the incident in some way the heart needs to know, and in so doing extracts the pain from it. Remembered again, it is imbued with the presence of Jesus or God the Father: he was there, he knew, he doesn't condemn me or reject me or hold me guilty, he felt all the pain, I was not alone, he came, he filled me, he took the terror out, he loves me.

If Dr Penfield's electrode could prod long-forgotten

incidents into consciousness so that they were relived, then it should not surprise us that Jesus – who lives outside time – can enter our yesterdays and the incidents that have deeply shaped us and still trouble our adult lives, and heal us.

Ministry to the unconscious often helps disable the defensive detachment underlying homosexuality. It often facilitates forgiveness – as we saw with Merrell – helps restore trust, banish fear, and correct negative imagery of God. It gets at the roots of crippled self-esteem.

Those who encounter Jesus in this way are able to say, with genuine conviction: "Surely he has borne our griefs – sickness, weakness and distress – and carried our sorrow and pain. With the stripes that wounded him we are healed and made whole" (Isaiah 53:4-5).

To tell those who struggle with homosexuality, relationship addiction, and other life-dominating compulsions they cannot stop, to read their Bibles and pray every day is like trying to kill an elephant by throwing stones at it. "You're new creatures in Christ now, confess it and believe it", "You've got power over sin so just stop it", "Worship the Lord", "Trust and obey", "Let go and let God", are not enough where unhealed unconscious pain is involved. Christianity that denies the reality of the unconscious has a way of becoming an empty system of rules, regulations and obligations.

For those of us who carry emotional pain repressed in the unconscious, the past is not in the past – as some Christians say. It is still with us, in the present. For the healing of addiction, Jesus the Healer has to enter our forgotten pain and comfort us, love us as if we were his only child, and set us free. And to *that* place he will often come, *not only* through the intellect (which comprises only half the Christian mind), but through the heart's native language – the imagination.

"You shall love the Lord your God with *all* your heart. This is the first commandment." The conscious, rational, analysing "head" by itself is not all the biblical heart – just as the intuitive, unconscious, feeling, symbolic "heart" by itself is not all the biblical heart. Nor is the heart carrying unhealed, unconscious pain that surfaces in compulsive drives to assuage it, *all* the heart: a whole heart. Christians bearing unhealed, unconscious pain (most of us), and Christians who deny the heart and live out of their heads (most of us), are not really able to obey the first commandment.

But there is more to the healing of addiction than simply the healing of buried pain – vital though it can be. In the next chapter we will look at other essential steps.

Note

1. From the *Living Waters* course manual used by the ex-gay group, Desert Stream.

Chapter Fifteen

FURTHER STEPS IN HEALING

To write about the healing of the homosexual is to write about the healing of all men and women. (Leanne Payne)

The power behind homosexuality has been that it masquerades as a bigger-than-life problem requiring new and different answers. (Sy Rogers)

With the right help, the healing of the homosexual is not just possible – it's inevitable. (Frank Worthen)

Paul sat opposite, literally squirming in his chair. He was straight. His pastor had sent him along for some help with sexual addiction and he had just been invited to take part for a year in an ex-gay healing programme. Paul was horrified crimson at the thought. Not just horrified but very embarrassed and indignant. He! – so obviously a virile heterosexual male – in with a bunch of queers. What on earth would everybody think? Paul never turned up, which was a pity because he had a great deal in common with his "bunch of queers". He was not a virile heterosexual male; he was an insecure and addicted one.

In this chapter we will see how people with same-sex attraction set about healing themselves – and discover again that we are like them. If people with an insecure gender identity who are searching for it in others of the same sex can be healed, then so can we who have lesser love needs that we are also trying to meet addictively. Obviously this chapter is not intended to be a definitive recovery programme for all people with compulsive habits; there are specialist programmes for different addictions. But many of the principles are the same.

So – if you have realized that you are in the grip of life-dominating addiction and want to break your dependency, what might you find you have in common with a homosexual struggler in the same position? Here are a few things.

THE NEED TO ACKNOWLEDGE

- That if will-power hasn't worked so far, it won't suddenly start now. Addicted people often believe that a little more will-power will do the trick. But the half of you wanting to continue is stronger than the half of you that doesn't. (The unmet need in you is stronger than the will to stop.)
- That you won't get out secretly all by yourself – even though God is all-powerful and you and God are a majority. Concealment and failure are often companions.

THE NEED FOR:

- *Personal motivation.* You are going to beat this thing not to please someone else but because you want to. (Otherwise you won't stick it out.)
- A surrender and appeal to a *kind and understanding* God, otherwise known as repentance (note the adjectives), following the realization that addiction is at base a spiritual problem: the attempt to fill your empty love-tank by attaching to things, goals or people.
- The support group. An essential part of any addiction recovery programme. They are usually addiction-specific but need not be. The support group is a "safe place", where everyone knows what you're like because they're like you. There's acceptance and understanding and you won't have to pretend any more. But a good support group will hold you to the highest and call you to account when necessary. Others there will have played your games so you'll have a hard time fooling people. You will learn from each other's mistakes and be encouraged by each other's successes. They will be there for you when the going is tough, and help counteract the isolation that is part of addiction.

If you find yourself experiencing sexual attraction to a group member, you make yourself accountable to the group leader and a trusted few (preferably not the person you're attracted to) and take it as an opportunity to find out what it is you're really seeking. Group members commit to not acting out sexually with each other but to converting the sexual signals back into emotional signals and getting these needs met in legitimate ways. Typically the support group runs courses giving a good understanding of the roots of the problem and effective responses, and that insight is a large part of healing. In such an atmosphere of acceptance, accountability, sharing of successes, failures and insights, healing prayer, commitment, friendship and discipline, there is progress.

- Accountability: someone to whom you give the right to question you about anything at all and to whom you promise to give an honest answer. (Did you read porn? Visit an adult bookstore?)

- Honesty: no more denial, and rationalization of your problem. It also means dispensing with the fantasies – my family (mother, father) were wonderful, my childhood was happy. You can't deal with what you don't face.

- Forgiveness: giving away the idea of hurting them for hurting you. Secular therapists also focus on forgiveness.

- Restitution: making amends.

- Patience: recovery is a process, not an instant cure. God is not coercing you, he's helping you. He doesn't condemn you when you fail. Healing is a process, not zap. There is no pill to take that changes everything. Healing is not just "no more sex". It is changing ways of thinking and reacting, and that can take time.

- A therapist or counsellor. People with same-sex attraction often benefit from exploration with a therapist of the *same sex* of the transference and counter-transference that often comes up. Typically the client begins to interact with the therapist as he interacts with the same-sex parent or peers, only this time the client is encouraged to mine the reactions for insights into attitudes propping up the homo-sexual response.

- A heterosexual friend or mentor. This is a valuable source of healing but often not an easy one to find. The therapist is often constrained by professional rules of conduct – not so the friend. Being able to tell all to a friend who is not fazed by anything you say, and doesn't get emotionally enmeshed or sexually involved with you, will give you a good dose of what you're needing – same-sex affection with nothing erotic in it. Specialist mentors in some cases, provided safeguards are in place, can be invaluable in work-ing through some tight spots in dependency.

THE NEED TO:

- Take responsibility for the addiction, your unmet need and your own healing.
- Refuse to *define* yourself by your problem. "Homosexual" is only a label, don't wear it. *Acknowledging the problem and accepting a label are two different things.* There is no difference between you and everyone else: certainly not on the "sin-scale". Any addict is just a person loved by God who is being healed of old wounds. You are a Christian, loved and valued by God: that is your true identity.
- Burn your bridges, close the escape hatch back to your addiction: you pledge to give up the sex (the alcohol, the food, the spending – whatever the thing is that masters you), *so that* the needs underlying the addictive placebo are forced to the surface.
- Dissociate from the old lifestyle in practical ways. It's hard to break ties with your gay friends but with rare exceptions they have a strong vested interest in helping you fail. Burn your porn and gifts and memorabilia that remind you of old lovers. Noel got rid of thousands of pounds' worth of furniture, and leatherwear when he decided to leave homosexuality behind.
- Know that as a Christian your will is free – to make the right choices appropriate to your stage of recovery.

- Deal with the addiction cycle – vital in recovery. Know your unique triggers and learn to avoid them. Self-talk: knowing what it is you're *really* wanting. Know that temptation is only temptation – not "sin".
- Refuse to worship the goal, e.g. for the person with homosexual drives heterosexuality is not the aim and object: it is a by-product of meeting unmet need and re-shaping ingrained responses, wrong assumptions and attitudes. *The obsession to be healed, or heterosexual, can become another kind of idolatry.* It can keep the focus on homosexuality in an unhelpful way. There is much more to your life than homosexuality.

In her book *Co-Dependence, Misunderstood Mistreated*, Anne Wilson Schaef says the Alcoholics Anonymous Twelve Steps programme is not only crucial for recovering alcoholics but for relationship addicts and "all other addicts". She says the programme brings about a "systems change" – the major change in "beliefs, behaviour, thinking and practice" that is essential in the healing of any addiction: not just the chemically addicted. The healing homosexual will also work through every one of these steps in one form or another. The programme stipulates:

- an admission of powerlessness over the addictive process/substance
- an admission that our lives have become "unmanageable"
- *surrender to God* as we understand him
- a "searching and fearless moral inventory of ourselves"
- *admission to God and another human being of* the exact nature of these wrongs
- agreement that "these defects of character" be removed
- a list of all persons harmed by us and our addiction
- direct amends
- continuing personal inventory and prompt admission of wrong
- a search for a closer relationship with God
- carrying the same message to others

Let's look a little more closely at the three most important things any addict will have to do.

REPENTANCE

Repentance has unfortunately become a word with negative connotations because of our wrong images of God. Really it is one of the most magnificent words in the human vocabulary; bursting with the promise of everything we have always needed. Repentance is the *sine qua non* of true self-esteem, the essential first step in any deep and lasting healing. It's "I'm sorry I've been so determined to live life my own way", and the return home to a waiting, compassionate and forgiving Father. The root of our human problems is not our addictions, it's our separation from God: our determination to live our lives without him and to meet our needs our own way. This disposition is called *hamartia*: sin – which simply means *a missing of the mark so as not to share the prize.* The only cure is God's pardon for our rejection of him, offered through Jesus. Our genuine apology is repentance. Repentance and God's ready pardon reconcile us to him. He wraps his arms around us and we become his favourite son or daughter. Without repentance we have no access to all the resources we need for healing. Without genuine surrender – the white flag raised to the Lover of our souls; capitulation to his gentle and rightful ownership of our lives – we only replace one addiction with another.

Despising ourselves, wanting to get rid of our addiction, even feeling sick of it for a while and wanting to turn over a new leaf is not repentance. In homosexuality it's not feeling miserable that the affair has been discovered, or that an affair is over, or even being disillusioned with homosexuality. Repentance is *metanoia*: a change of mind and heart, a 180° round-turn, the decision to follow Christ, knowing you can't even do that without his help. But that's alright.

A word of warning: people who "repent" before an image of an angry, remote and punishing God do not really repent; they merely set themselves up for failure by chaining themselves in fear to a set of rules.

TAKING RESPONSIBILITY FOR OUR ADDICTIONS

Taking responsibility for our own behaviour is an essential pre-requisite to healing from any stubborn habit, says Erwin Lutzer in *How to say No to a Stubborn Habit.*

In the healing of compulsive behaviours this applies at two levels. First – and it seems unfair – we have to take responsibility for our early responses to the pain or trauma that we try to lessen through our addictions. The point is: *no one else but we made the responses we did*: perfectly understandable, reasonable responses given our young age and lack of objectivity and our fear, but the wrong ones nevertheless: withdrawal of trust, rejection, unforgiveness, hostility, anger. Later, driven by these unconscious wounds of earlier years, we were still the ones who continued to make the wrong responses and choices that fed our addictions. Ultimately no one else did.

Second – as we heal we must stop blaming other things, circumstances, and people, for our relapses. The truth of the matter is the relapse happened because we let it.

Turning Point, an ex-gay group, has the following poem available for those homosexuals working through change, but it has a far wider application.

> There's a deep hole in the sidewalk.
> I fall in.
> I am lost…
> It is hopeless.
> It isn't my fault.
> It takes forever to find a way out.
>
> I walk down the same street.
> There's a deep hole in the sidewalk.
> I pretend I don't see it.
> I fall in again.
> I can't believe I'm in the same place.
> But it isn't my fault.
> It still takes a long time to get out.

I walk down the same street.
I still fall in…
It's a habit.
My eyes are open.
I know where I am.
It is my fault.
I get out immediately.

I walk down the same street.
I see the same deep hole.
I walk around it.

I walk down a different street.

(*Autobiography in Five Short Chapters* © Portia Nelson from *There's a Hole in my Sidewalk*. Beyond Words Publishing, Inc. USA.)

FORGIVENESS

Without forgiveness healing cannot happen. Unforgiveness is punishing those who have hurt us; hurting them for hurting us, making them pay, getting even, holding our pain in their faces all our lives. Forgiveness is releasing them from the debt they owe us. Forgiveness is realizing they did it wrong, and there were reasons why they did; just as we did it wrong, for our own reasons. We can afford to forgive because God is able to restore us. Forgiveness does not mean we have to close our eyes to their behaviour, or continue to sit back and take it, or never challenge it. Forgiveness does not mean the incident is erased from memory. It does not mean we have to become best buddies with the person we have forgiven.

Even the secular therapists acknowledge the importance of forgiveness. Real forgiveness is never instant. It is a goal we set our face towards. The wounded person who immediately says "I forgive you" is forgiving without emotional integrity, say Minirth-Meier in *Love is a Choice*. Real forgiveness often only occurs out the other side of the grieving process, after a lot of anger, hostility and tears have been drained off. Often inner healing is necessary before forgiveness is even possible.

Unforgiveness biases us, so that we imagine offences where there are none. It stops us seeing another's good points. In the same way that we become like Christ as "we contemplate the glory of the Lord", so we become like the person we fixate upon by refusing to forgive; this is particularly true of children towards parents. We need to forgive for our own sake if not for the offender's. The Bible is clear: unforgiveness tortures us (Matthew 18:34). God having forgiven us insists that we forgive others to continue receiving his forgiveness. We must also forgive ourselves.

In homosexuality forgiveness can take the power out of early defensive detachment. Sy says he went through the "obligatory forgiveness thing with his parents: 'I forgive them, God, they know not what they do', when really my attitude was, 'Get them God, make them pay!'" It took him some time to admit he still hated his father. Then he settled on a 50/50 bargain, "I am responsible for 50% of the failure in our relationship, I was only a poor child-victim. They were the adults." But God wouldn't let Sy away with it. He finally broke down before his parents asking their forgiveness for "failing them, shunning and scarring them", and asking for their love and trust again. "They opened up just like that!" he said. (Sy's story, Chapter 7.) A "much needed life-changing inner healing" helped him to forgive.

Forgiveness helped Starla overcome an irrational fear of men. Starla was raped when she was twelve, an incident that reinforced a growing lesbian orientation that culminated years later in a five year live-in lesbian relationship, an alcohol problem and a hatred of men that led her to the verge of manslaughter twice in her life.

By the time God asked her to forgive, Starla was a Christian and had left her lover. She was cooking for two men on an isolated ranch when she suddenly realized she had an irrational fear of men. "I took it to the Lord and almost got an audible voice. He said, 'Well, you have some forgiveness that needs to be done.' I said, 'OK God, I can do that.' He said, 'You need to forgive the man who raped you.'" Starla was stunned.

I had 53,000 good reasons why I didn't need to do that. It was unfair, unjust. I said, "No God, I will not." A couple of rough weeks of wrestling followed. I wasn't willing. And pretty soon, God stopped talking altogether. I would talk to him and he wouldn't talk back. It went on for three days, it was awful. I said, "Why aren't you talking?" He said, "Cos I tell you things and you don't care to know." I said, "I do." He said, "You want to know but you don't want to do anything about it." Finally God got it down to a level where I could understand it. I started with no feelings whatsoever and three days of fasting and prayer. I told God, "I'm doing this because you have asked." Then I realized it was like setting up boxing for concrete. I set up the boxing, he poured in the concrete: the emotions.

The forgiveness process ended up going a lot further than Starla ever imagined. "I ended up praying for the man's salvation and forgiveness, renewal in his family, the whole works." Afterwards she noticed that her fear of being victimized by men diminished. "I could relate with them, even trust them. I felt less vulnerable, stronger, but not an independent defiant strength."

Ann said she noticed a "dramatic" link between her forgiveness of her mother and her ability about a week later to wear feminine clothing. "I felt comfortable in women's dresses and clothes I had never felt comfortable in. I started to enjoy men looking at me instead of thinking they were only looking at me to abuse me." She described it as the single biggest step in her healing.

SELF-ESTEEM

Image of God, and self

Unmet need and low self-esteem lie at the root of addiction, not the least homosexuality. Self-esteem starts to repair when we realize, first, how much we are loved and valued by God. But many homosexuals see God as an angry critic of their condition. To get any distance at all in healing we have to begin to believe that God is not a larger-than-life replica of our own father or worse: he is not cruel, angry, punishing, unfair, remote, unsmiling, indifferent, impossible to please. He understands and is sympathetic. He can be trusted, and approached for help. He is on our side regardless of mistakes and failure, is patient and gentle. God is our best and most faithful friend on our up and down journey out, not our enemy.

Self-esteem is low not only because of wrong ideas about God and gender identity deficits. Homosexuals have taken on board messages of rejection they have heard for years. Inwardly they reject and hate themselves. But the flipside to low self-esteem is arrogance, contempt, superiority, and anti-authority attitudes. "We either believe that we are nothing, the lowest of the low, or we fight back, trying to gain some sense of self-worth, but through pride and arrogance," says Frank. Low self-esteem leads to many things, but ultimately to wrong self-love and the grandiose self-image; or the obverse, masochism and the need to be dominated.

For our self-image to recover we all have to start seeing ourselves as God sees us: as unique individuals, infinitely precious and worth dying for. "It's not saying, 'I'm worthless' or 'I'm wonderful'," says Frank. "It's grasping our value as being equal to Christ's life, because that's what God paid for us." We have to start seeing who we really are in God's eyes, even while we struggle: accepted, Not Guilty! holy, pure, a new creation, chosen, the apple of God's eye.

Image of others

The homosexual has become used to living in a self-protective way: rejecting people before they reject him, or using people to gratify his need for acceptance, affection and value. In his insecurity he constantly measures himself against others: those he is better than, those better than he, those he feels he could never measure up to, those he feels he's too good to relate to. In this process people become things. With males in particular, sex becomes the addictive substitute, instant gratification replaces the hard work of building a relationship and the dehumanising process continues: people become "tricks" or "numbers". The homosexual may start out with "idealistic dreams of life-long loving companionship but this usually degenerates into impersonal sex, gratification from others: a snare of using and being used", says Frank.

As we begin to learn how much we are loved and valued by God we begin to realize we have intrinsic worth and that others have too. As we begin to treat ourselves and others with new appreciation and respect, others begin to respond in kind. A positive cycle begins.

THE ADDICTION CYCLE

Temptation

For the homosexual person, for any addict, temptation is the starting point of the addictive cycle. But temptation is only temptation. A homosexual thought or image or desire is not sin, it is only temptation. James 1:15 makes it quite clear: "the evil desire, when it has conceived, gives birth to sin" – not before. Jesus was also tempted in every way we are, but never sinned (Hebrews 4:15). "Since Jesus was a man, a human being, I concluded he knew what sexual temptation was," says Sy Rogers. "He was tempted but he didn't sin. I was encouraged. God didn't see temptation the way I did. It meant that I could be tempted but still say 'yes', or 'no', to sin."

For homosexuals, temptation, if it is entertained, is the start of a ritual that is almost impossible to stop, except at the earliest stages. Frank Worthen describes the cycle (similar in all addictions). It starts with a mere suggestion, a thought, an idea (temptation), which if not rejected arouses a diffuse impression of pleasure, curiosity and interest and a little mild fantasy: I wonder what it would be like if... Unchecked the fantasy gains shape and focus, desire is aroused, and guilt. At about this point "sin is conceived" (James 1:15). Then the scheming starts: working out the details of the gratification plan, allowing for every contingency. At this point all systems are on "go". Then the plan goes into action: the right clothes (or lack of them), being in the right place at the right time so the encounter will probably happen, setting up alibis, the beginning of seduction. Then the act. In minutes it is over – and the price paid is immeasurable. Ex-gays testify: you feel empty, short-changed, cheated, a failure, guilty and separated from God. And a voice whispers, "You've blown it now, you'll never make it out." The memory selectively erases the negative, spurring on another attempt. We begin to think how the next encounter will be better if subtle changes are made to the plan.

Triggers

For the homosexual (for all of us), there are times he is more vulnerable to temptation than others. After tempting Jesus, Satan left him alone for a time, awaiting a more favourable opportunity (Luke 4:13). The ex-gay movement talks of triggers, and uses the acronym HALT: hungry, angry, lonely, tired, to identify the major ones. But there are also others: fear, rejection, boredom, homesickness, depression, discouragement, hopelessness, feeling disparaged, a desire for power, envy; certain music, smells, sounds, images. How do we deal with the triggers? Knowing what they are is the first step; some of them will be unique to us. Here is a second step.

DISCIPLINE

Avoid the tempting spots. Take a different route home, not past the video store. Don't buy that magazine. Don't watch that TV show. James found it helped to visualize Jesus standing between him and his temptation and to busy himself doing something else. Steve went looking for company whenever he felt the urge to masturbate. For those who have used sex to meet their needs for a long time it can be a tough struggle. Says Sy Rogers:

> There were times I had to grip my chair and say, "Yes, maybe I want to give in, but no, I won't. I won't. And nobody but me can make me. The devil can't make me." I used to say to Satan, "I'm not going back into homosexuality and you can't make me."

Getting out of any addiction is not easy. The mind and body have been taught to expect the emotional and sexual high. From a simply neurological point of view millions of nerve cells have to learn a new normalcy, even where no chemical addiction is involved. That can take time. "Withdrawal symptoms are real and one way or another they will be experienced," says May in *Addiction and Grace*. "If we can both accept and expect this pain we will be much better prepared..."

There are other ways to break into the addictive cycle at the temptation stage.

DISPLACEMENT

In the book *Brain Lock* which looks at ways people with Obsessive Compulsive Disorder (OCD) can break into the repetitive compulsive performance of rituals to try to prevent imagined disasters, the author, Jeffrey Schwartz, discusses a four-step process which is proving highly effective in combatting OCD: Relabel, Reattribute, Refocus and Revalue. "Relabel", means "this is not me, it's my OCD"; "reattribute" includes the refusal to classify yourself as intrinsically "bad" because of what is happening, "refocus" is to refuse to do the ritual for at least fifteen minutes and to *actively* do something else enjoyable, and revalue is evaluate the effects of those responses and to see OCD's tricks in a new light.

These are helpful tools in dealing with addictive drives.

To relabel is to say: Sex is not what I'm really wanting. The roots of this are non-sexual. I don't have to do this. This is not inevitable, I have an option. I am just getting into an old pattern. I'm going to be miserable afterwards. God I choose you!

To re-attribute is to say: I'm tired; I'm feeling lonely and rejected. Is what I'm wanting affirmation? A sense of belonging? Someone to tell me I'm OK?

To refocus is do something else you enjoy. It's sometimes called displacement – putting something else innocently pleasurable in temptation's place, thereby pushing the thought out with something else while it is only a suggestion. Simply trying not to have homosexual thoughts is about as productive as sitting in a corner for 30 minutes trying not to think of a blue giraffe. Displacement can be calling up a friend (a good antidote to loneliness), going for a walk, listening to an uplifting CD, burying yourself in a good book, doing a favourite hobby, playing a computer game. It's only temporary but it can get you past the vulnerable time.

POSITIVE FEEDBACK

Confidence and healing take quantum leaps when success feeds into the picture. Kevin used to be sorely tempted by pornographic bookstores. On this occasion he was lonely (a trigger) and without group support. It was his first major test by himself. He was on his way home, and decided to detour past the bookstore. But he didn't go in, he drove past, then circled back several times, not wanting to park in the parking lot because he had a Christian fish logo on the back bumper.

> It was clear I was caught in the addictive cycle. My first step was to be honest about my feelings: I was lonely, and part of me really wanted to see that porn. But I didn't want to be wanting to.

The Bible was lying beside him on the car seat. He picked it up and read it; it didn't help.

> I stepped out of the car, I got back in the car. I put the keys in the ignition. I took them out again. I was praying all the time, "Oh Lord, you know how close I am to doing this. I know you have the power to save me. Please help me, strengthen me." I tried to focus on the passages of scripture I knew: I am dead to sin. Satan cannot force me. This is a choice! I had just enough strength to put the keys in the ignition, start the car and leave.

Later he wrote in his journal, "Thank you Lord for not letting me shut down on you."

> I was right up to the edge but I realized I could say "No"! Had God given me an incredible surge of strength or not let me get right to the edge it would not have had the same strengthening impact. Because it was so difficult and I did it, I knew I could do it next time.

His next success story occurred when he was "very tired and isolated" (two HALT triggers), and attracted to one of a gay couple living in an apartment above him.

> I was lounging at the poolside when this guy came to the balcony and invited me up. I knew it was dumb, but I went up. We were only about 30 seconds into the conversation and he propositioned me. I wanted to give in because what was being offered to me was all part of my fantasy struggle. All I could say was, "Think of your lover, someone might find out." Then I looked in his eyes and there was something dead there. I croaked, "God will know," and left. I collapsed and called my small group leader, "I need prayer right now. I'm a mess."

This was the last major struggle Kevin had with sexual temptation. "Again it was because I realized I could say 'No', though I should have said 'No' at the poolside." Two and a half weeks later the man was found dead of a heroin overdose. Sexually promiscuous and a habitual drug user, the man was in the high-risk category for AIDS.

Ann took a big step when she also realized she could say "No". Out for dinner, in the "perfect romantic set-up", with a woman who wanted her to keep going, she said, "I can't. I can't do this to Jesus." "I was able to step back, and as I did I realized I could say 'No' again." In this way homosexual desires gradually weaken. Sy Rogers calls it a starvation process. For Sy, a former transsexual, planning a sex-change operation, that process took several years. "I had been cultivating these appetites all my life," says Sy. "They didn't just vanish overnight."

THE WILL AND THE POWER TO SAY "NO"

It helps in displacement, discipline and self-talk to know that the redeemed will is free. Every addict needs to learn Romans Chapter Six by heart. It is a triumphant declaration to the Christian with an addictive struggle: your will is freed from captivity, you are no longer a slave to your desires, you have the power to choose right over wrong. The Christian who continues to use Romans Chapter Six like the battering ram it is – as he takes ground in other ways – will make progress.

When it is all boiled down, says May, people who stop their addictive behaviour do one thing: they simply do not entertain the next temptation.

DISCOURAGEMENT AND PATIENCE

Healing has its setbacks and discouragements. But this is the time to run towards God, not away from him. One of Satan's most effective lies is "God won't want you back now". But does a parent berate and criticize a child who stumbles when he is just learning to walk? God understands, he knows you're trying. He's waiting to forgive you. Just ask. You don't have to earn his approval by succeeding all the time. You have it already. Anyone working his way out of addiction has to be patient with himself. Debbie, working her way out of lesbianism is making steady progress, but it's slow: she has a lot to work through. Disconsolate, she lit up a cigarette one day and then berated herself that she couldn't even give up smoking. It was then she said she heard "as clear as that, the Lord say, 'Give yourself a break!'"

We are often harder on ourselves than God is. For those with distorted images of God, sometimes the sense of his love for us is all that's needed to stop a wrong step. Shawn says in a Desert Stream newsletter that his own attempts to "stop himself" in his struggle with porn were "consistently futile", though he was no longer homosexually active. He was literally planning his evening's kick when a voice broke into his planning: God's. "It was very quiet but very stern," Shawn said. "'Even if you do, I still love you.'" It stopped Shawn dead in his tracks.

> It wasn't what I expected to hear from God. My temptation was being fuelled by the false belief that Jesus didn't like me (because I was tempted) and that I might as well act out since I was "bad". When I heard those words Jesus suddenly came into the very midst of my struggle. I was loved. I was no longer alone. He wasn't even angry at me! I came out of my self-pity… The decision, though I wrestled with it was an easy one… needless to say, I didn't act out.

One of the causes of greatest discouragement to ex-gays is the fear that attraction exists when it doesn't. Because the ex-gay person does not know how straight males relate, he can mistake normal curiosity, interest, mild comparison, and "just looking" for homosexual attraction. "All people notice attractive people," says Frank, "no matter what sex they are. I can acknowledge a nice looking guy, a good body and a good personality and maybe like a guy like that for a friend. But there's no way I would want to go to bed with him."

DELIVERANCE

Some groups encourage renunciation – in behaviour and imagination – of Baal or Ashtoreth (the biblical male and female gods of sexual orgy that constantly ensnared Israel, finally to its own destruction). When these are renounced by name, often, as a result "phallic demons" leave, says Leanne Payne. Deliverance must be used wisely. To attribute homosexuality solely to a demonic spirit of homosexuality and try to cast it out is as silly as trying to cast out someone's legitimate hunger for gender affirmation, parental love and peer acceptance. Whatever deliverance may occur from spirits attaching to the homosexual condition, some of it may need to wait until the emotional-psychological wound that has provided demonic lodgings in the personality, is receiving attention.

CHURCH: A TWO-WAY STREET

Healing homosexuals are often critical of the church; some are as judgmental of the church as the church has been of them. But God is as long-suffering with the church as he has been with them. The church also has to learn to love and identify with people who are homosexually attracted. In this the healing homosexual can be its teacher. Many in the church do want to help, but don't know how.

It's easy to blame the church. In fact many homosexuals who anticipated rejection from their churches when they owned up about their orientation and behaviour, didn't in fact get it. The church's lack of understanding is often an excuse."

Says Sy:

When I first began going to church I felt like I was going to feel very sorry for myself because people were failing me. I thought, *I'll show those Christians they don't love me enough*. But I'll tell you what! The Lord basically grabbed me by the collar and he let me know, "Who are you going to serve, me or yourself? You're not the centre of the universe. I didn't put all these people here just to stroke you. You're going to have to grow up and understand that maybe other people aren't going to understand where you've been. I know what you need. You live your life before these people and in time, as you persevere, they're going to see that what I've done in your life is real." Well, when God speaks to you like that you just hush your mouth.

Sy spent an isolated year. "Yes, I was lonely but that didn't give me an excuse to sin. If I had allowed my immaturity to prevail I would have gone back into homosexuality." As he stuck with it people began to make approaches.

Men weren't so afraid of their reputations being soiled. They began to take me to restaurants and on camping trips and spend time with me and give me the love and affirmation and nurturing that I had craved for years and tried to satisfy through sex. I found God began to meet that need through the mystical relationship of friendship. God clothed himself in flesh – his people – and they became ingredients in my healing. Slowly the men began to treat me like one of the guys because, revelation of revelations, I was one of the guys. My homosexual orientation basically died then and a new confidence in my manhood that I'd never had sprang up – and a new view of women: no longer a threat to the little shred of manhood I had, but as a complement. I was no longer terrified by the possibility of a romantic relationship.

Love in Action and the Church of the Open Door enjoyed a healthy and mutually enriching relationship for years but it wasn't always that way. When Frank began attending, as a new ex-gay, he found the church was "normal: unloving, and very dead". Some people were receptive, others horrified that he and a few other Christian men with a homosexual orientation were attending. "We turned things round," says Frank.

> We became servants of the church. It was a hard transition to make: it took five or six years to push a way in there. You have deal with your own rejection, get solidarity from each other and tell yourself you're not a second class citizen, your background is no worse than any other, that you're where God wants you, and take your rightful place.

Gays must forgive the church. Dee described an incident at an ex-gay conference in which "a man from the church got up in front of us and said, 'I apologize to you for my judgmentalism, and now I want you to have the chance to forgive the church.' It completely broke me up," said Dee, who is still working his way out, "because I realized I had never forgiven the church for treating me so harshly."

SAME-SEX FRIENDSHIPS AND THE CHURCH

The two men were Christians in their early twenties; two average New Zealand males wearing their tough-guy disguise. They had just listened to the testimony of an ex-gay for 30 minutes. "If you knew someone in your church was struggling with homosexuality would you be his friend?" I asked. Each shot the other a quick look; neither answered. Then one of them smirked. "Not really, I wouldn't want him getting sweet on me." The other agreed.

It is tragic that so many straight males go into hiding when homosexuals seeking a change of orientation need their friendship so badly, because healthy non-erotic friendships with others of the same sex are crucial in homosexual healing. Christians must learn to offer genuine friendship and show ex-gays what normal relating feels like, because they don't know. Homosexual love is the search for same-sex acceptance, friendship, security, and gender identity. When they begin to absorb this from genuine friendships with mature straight men, they are getting the vital ingredients of their own healing. May I say to straight men and women in the church: You must allow the homosexual struggler to make mistakes in his/her same-sex relationship with you. You may have to help him work through a possible struggle with homosexual feelings over you. That's OK. He only eroticizes what he idealizes. It doesn't mean you are homosexual. If you end the relationship because of it, you deny him, and yourself, a chance to grow. The truth is he is far more frightened of messing up the relationship than you are of entering it.

Ed

Ed was a Christian with homosexual desires. He had come a long way, gaining some ability "to be one of the guys", but he still had "three towering fears": the fear of seeing male nudity, of getting sexually involved with a man, and of falling in love. Terrified to show physical affection or hug another man in case he fell in love, he limited his contact to "punching on the shoulder". But he was wisely counselled to try showing physical affection so that he could face and deal with whatever might come up. So Ed plucked up the courage to try two things: to start hugging, and to try to build a friendship with two Christian guys, Rob and Mark, whom he had avoided up till then because of their good looks.

He said it put him through a "shaky" period, struggling with "memories, associations and confused feelings". He prayed as he never had before that God would help him keep the friendships honest and clean. "God was faithful." His friendship with Rob and Mark grew strong; they were closer than the gay he had been in love with. Rob and Mike stuck with him. "We developed a trust, honesty and openness that was overwhelming."

Then a major test: On a trip Ed was forced to share male group showers with Rob and a few other men.

Fear gripped me as I realized that, for the first time since salvation, I would be exposed to male nudity; and sheer terror as I realized that Rob himself might be one of those in the shower room. "But God," I screamed silently, "I'm not ready!" Evidently God had another idea. As I was confronted with this situation that I feared more than any other, my heart leapt to my throat. Then, quite suddenly, the peace of God settled on me with a precious revelation: "He's a Christian, YOU'RE a Christian. He's not into that... YOU'RE not into that." And more directly, "Just because you see it, doesn't mean it's yours." I realized that Rob's body belonged to him and to the Lord... that someday it would belong to his wife. But it definitely did not belong to me... with a quiet heart I realized that I had passed the test.

But the next awaited. Ed was horrified to realize when he saw Rob a few weeks later that he had fallen in love with him. "Where to now God?" I pleaded.

I was about to run out of the friendship, away from what I feared. But then I heard God's still, small voice again: "Son, I don't want you bound by sin, but I don't want you bound by fear either. Stand fast in the liberty in which Christ has set you free and don't be entangled again in bondage. Face it son, then deal with it."

Ed did. He found Rob and asked for prayer. Because Rob stuck by his friend – even as the object of Ed's struggle – Ed pulled through. Rob remains a special friend. "God would not allow me to remain imprisoned by these fears, so he confronted me with each one and brought me through," says Ed.

Chad (Chapter 6) broke down when he told me that his straight Christian flat-mate hugged him when he finally revealed his homosexual inclinations. "Doesn't worry me a bit," his friend said, "I don't have that problem. I'll give you a hug anytime."

John, a former homosexual and female impersonator, says the acceptance and love of straight men at the Church of the Open Door, base-church for ex-gays on the Love in Action course, was vital to the men in the programme.

All your life you've been told that you're a failure as a man. You feel totally inadequate, you don't feel like a man, you don't know what a man's supposed to be like. So when straight men can look at you and not be afraid to put their arm around you and say, "I love you", that heals a lot of wounds. And when the pastor hugs me and says, "I really love you", it does wonders for me. Unfortunately those Christian men are few and far between.

Mike Riley, pastor at the Open Door, says he and other key men in the church set the tone by example rather than from the pulpit.

We had a few things to work through, but only because we didn't understand what's going on with an ex-gay. What are you allowed to do? What's taboo? You go into the bathroom. You're there with three or four guys from the course. Do you go into a stall and close the door, or do you use the urinal like everybody else? I basically took the line: I'm going to treat these guys like anybody else. Most of us have taken that approach. We haven't communicated it, but how can they not see our example.

Gifted in many ways, the ex-gay contingent at the Open Door in 1992 was approximately four in ten in a congregation of about 250; ex-gays have felt so welcome there many stayed put.

Learning to relate honestly and form non-erotic friendships with other ex-gays in his support group is the first step in healing. The second is acceptance and friendship from straights of the same sex, especially from Christian straight men. The man who is beginning to feel like one of the guys and more at home in the company of straight men – the ex-lesbian who is becoming comfortable with the idea of herself as a woman – is not far from the next step.

DATING AND MARRIAGE

Slow and steady is the motto, for there will be frustrations. For men this is the time when "mother issues" will tend to come up.

For the ex-lesbian her concepts of men, usually coloured by sexual abuse, or male passivity, will come up. Neither will have much idea how a man or woman is meant to act or feel towards the other.

Gays and lesbians have missed out on that roughly six-year period in normal growth where men and women find their feet with the opposite sex. Ex-gays have to pick up at about age twelve, though obviously it will not take six years to recover that lost ground. The first feelings of sexual and emotional attraction to the opposite sex can be intoxicating for ex-gays: the first tangible signs of the real thing. But it must not lead to intimacy, because intimacy means commitment, and they're not ready.

Dating is a high-pressure word for ex-gays with a developing but still insecure heterosexuality. Romantic relationships do best to start out as friendships. Kevin (page 249), his homosexual struggle largely behind him, says he now feels secure enough to be able to ask a girl out but only if he is not thinking of it as a date. (He was grateful to be reminded that most straight men are nervous about dating.) "If I date I have to act a certain way, and I don't know the criteria." But he is confident that as he becomes "more secure in his manhood", relationships with women will begin to happen naturally. Until then he is happy enough having breakfast from time to time with a female co-worker.

Ex-gays often find the beginnings of the romantic encounter a time of fresh homosexual struggle. It can throw up memories of old gay liaisons, times of special intimacy; experiences get compared, particularly if the relationship is becoming boring and bogging down in mutual problems. The intense emotional highs and lows of the homosexual relationship can make cautious heterosexual dating feel tame.

Jim and Donna, although they are not dating, are having to work through the typical sorts of issues that arise. She is a former lesbian, he ex-gay; they work together. Jim was very close to his mother, had put her on a pedestal and hated to disappoint her. He also had a passivity problem: part of his insecure masculine identity. Jim is treating Donna the way he treats his mother, which means he doesn't want to disappoint her, defers to her too much and backs down if she doesn't like something. He won't initiate or make decisions. This revives Donna's old "strong and stroppy" lesbian patterns, making her feel disgusted with herself, and disgusted with Jim for being "weak and ineffectual". But Jim does not want to be like that – because it will disappoint Donna and because he wants to be "a man". So he over-compensates. "He completely takes over and makes decisions without me," says Donna. "So I back off and let him do it without me; I become completely passive." Jim and Donna are "working on it".

Kirsty found the same: an ex-lesbian she has a romantic friendship with an ex-gay with a passivity problem.

> I don't want to be in control but he leaves everything to me, which means I stay in control. If he says, "Whatever you want" one more time, I'll scream. I don't want that any more. If he would just say, "I want to do this", I'd be more than happy to oblige.

MARRIAGE?

Yes, the ex-gay can be as happily, more happily, married than many heterosexuals, mainly because as a healed homosexual he has faced and dealt with many of the anxieties and insecurities that lie behind many heterosexual problems.

But marriage is no cure for homosexuality (nor is it proof of healing), and the ex-gay courts disaster if he marries too soon, which he may do for several reasons: to prove to himself – or others – that he is healed; because his counsellor was too hasty; because the church put pressure on him, or because the woman he was dating did. All are fatal.

"The best marriages of ex-gay men to straight women occur between five and eight years after a solid commitment to change," says Frank. "Marriages after three years have a lot of ups and downs. We say a guy is ready for marriage when he no longer seeks protection (fathering) but wants to protect."

Everyone wants to know what a healed ex-gay is like in bed. Generally better than a lot of heterosexual men: less selfish, more sensitive, gentle, desirous to please. Is he turned on by his wife's body? Yes, slowly and steadily. Is he capable of good old male lust? Who says he's meant to be? The Bible certainly doesn't (1 Thessalonians 4:4). Having beaten homosexual lust, Sy thought heterosexual lust was the proof of his healing. He waited for it but it never came. "I kept waiting for God to zap me into a hot-blooded Don Juan. It didn't happen. Where was the fire? Why didn't my hormones boil when an attractive girl went by?" When Sy fell in love with a woman for the first time, it was after months of friendship, and with the woman who was to be his wife.

> I fell in love with Karen – not her body. I fell in love with her integrity, her love for God, her strength, her convictions, her personality and temperament. I wanted to be with her, and I couldn't imagine spending the rest of my life without her.

His sexual interest in his wife developed quite normally, he said, after he had experienced for himself what heterosexual sex was like. Sy "fell in love" the way heterosexual men are supposed to. For Sy sex is now an "enjoyable, pleasurable, wonderful slice" in his "pie of life".

Does the wife of an ex-gay have to worry continually that her husband is being tempted by other men? No. Provided she didn't make the mistake of marrying him too soon. If the spade-work has been done, if he is capable of forming good *non-possessive* same-sex friendships, if he hasn't been sexually active for three or four years, if he is no longer struggling with porn, masturbation and sexual fantasy, he will be tempted far less than the average Christian heterosexual is tempted to look twice at another woman. "Some little thing may zing 'em periodically" says Alan Medinger, an ex-gay leader, "but the power's gone out of it, and it's really nothing more than a nuisance." Most healed ex-gays say the temptations they experience have merged into the mainstream of human temptation and are no longer specifically homosexual in character. Ex-gays still often feel the need for males "bigger" than themselves to say, "You're worthwhile, your life counts and you're OK." For a former homosexual – because of years of conditioning – this can be one way the irritating "periodic zing" can occur, but it progressively does not, simply because it is only male affirmation they are seeking – as it has been all along – and now they know it. But many straight men seek affirmation from other males. Everyone is tempted in a former area of weakness until he becomes strong. It is no different with the ex-gay.

Male ex-gays, although they are over their sexual struggle, can still struggle with an ache for one exclusive intimate friend – the emotional need for connection that underlies homosexuality. If they have not grown past this when they marry, wives will be hurt by their "emotional adultery". Bruce's wife was upset when they returned from honeymoon to see he was more excited over his male friend than he had been with her all honeymoon. In this respect Bruce married too soon. Ex-gays are usually over the emotionally dependent stage after five years.

Women marrying ex-gays should not put pressure upon them to perform sexually. Most men are nervous about their nuptial night; the ex-gay more so. Frank advised one ex-gay not to marry the woman of his choice.

> She said to me that once he married her he'd be a lion in bed. She was putting so much pressure on him he was bound to fail. I've asked many women, "Do you love this guy enough that if sex never happened you would still marry him?" If they say, "Yes", I know they'll have a good sex life.

Before male ex-gays marry, they should have made significant progress on their ambivalent relationships with their mothers, or wives will have a roller-coaster ride. Most ex-gays have found mothers dominating, suffocating, and emotionally demanding at the same time as they often have them on pedestals and are close. This can reflect in a love-hate, mother-son, relationship with their wives. The lesbian marrying too early will transfer to her husband her unresolved anger, fear or frustration with her father, or other male figures.

Ex-gays marrying too early can make bad choices, frequently marrying women like their mothers: often "rescuers" who will mother them and make their decisions for them – a fatal choice for the ex-gay who must grow up as a man, overcome his passivity, take responsibility and initiative. Because of her own crippled self-esteem, a wife in this category will fight his recovery to keep him needing her. Ex-gays who marry too early can often choose unattractive, overweight women who do not daunt them sexually, or women with poor self-esteem and weak identities. An ex-gay marrying a woman like this, if he continues to heal inside the marriage, and she doesn't, risks ending up a disappointed man. An ex-lesbian might choose a male "rescuer" or a passive or abusive man. It is very advisable to wait.

MASCULINITY AND FEMININITY

An ex-gay wants to be a man; the healing lesbian's goal is to be a woman. The ex-gay makes a mistake who feels he has to conform to any of the various secular ideals of masculinity – which usually focus in some way on power. But there are many false models of femininity around too, not least in the church. What exactly is a man, what is a woman? Check back to Chapter 3 for definitions of masculinity and femininity.

I leave the last word on masculinity to Sy, whose life-long attempts to be a woman made masculinity something of an issue for him.

> We're never told in the Bible how macho Jesus was, how deep his voice, how broad his shoulders, how thick his beard, how big his biceps, how tight he wore his blue jeans. He never even dated. But of all the men who ever lived, he had the most intact masculine identity. And, everything he did pleased the Father. If everything I do pleases the Father, then I believe it will be reflected outwardly as manliness and transcend every cultural stereotype.

LESBIANISM

For further discussion I refer readers to Jeanette Howard's book, *Out of Egypt*. Everything treated in this chapter so far and in Chapter 14 applies to women with same sex attraction, as will Chapter 17. The lesbian differs from the male gay in that:

- The male homosexual struggle is with his sex drive: learning to translate sexual signals back into the basic need for affirmation. The ex-lesbian has to do the same with her intense emotional attachments. She has a hard time seeing that relationship addiction without sex is wrong.

- Where male gays are often emotional, a lesbian's emotions (apart from eruptions of hostility focused round jealousy) are often deeply repressed. It is part of her armour: if you can't feel you can't be hurt any more. She knows she is healing when she starts to feel again.

- Whereas male gays are rarely hostile to women, the lesbian is often hostile to men – usually the legacy of the high levels of male sexual abuse in lesbianism. Because of abuse, lesbians find it hard to trust God – a male figure. "For lesbians it helps to see the feminine side of God," says Sy. "He's your advocate, compassionate, responsive, he was there when you were hurting. You just didn't know to go to him."

The lesbian's greatest struggle as she moves towards wholeness is the recovery of trust lost through years of disrupted attachment to the same-sex parent, a series of relationships, and, often, sexual abuse. To stop manipulating and controlling others in an effort to gain love and to protect herself; to become open and vulnerable; to begin to feel again, is something she will probably not be able to do without inner healing.

ENDING THE RELATIONSHIP

Lesbians – like relationship addicts – will rationalize their need to stay in the present relationship. They will want to stay together as "just friends" but it will tend to slow down their progress. They often have to get away from each other even to begin to see objectively the neediness that was keeping them together. "A complete break with a lover is often the only way that one is able to leave a relationship at all," says Starla Allen (page 243). The only question is when. An ex-lesbian who leaves a relationship faces grief, loneliness, fear and doubt. Lesbian relationships must not break up before there is substitute support for her, says Starla. "Their relationship has been so exclusive, so emotionally all-in-all, that she has nothing to fall back on. She is often in financial difficulty because so much was jointly owned." The lesbian who leaves her lover to start the healing process needs friendship, spiritual support, help in finding new housing and possibly with budgeting. She also needs space to grieve the loss of her lover.

The choice to get out

Because of the intense emotional security the lesbian relationship provides, those lesbians who leave it do so because they choose to, not always because they want to. Male homosexuals are more motivated to change than lesbians because promiscuous sex is more disillusioning than intense emotional relationships. "Gay men coming to us will say, 'I feel used, abused, a commodity'," says Jeanette Howard. "Women don't say that. They say, 'They really loved me. I'd never experienced love like that in my life.'" Jeanette was one of them: "I wasn't desperate to get out. I didn't find lesbianism destructive; I didn't feel used or abused. I felt cared for and secure; it met many of my needs. I only got out because God said, not because I wanted to." Says Ann, "I got out because Jesus was more important to me. I didn't expect restoration of my sexuality, only celibacy and struggle. No-one told me you could change."

"If a lesbian says, 'I'm coming to you because God said, "No!"' Then there's a good chance of healing," says Jeanette:

> If she doesn't, what she's really saying is, "Relieve my pain till I find someone else." Usually what they're after is a painkiller, not change. If that's what's motivating them they'll co-operate till the pain lessens enough, and then they'll be back into it.

THE CHURCH AND THE EX-LESBIAN

Christian women must be willing to offer a healing lesbian healthy, unpossessive, unerotic friendships. They are as vital in her healing as in the male ex-gay's. Jeanette, in a paper on lesbianism, looks at a few things the healing lesbian will also be doing when she is around Christian heterosexual women.

If you are a woman she will be watching you to see: Do you like you? Are you happy with your appearance? Do you care for yourself (hair, make-up)? Do you like and trust other women? Do you like and trust men? Do you hug other women? For how long? What do you talk about? Are you competitive with them? Do you respect men? Fear them? Do you trust them?

If you are a man she will watch you like a hawk, noting how you describe your mother, sister, wife to other people (with respect, disdain, or indifference), she will scrutinize your relationship with your wife (are you attentive, loving and supportive?), and observe how you relate to women in general (are you courteous, sarcastic, dismissive?).

A woman emerging from the lesbian lifestyle may look and act awkward, she may ride a motorbike, wear plaids and jeans – and drop earrings. Men: you should open car doors for her, offer to carry heavy items, compliment her on her appearance – and not be surprised if she snarls at you. She is questioning your motives, embarrassed at being treated like a woman. But she will be wooed by your kindness, compassion, understanding and persistence. Outwardly she won't reveal a thing, but internally she will be responding.

You will have to deal with rejection, anger, bitterness, the need to control, her lack of trust. She will be loud, sullen, violent, lethargic, she will love and hate you with equal intensity. She will need inner healing, confrontation, honest communication. You will have to be firm, gentle, and long suffering. She will emotionally attach to you, then violently detach. But one day she will amaze you all by turning up in a dress.

"Underneath the rough exterior," says Jeanette, "is a little girl asking you to listen to her and to love her into healing. Help her become the woman she was intended to be from the beginning."

OF THE SAME CLAY

Even if we cannot see how like the homosexual we are, healing homosexuals soon do and it heartily encourages them. "One of the things that we find when we get to the church men's retreat every year is how screwed up the straights are," says ex-gay John. "The things we've had to work through and think about they haven't even started work on. They are so messed up."

"I had this romantic notion that straight women glided gracefully though life with hardly a care in the world," says Jeanette. "That illusion was shattered during a sixteen-week discipleship course I led. I was amazed to find they were actually more screwed up than I was."

"Ex-gays are often surprised to find that regular folks have also experienced rejection, hurt, insecurity, frustration, loneliness, self-pity and lust," says Robbi Kennedy, an ex-gay group leader. "Discovering that, helps them put their lives in perspective and makes them less isolated."

Christians will be able to help homosexual men and women when they can turn to them, and say with honest conviction. "You know, you're right, we're no better than each other!"

Let's look next at one particular obstacle to the healing of addiction.

Chapter Sixteen

PRESERVATION OF THE MARRIAGE – A BARRIER TO HEALING?

Wayne was a born-again Christian – but that didn't stop him breaking Michelle's nose during a church service. Once her head was split open, another time her neck fractured. Finally she was nearly drowned in a bath with a dog chain around her neck after she had just come out of hospital after stomach surgery.

"He got me back to my place," she said. "He put a dog chain and lead round my neck, and I had them on for four hours, pulled tight. He tried to drown me in the bathtub with that chain on and the kids screaming. I stopped fighting and passed out and vomited and he pulled me up. Then he dragged me out and raped me."[1]

Severe hidden addiction – child abuse, wife battering, promiscuity, rage, misogyny, homosexuality – scars the family for life and violates marriage vows to honour and cherish. It turns Christian marriages into hell-holes, not holy, loving relationships meant to reflect the relationship between Christ and his bride.

When marriages are under strain from addictive abuse the first instinct of the conservative church is to keep the marriage going, prop it up somehow, because of its belief in the sacred matrimonial vows: "until death us do part". This is understandable and perfectly reasonable when the abusive party is prepared to do the hard work that changes things. But if he or she isn't? If the abuse is denied? Kept secret? What then?

KEITH AND KAREN

Turn back for a moment to Chapter 2 and refresh your memory of Keith: relationship addict and "rageoholic". Now meet Karen, his wife. Karen's father was schizophrenic and she spent much of her childhood and adolescence dodging his violent rages and living with his wild mood swings, eccentric public behaviour and periodic psychiatric committal. Karen's mother worked 18-hour days to rescue her husband from debt and keep the family above the poverty line. A nurse by training, she nursed her husband one day and hid from him the next. It was a miserable marriage. For Karen a man's needs came first. It was normal that men dominated the home, were abusive, sick, and selfish and that women made the best of it, tried to help, but never left because men were a woman's only security. Karen escaped from home as quickly as her first romance provided the opportunity to marry and got herself hooked up with a man with another life-dominating problem – alcohol. They married because she thought her love would help him. There were two children. For ten years he sexually and physically abused her, while she left him twice and returned twice, won back by his tears, pleading, gifts and promises of reform – and her fear of life without the security of his income. The third time she left him for good. She had been a Christian for one year and was living on welfare and recovering from back surgery when she met Keith.

Karen's response when one close Christian friend begged her not to marry Keith was almost predictable: "He was a bit eccentric but I thought his problems weren't that bad; that with a good marriage relationship they would disappear", which was what she thought when she married the first time. From a poor, insecure home she was attracted by the security promised by Keith's professional salary. She was also fooled by his "generosity", "loving" attentions, and regular church-attendance into believing he was a Christian.

Keith was a misogynist – the name given to men who seem to hate the women they love. Dr Susan Forward in her book *Men who hate women, and the women who love them*, describes the misogynist as a man who has learned in his early life that women have the power to hurt him, engulf him or abandon him. He has also learned that the way to control women is to demean, scare and hurt them. At the same time he expects the woman in his life to meet his needs. Fearful of abandonment he attempts to bind his wife to him by weakening her – by stripping her of her independence and confidence – to make her dependent on him.

Keith also responded to women who needed looking after, as his home life had taught him. He often told Karen she was his Pygmalion Project: he found her flat on her back and nursed her to health; she was penniless, alone, and needed the social uplift he could give her. During their courtship he tried to buy her, and once they married he believed he owned her.

Chapter 2 described what happened to the marriage.

Four years into the marriage Karen was desperate. As a Christian she no longer believed divorce was an option, so she sought help at church. She made four appointments with the pastor to explain what was going on, but it led nowhere; he didn't seem to believe her. Nor would he speak to Keith and Keith himself refused to get any counsel: he said he didn't have any problems; they were all Karen's. The elders assured her that submission and loving service were the scriptural things to do. Keith seemed a nice enough guy: bit of a loner but pleasant, professional, respectable, not too involved but a regular attender. Whenever anyone visited, Keith was charming and attentive. Karen's story seemed rather far-fetched.

Karen slowly gained the courage to begin challenging Keith about his behaviour, but he denied everything she said, until Karen began to feel she was slowly going mad: as if she were just imagining and inventing everything. He told her she was slowly going insane and would end up in a psychiatric ward like her father. There was "absolutely no change in him. We had normalcy about two days a month," says Karen.

Karen began to insist Keith come with her to marriage counselling sessions, but he either said there was nothing wrong with the marriage, or that any problems were her fault; or ran away, cried and sulked and threatened to make her name "mud" at church if she left him; or hung on to her desperately telling her how much he loved her. Finally, under duress, he attended one marriage counselling session in which he said he was "quite happy in himself" and that the marriage was good. Nine months later, after realizing Keith was deeply opposed to any self-examination or change, Karen left him – before she "did something desperate".

Once her church learned her whereabouts the phone calls started, warm and friendly at first, but soon obvious attempts to bring about a return to Keith. In the meantime Keith was going to church every Sunday with their young son, sitting in the back row and crying. People sent him notes and messages of Christian comfort. Compared with this heartbroken man bringing his little boy to church, Karen appeared fickle, a deserter, a woman who obviously married easily and left lightly. There was no question Keith loved her: look how desperate he was to have her back. Her place as a Christian woman was clearly alongside her husband. The pastor wrote outlining her options: either she return to the marriage or relinquish her ministry with the church. Her solicitor, a Christian man, advised her not to proceed with legal separation. Her circle of Christian friends shrank: some of them became openly rejecting. After several months Karen left the church.

An inside look

Karen recognized her codependent behaviour and stopped protecting Keith. She gained her courage from her growing relationship with God and a few Christian friends. But Keith's denial, rages, ridicule and accusations only intensified as time passed. After Karen left, Keith went to counselling and the counsellor began to explore his early life; after two sessions Keith cancelled all further appointments. Karen's church did not take a second look at the man she had married: she had walked out on a Christian man when there had been no adultery: that was enough. Karen no longer believes God led her into the marriage. She now believes she led herself into it and thought it was God. She was too locked into her "patterns" at the time to see what was really going on, she says. For three years she "submitted" and "served" because she was told this would change Keith's heart. It didn't. He became worse. She wanted the marriage to grow but when she began to challenge Keith his behaviour became still worse. She believes God finally led her out of the marriage because it was not a marriage and was not going to become one.

THE CHURCH'S PREDICAMENT

When the church is faced in marriages with compulsive, abusive male[2] behaviour it tends to intervene in favour of the man in ways that protect the marriage rather than threaten it. There are at least two reasons the church intervenes in this way.

One: Its attitude to women

Pastors, ministers and priests are rarely deliberately heartless towards women, but most church leaders are men; so are most members of the church's doctrinal and policy-making bodies. Male empathy can understate the level of male abuse.

Two: Its commitment to marriage

The church is one of the few remaining champions of the institution of marriage as faithful life-long monogamy – which is right and proper. But when this commitment is combined with notions of the "suffering saint"; the hidden nature of abuse; a prevailing male perspective on the role of women, headship and submission; preservation of the marriage at all costs can be a vote in favour of perpetuated abuse.

Let's look at the suffering saint and headship and submission.

THE "SUFFERING" SAINT

In her relationship with an addicted man a codependent[3] woman can *appear* to be displaying and developing Christian virtues. After all, love hopes all things, bears all things, believes all things, suffers long. Greater love has no (woman) than this, that (she) lay down (her) life… the Bible says. There is a litany of right-sounding phrases that appear to bind a woman to an abusive relationship: suffering with Christ, dying daily, taking up her cross, forgiving seventy times seven, submitting, allowing tribulation to work patience and endurance. She is being a missionary to her husband.

"If someone strikes you on the right cheek, turn to him the other also", is an injunction meant to apply to treatment of enemies not to a love-pledge. Apply it to a marital relationship and it only trains up children in the way they will go. "I don't think what I'm going through is any worse than what the disciples went through," says one woman married to an abusive Christian man. "There's a lot of torment in the Psalms; Job went through a lot. My reward will be in heaven. If I stand faithful my children will follow me." But her young son is already treating her the way her husband is.

The codependent woman involved with an abusive man is not really giving or loving; she is hooked into a desperate exercise in raising self-esteem. She is not "denying" herself, laying down her life, or taking up her cross. When he abuses her she is not experiencing persecution for righteousness sake. A woman married to an abusive man often has confused and distorted notions of Christian suffering. Christian suffering that comes from carrying the cross is when "His Light in us collides with the darkness in this world – the ignorance, hate, lies and delusions within the souls of men, and we know conflict," says Leanne Payne in her book, *The Healing Presence*. (Karen began to experience true Christian suffering when she began to confront Keith rather than "submit" to him.)

The codependent is an inwardly emotionally starved person who is bending her outward "strong, coping, together" mask to the task of dying to self, suffering with Christ and taking up her cross. It's an absurdity. Jesus came to remove the mask and heal the person in pain behind it. Only the healed "real" self can take up the cross, but in the codependent the real self barely has an existence. When she takes the submissive role in an abusive relationship it is submersion not submission. She will do anything to keep him loving her.

Christians can easily get caught in the trap of codependency (aiding and abetting abusive behaviour), by being nice, kind, loving, forgiving, gentle, caring, peacemaking, humble, serving, unselfish; the kind of people Christians think the Bible says they should be. But there is plenty of room in scripture for assertiveness, tough love, justice, mutuality in relationships, respect and confrontation. Jesus did come to bring peace on earth, but only after he had brought a sword (Matthew 10:34). He came to divide light from darkness, truth from error in the hearts of men and women; if need be with the effect of dividing families. Love, the Bible says, rejoices with *truth*. The Christian *is* meant to care and help and serve, but not when its effect is to prop up someone's addiction in a desperate attempt to gain love.

HEADSHIP AND SUBMISSION

Modern Christians might no longer use the words male headship/female submission, but male superiority/female subservience has been, and in some parts of the church still is, well entrenched in the thinking of many Christians. It can foster dependent, rescuing behaviour in women and abuse in men.

For centuries a little Hebrew word has been mistranslated in the Old Testament. Jessie Penn-Lewis, in her book *The Magna Carta of Women*, considers it "the most serious mistranslation in the English version of the Bible", the one "lying at the root of all the misinterpretations of the words of Paul in the New Testament" as they relate to male-female relationships.

The little word is *teshuqa* and it appears in one critical verse of scripture as part of the consequence of man's fall away from God. Your desire shall be for your husband, and he shall rule over you (Genesis 3:16, RSV). *Teshuqa* simply means *turning*, but is translated incorrectly "desire" or "craving", "stretching out after", and "longing". The correct rendering of the passage is simply: You *are turning to* your (man) husband.

But there is another mistranslation. The words "shall be", in "… your desire *shall be* for your husband… " are not there in the original Hebrew. In other words there is no "must", there is no imperative. It does not say, "Your craving must be for your (man) husband."

The verse – incorrectly translated – goes on to say: "and he *shall* rule over you", "shall" here again equalling "must". Some versions use "dominate" and "master" for "rule" so that with the full bias aboard, the incorrectly translated passage reads: *Your craving, your stretching out after, your longing must be for your (man) hus-*

band and he must rule over, dominate, master, have dominion, have power, over you.

Which is the way millions of Christian men and women over the years have understood the passage, which is frequently cross-referenced to 1 Corinthians 11:3: "...the head of the woman is the man", thereby loading that passage too with all the bias of Genesis 3:16. Where Christian men have notions of superiority, mastery, dominion, and power in their heads – reinforced by the culture – they are not quick to denounce female dependency on men, caretaking behaviour, or abusive husbanding.

God was *not* saying to Eve, "You must crave and long for your husband (man) and he must rule over you." *He was saying with sadness, "You are turning away from me towards your husband (man) and he will (simple future) have power over you."* God was simply looking down the time-line and commenting on the inevitable. What we turn dependently towards, we give power over us. Ever since Eve, women have turned to men rather than God for fulfilment and love. In principal the emptier the love-tank the more slavishly they have turned, and the more abusive the men they have turned to. God wants to strengthen women so that they "turn towards" him again for love and fulfilment. The mastery of a woman by an abusive man is a miserable domination. No male "rule" of that sort was ever ordained by God. In relationship addiction women have turned away from God to meet their needs for love. There is no blessing of God upon it.

Obedience

The New Testament Greek word (from *hupo* and *tasso*) often translated "submit" or "obey" has been most discussed in relation to husbands and wives, but the word is also used of the attitudes of all believers to each other, irrespective of sex. It is a word with a particularly Christian use; it had no secular usage. "Wives, submit to your husbands as to the Lord" (Ephesians 5:22) means no more than "the Christian grace of yielding one's preferences to another where no principle is involved," says Penn-Lewis.

In their book *Battered into submission*, James and Phyllis Alsdurf quote surveys of abused women who sought help from clergy. In the Roman Catholic, Greek Orthodox, and conservative Protestant churches, priests and ministers "were of little help" because they felt threatened by conflict that might lead to separation or divorce. Women seeking help were subtly blamed for the abuse, the authors say, and reminded of the admonitions of St Paul and told to "try to be a better wife", "be more considerate of him", and "obey him". Leaving the abusive marriage was sin, or desertion. Women were advised to see the abuse as "an opportunity to suffer for Jesus' sake". Almost without exception women reported that pastors focused on getting them, not their husbands, to change. One in four of 500 United States pastors surveyed across 34 denominations said they believed that wifely submission was the answer to male violence.

Well-meaning Christians wanting to save the marriages of couples in abusive relationships are doing far more harm than good, when they regurgitate formulae about obedience, submission, and headship, death to self, servanthood and humility, and offer fascinating little secrets to women. The Christian relationship addict in an abusive relationship needs to *teshuqa* to Christ for the love she is seeking, and not continue to let her partner abuse her. Even Christ is not asking that of her – as we will see now.

True love

The correct meaning of headship is not rule and domination but servanthood: love that sacrifices itself, that is nurturing, cherishing and supporting (Colossians 2:19). A healthy woman is capable of answering warmly and willingly and joyfully to a man who loves her this way. *Scripture does not expect a woman to respond where she is not loved:* her response is contingent on the attitudes and behaviour of her partner. It comes through clearly in the original Greek: … each one of you (husbands) also must love his wife as he loves himself *in order that* the wife may reverence her husband (Ephesians 5:33), not as many translations put it: and the wife *must* reverence her husband. Telling a wife she should obey and submit and adapt to a man who, rather than loving her as Christ loves the church, is only capable of an obsessive, hostile, abusive relationship with her (like Keith), is asking her to do what Christ himself is not asking.

HEALTHY SELF-LOVE AND MARRIAGE

The *first* commandment and therefore the most important thing we can do in life is "to love the Lord (our) God with all our heart, and with all our soul and with all our mind" (Matthew 22:37). But God is fair; he doesn't expect us to do that until we are assured of his love first. We love him because he first loved us (1 John 4:19).

The second greatest commandment to us all is to love our neighbours *as we love ourselves* (Matthew 22:39). The Bible also says: the man "must love his wife *as he loves himself*". So loving ourselves is the second most important thing we can ever do in life and crucial for our marriages: the man who is incapable of loving himself is incapable of loving his wife as he ought, thus making it difficult for her to respond as she ought.

It all goes back to love-tanks and masks. True self-love is being totally comfortable without the mask. It is knowing we are loved and valued by God, as we are, as if we were his only child. There is no need for compensation, or timidity – or addiction. Loving ourselves *because* God loves us, is the first step on the way to loving others with the secure, expansive, unthreatened love of 1 Corinthians 13, which is not jealous or rude, or haughty or selfish, or irritable or touchy, and not demanding of its own way, but is patient and kind. A man who can love like that will be a man who loves his wife as he ought, and normally she will be respectful and responsive as a result.

This is a rosy and idealistic picture, but it is the picture God has in mind when he speaks of marriage: two people knowing themselves loved and valued by God, so able to love and value themselves and each other: the husband initiating in love to his wife, the wife responding in love to her husband – like Christ and the church.

Clearly, the church is not now the ravishing and exalted creature who will one day wed the long-suffering and perfect bridegroom. Neither are we nearly perfect husbands and wives when we marry. But two imperfect people who love God and are struggling together to overcome damaging legacies of the past so that they can love themselves and each other as they ought, can be assured of the Holy Spirit's help, a deepening love for each other and increasing success. This is a marriage consistent with the model of Christ and his imperfect, chosen bride, and hence deserving of the name.

But what if the relationship called marriage is hostile to the model? What if two people – a woman with unmet needs for love and an abusive man – read each other's cues, "click" into each other, get a minister to make them man and wife, and then begin a life of mutual destruction? Do we say God joined them together?

RELATIONSHIP ADDICTION AND GUIDANCE TO MARRY

When women are attracted to problem men what happens to divine guidance?

Jackie

Jackie fell for Clive, a tall, quiet, good-looking, wealthy widower with warm, twinkling humour and two small children. It was Jackie's second marriage at the age of 27; her first ended after five years of her first husband's unfaithfulness and physical abuse. Jackie became a Christian after her first marriage and Clive became a Christian early in the courtship (it turned out later) to satisfy Jackie's insistence that they should not be "unequally yoked". The commitment seemed authentic (the pastor was happy with it); the rest of the church was excited. He married them in a happy church service.

It was all over in a year. Clive's Christian façade disintegrated within weeks: he forbade church going, prayer and Bible stories with the children, and any playing of Christian music. He became tyrannical, cruel, baiting and cold. He seemed to hate her. He was deliberately cruel to her horse. Their sexual relationship stopped – he pushed her into another bedroom and told her not to come crawling for his affection. But visitors always found him charming, quiet, and mild. After a year, when she was sick and emotionally devastated, he took her to the lawyer and forced her to sign legal separation papers.

Jackie had done it again. Repeating old patterns she tried to extract love from men who were outwardly charming but selfish, abusive, and hard. But when Jackie married Clive she believed with all her heart that God was leading her. She could point to scriptures that had "spoken" to her and other signs that showed the smile of God was upon them. Jackie continued to believe God had led her into the marriage and spent the next few years praying for its restoration and struggling every time she saw Clive. But Clive took another woman in, and divorced Jackie after the statutory two years. The experience took a considerable emotional toll on Jackie. God had misled her or seemed indifferent to what had happened.

Another relationship followed this one some years later. This time the man was not a Christian, and he and Jackie were soon sexually involved. He was visibly arrogant, aloof and emotionally cold. "It made me shiver just to shake his hand," one woman said. But Jackie made excuses for him: his aloofness only hid inferiority. She became defensive and angry when Christians warned her about the relationship. She said she had waited and waited for God to bring her a Christian husband (she was then approaching 40) and he hadn't, so now a flesh-and-blood relationship with an agnostic was better than a relationship with a distant demanding God whose love she had never felt. After eighteen months it was all over. Then there was a series of other short-term sexual relationships.

Jackie was responding to her own needs for male love and to signals certain kinds of men flashed her. She probably spiritualized her relationship with Clive because she did not understand her own drives and because all she had ever wanted was a happy married home life. In the process God became a callous and emotionally indifferent figure, like her own father. God wants to heal her distorted image of him, but she is too hurt and angry now to trust him. And in the meantime she is drawn into more relationships that hurt her.

Patty and Blake

Patty was engaged on her second date – the swift commitment that characterizes the "click" of intermeshing agendas – and several months later married a homosexual man. She didn't know he was homosexual when she married him. She thought it was God's guidance. So did everyone else. She had been a Christian a few months; Blake for several years. He was "very spiritually minded, read the Bible and prayed and said he wanted to have a good Christian family and be a good father". He was also handsome and very intelligent.

The marriage was an "awful" six years of crying and depression, which Patty feared might end in his murder at her hands, but actually ended in a legal annulment of marriage: the marriage was never consummated. Blake manipulated her emotionally: telling her he loved her, promising her it would work out, and buying her gifts, but he was homosexually active. He often locked her out of their bedroom. From time to time she discovered cabinets full of male porn. She became codependent: shielding him from the consequences of his behaviour, letting him swear her to secrecy about his homosexuality (on grounds that their relationship would never work if she told anyone), not seeking counselling for herself in case it exposed him and damaged his career. She worked to put him through college only to find later that he had dropped out and continued to take money from her under false pretences. He bent her to his will by laying heavies on her about submission. He refused to seek help. Patty became sick with constant abdominal pain.

When Patty finally broke six years of silence and went to her pastors for advice, they believed her because they had known Blake before Patty had. They asked her to give them time to think about it and return in two weeks. When she did, says Patty, "They opened the Bible and read… 'what God has joined together, let man not separate.' Then they said, 'We don't believe God ever joined you together.'" Several days later Patty moved out.

Patty is no longer mad at God for "misleading" her into the marriage. "I was for a while, but now I believe I took a wrong step and it wasn't what he wanted for me at all."

SEPARATION AND DIVORCE

About 75% of marriages in which separation occurs end in divorce, which is one reason so many pastors and ministers are reluctant to advise separation for women in abusive marriages. But in some cases separation is exactly the jolt the abusive partner needs to break the wall of his denial and do something about his problem. As the abusive husband of a friend of mine said to her: "When you left me you shocked me into next week. But if you hadn't I would never had seen I was doing anything wrong." There *are* success stories as a result of separation. (In many abusive marriages the divorce figures are only so high *because* so many abusers refuse treatment.)

The Bible allows for separation (1 Corinthians 7:11). And God exiled Israel to Babylon to think over her behaviour in a hard place and have a change of heart about her relationship with God: her husband and lover.

But what if the abusive male claims the name Christian, has no intention of leaving the marriage, claims never to have committed adultery but remains abusive – like Keith. What if there is no change after x years of separation? What do you do when the only traditional scriptural "out" is adultery or desertion by the unbelieving spouse? Tomes have been written on the subject.

"If a woman comes in telling of… every conceivable inhumanity and is simply and grandly told that unless there is adultery or desertion she has no biblical basis for divorce, that is an attempt to turn the words of Jesus and Paul into a new legalism,"[4] says Richard Foster in *Battered into Submission*, by James and Phyllis Alsdurf.

"Fidelity," argues Lewis Smedes, "is not achieved simply by staying out of other people's beds."[4] It is a nonsense that the letter of the law should allow a woman to divorce a man who commits adultery once, but not permit it if he cruelly abuses her for years.

"Preserving the external semblance of a marriage without the inner reality of marriage as God intended it to be and rigidly condemning divorce can be traced to moral pride,"[4] argues Allen Verhey. Theologian Karl Barth comments: "In certain cases… dissolution by divorce is a recognition of the fact that God has already brought the marriage under the judgment of nonexistence."[4]

"God's intent from creation was not divorce but companionship," say James and Phyllis Alsdurf. "But there is the continual conflict between God's intent and man's sinful choices."

A person might not commit adultery but kill instead, and both are violations of the law, says James 2:11. In some abusive relationships killing is going on. They are not love covenants, they are death traps: physically, psychologically, and spiritually.

A point can be reached in a relationship when darkness and light become so polarized (regardless of the label Christian) that it is bordering on blasphemy to pretend it mirrors the holy, loving relationship between Christ and his bride. In some cases of intransigent abuse, where a wife has left, compassion, mercy and justice rather than lofty judgments based on the moral law are called for. James 2:13 tells us to judge with mercy, because mercy triumphs over judgment.

There is bright hope for any marriage in which both parties bite the bullet and work at change, but there is little hope for the marriage, such as Keith and Karen's, in which one partner actively obstructs the process of "cleaving" and becoming "one flesh" – God's original intention for marriage. How can a marriage reflect the relationship between Christ and his bride when one party is hostile to the model – particularly when the male, as initiator – is violently hostile? God hates divorce but he also hates violence: "I hate divorce *and* I hate a man's covering his wife with violence" (Malachi 2:16). The obsessive manipulation of misogyny, for example, is psychological violence. It can reduce a woman to emotional rubble.

Significantly, *Battered into Submission* comments: one denomination's policies on divorce changed when, over the course of one year, daughters of six "top echelon leaders" were divorced. This need not necessarily be self-serving, as one Christian woman said who finally fled her marriage after years of abuse and submission (that only made the abuse worse): "I believed the verses (about submission and giving and loving) because it was scripture, and scripture doesn't change. But what eventually happened was that my perception of what they meant changed."

Better never to get into such a marriage in the first place.

THE DIVINE WARNING SIGNS

Christian women who get into abusive relationships sometimes remember, with hindsight, that there *were* warning signs of an imminent mistake. Patty, for instance, was vividly warned in a dream the night before her first date with Blake – a dinner date at his house.

> I dreamed we were in a house and Blake was sitting in a chair and there was another man standing behind him – a man who also went to church – and this man had his hands on Blake's shoulders. The two of them were ridiculing me, running me down. There was a closet and they wanted me to go over to it. I went over and opened it and it was full of the most disgusting, vile refuse. And they said, "Clean it." It was a terrible, terrible feeling. I woke up and when I did I was completely drained and I felt like throwing up. I thought, *There's no possible way I can go out.* I was sick. But he didn't have a telephone so the only way I could tell Blake I wasn't going to come to dinner was to get someone to drive me over to tell him. But when I got there, he said, "Well. you're already here, why don't you stay. It's OK if you don't feel well, I'll take you home" – so I stayed. I ignored the dream because everyone has dreams.

Patty's dream was prophetic. Blake did dump his refuse on her. The pastor who encouraged their marriage knew of Blake's homosexuality and was later dismissed from office himself for sexual immorality. Patty says he was the man in the dream with his hands on Blake's shoulders. God *was* warning her but as a rational Westerner she didn't take the dream seriously – though "If someone else had warned me," she said, "I would have listened because of the dream."

HOW TO CHOOSE?

So how does a woman with low self-esteem who is searching for love, avoid getting into an abusive relationship? How does she go about marrying the man of God's choice? First she needs to know herself: does she get into all-absorbing relationships of any kind? With problem men who treat her badly, or problem men she believes she can help, or is it milder: just to be noticed, special? Are there reflections of life at home?

She will probably benefit from prayer-counselling to bring God's love and healing to the empty places that lead her into these relationships. She will need to get her inner imagery of God the Father straight so that she will hear clearly when she asks him about a mate. "If you want to be certain you are listening to God, you must know the Father heart of God," says Joyce Huggett in *Listening to God*. "To distinguish between God's voice and Satan's is to become acquainted with what lies in God's Father heart."

She will need as long as it takes to develop a steady relationship with God and to make sure she can identify, and choose not to become involved with, certain kinds of men.

Then, I suggest that she ask God, her *kind and gentle* Father, to show her the man she is to marry *before* she is emotionally involved. In our romance-saturated culture this sounds ridiculous but it is not nearly as fatal as letting inner need override the Holy Spirit. She will probably find that the man God chooses will not be anything like the man she would have chosen for herself.

Of course God leads us all in different ways. Some people are drawn to each other and find God has been leading them in their very attraction to each other. But for the former relationship addict such a course is a risky one.

I should make it clear that I am enthusiastically in favour of committed, long-term, monogamous relationships and categorically not a proponent of easy divorce. There is bright hope for a marriage when *both* parties individually sort themselves out. But *abusive* marriages in which one party will not admit to a problem, present the church with thorny questions to which it must provide answers.

When a couple gravitates together (like Keith and Karen) for the dark reasons that are part of unmet need and addiction do we say God joined them in "holy matrimony" or did they?

If a relationship addict *teshuqas* to God to find the love she craves, and her husband – who calls himself a Christian – refuses to get help and continues to abuse her psychologically and/or physically, at what point does it become blasphemous to sustain the marriage on grounds that it reflects Christ's love for the church?

Once the glue that bonded an abusive man who refuses to change and a dependent woman, starts to fall apart upon the healing of her dependency, why don't we let her go?

There are times when separation is part of the healing of addiction: times when an abuser will not be brought to his senses and start taking responsibility for himself unless she goes. There are times the love-starved relationship addict must extricate herself from the problem man to whom she is addicted, to even begin to develop the self-esteem to refuse to be abused any more. And sometimes divorce is the consequence – because the abuser refuses to sort himself out and a healthier woman now refuses to return to her old habit of helping him; or because he has already gone looking for someone else who will.

Marriage is meant to be a holy, healthy, intimate, cherishing, joyful reflection of the relationship between Christ and the church. It is not meant to be an institution behind whose walls abuse continues to be perpetrated in the name of religion.

Notes

1. The Australian Women's Weekly (September 1992).
2. Of course, not all abusers are male; but when they are, the conservative church is more likely to turn a blind eye.
3. Surveys show 70 to 80% of battered women, for example, see themselves as rescuers and caregivers – responsible for their husbands' emotional and spiritual well-being. They interpret their violence as evidence that their husbands need their help. They fall into our definition: codependent (James and Phyllis Alsdurf, *Battered into Submission*, pp35-36).
4. Ibid pp119-121.

Chapter Seventeen

HEALING OF RELATION-SHIP DEPENDENCY

When we talk of healing relationship addiction we are talking of tackling three things in particular: fear, anger and the need to be in control. The ex-gay and lesbian, anyone being healed of long-standing problems of a compulsive nature, will also have to face fear and anger. In facing anger we are also talking about being real, not religious.

Fear and control

The deepest emotion of the relationship addict is fear: fear of abandonment and the loss of love, much of it unconscious. Fear can often be traced back to home life. It may have been chaotic, ruled by the tyranny of the "isms", abandonment implicit in the abuse and behaviour of parents. Or it may have been a home in which the child learned that caring for others was the way to be loved, or a home in which love was simply lacking or rejected. Whatever: when we *teshuqa* towards people or things in the attempt to fill our empty love-tanks, the threatened loss of that person or thing is all that is needed to revive all the old unconscious fears.

Fear is why the codependent person is so controlling. To ask the codependent to stop being strong, responsible, all in all to everyone, and in control of everybody and everything in the attempt to be needed (loved), is to take her back into her original chaos without her defences. She can't do it. Behind the strong mask is "the child screaming because no-one needs her or wants her", says Willa. "To die to control is to die to self-protection, but that will only come when she is able to see Jesus walking with her into her deepest fears." This is *the* crucial experience for the relationship addict. Without it she will not be healed.

For the codependent a consistent imagery emerges when Jesus comes to walk with her into her deepest fears: that of an abandoned child (the "true" me), and the codependent mask (the "false" me): very much the picture of Fig 1 (Chapter 4). Jesus interacts with and comforts the abused or abandoned child, the "true" me, that was forsaken for the rescuer's mask in the bid for love and approval. For the emotional dependent, he comes to the abandoned child crouching inside, silently screaming through her clinging relationships for love, security or comfort. Often the adult reconciles with the rejected inner child, and the child is incorporated into the adult personality.

The "inner child" is in danger of being trivialized by pop psychology, but she is not some imaginative fancy. She is, as a sexually abused acquaintance of mine wrote in a poem, "the little lost girl of so long ago, frozen in time, locked in a time warp, silently screaming, pleading for escape". She is "the child of God within us," says Willa, "that precious soul that God created who was never allowed to grow."

"God never nurtures or heals or comforts the false person," says Willa:

> He doesn't heal what he didn't create. The codependent may feel God doesn't love her, or that he has abandoned her, but he hasn't. It's just that he's not going to help her keep living that way. It is she who has abandoned herself.

JESUS IN OUR DEEPEST FEARS

Philippa

Philippa was emotionally dependent, the product of an alcoholic home. Predictably she made a disastrous first marriage to an alcoholic. Her second was to a gay man, upon whom observers said she had "a sickening emotional dependency". She had "no identity of her own". Small wonder: Philippa's childhood was dominated by an alcoholic and violently abusive father, and filled with "terror, anger, and a desperate relationship" with a God she could not understand.

As Philippa prayed with counsellors she saw "a bright beautiful light" that took her to the bottom of herself, like an elevator. "Finally the light and I stopped and I was in a large room. Jesus was sitting near the centre of the room and he told me to come and sit on his lap." Standing menacingly behind Jesus was the fear that had always been part of Philippa's life – but which Jesus banished with a gesture. Cowering terrified under a bench was a dark, wizened, little girl who Philippa recognized as the little girl who had "suffered the fear, anguish and terrible hurts of the years", who tried to protect her mother and was full of "rage, depression and grief". She realized this little girl was a "false self, an empty shell". Jesus coaxed this little girl out from under the bench with loving words, "I love you Philippa, you're safe with me, I won't let anyone hurt you. Please sit on my lap." Jesus explained to Philippa that hiding behind the wizened little girl was a "radiantly beautiful little girl" – the true self – whom fear had "kept bound and helpless, unable to grow and learn and understand". Jesus wanted Philippa, the adult, to let the false self go, so the real self could begin to grow. Only as Jesus wrapped his arms around her did Philippa find the courage to tell her false self she was now superfluous:

> I was very afraid and sad because the false self was very, very real to me and the beautiful girl wasn't. I felt great pain as she left. But then peace and light filled me and the room and the beautiful little girl began to dance and sing to beautiful music that somehow filled the room. I was overwhelmed with unspeakable happiness.

Jesus then told the beautiful little girl that they were going to scenes from her childhood and she would see Jesus in them. "He took me in his arms and it was as if we were again on an elevator." They stopped at many floors and at each stop Jesus and the little girl relived a tormenting childhood memory, from which Jesus extracted the fear by being there with her and comforting her.

When they returned to the top floor the adult and the child merged for the first time. "I knew the child within had been truly birthed and now would have to be nurtured," says Philippa.

This experience went to the heart of the fear in which Philippa's relationship addiction was rooted. God found, and comforted the unloved child and showed Philippa her true self as he saw her – "the beautiful little girl". In the discovery of "the beautiful little girl" the correction of her crippled self-esteem began at its very root: Philippa began to see herself as God saw her.

Jesus walked with Daphne (Chapter 10), into one of the childhood experiences behind her clinging relationship to Jeff. Daphne, also the product of an alcoholic home, saw herself at age six, sitting by a rubbish tin at school while the whole class trooped by, throwing paper at her and telling her she was rubbish because she hadn't pleased the teacher. For the rest of that year Daphne was neurotic about pleasing the teacher, and gradually deeply accepted the idea she was rubbish while she equally deeply repressed the incident. When she married her homosexual husband, Jeff, he treated her like rubbish and she let him because all she wanted was to please him. As she relived the rubbish tin experience at school, Jesus said to her, "You don't have to please Jeff, the teacher, or anybody."

The inner healing experience helps change the harsh God of the relationship addict's inner imagery into a gentle, compassionate Father who comforts and cherishes – someone to whom she can continue to turn in her recovery. The codependent begins to realize she does not need to be needed to know that she is loved. She *is* loved, greatly loved, by God, but for herself, not for her strong, responsible, indispensable persona. The emotional dependent begins to become dependent on a God who thinks the world of her. In his love she begins to believe that she and her opinions matter.

For those whose fathers were never there to approve and gently affirm their daughter's budding womanhood, Jesus can appear in the inner healing experience as a tender, adoring bridegroom, lovingly affirming her femininity. The Song of Solomon is written for the healing relationship addict: Behold you are beautiful my love, behold you are beautiful... your voice is sweet, your face is lovely... you have ravished my heart with one look from your eyes...

The relationship addict who has experienced the tender love of God in these ways can start to go to work more consciously on her self-esteem, as Carrie did, and her diary records:

> Jesus, you are the main reason I feel good about myself. You love, esteem, nurture, approve and accept me. I am your daughter, your masterpiece. You are my maker, my friend, my lover, my redeemer, my Saviour, my life. Lord, I never knew how flimsy my relationship was with you until my relationship with Tait fell apart.

IDOLATRY

Idolatry is turning to someone other than God to meet your deep need for love. Idolatry is loving someone else with all your heart, soul, mind, and strength, no matter what you might say about the central place God has in your heart. Relationship addiction is idolatry. Confession of idolatry is much easier once the tender love of God has been experienced in healing encounters.

RELINQUISHMENT

Relinquishment is the antidote to control. Secular writers on recovery from codependency say relinquishment is the *sine qua non* of healing. By relinquishment they mean stopping caretaking behaviour and leaving all the consequences and "what if's" with "a force higher than yourself". But God as an impersonal higher power cannot be trusted like the one who has entered childhood fear and healed it. It is only as she discovers God wants to be intimately, powerfully and compassionately involved with her that the relationship addict begins to *teshuqa* to him to meet her needs for love. And it is usually only then that she is able to begin to relinquish the relationship that means so much to her. Let's look at Christian relinquishment.

Willa was born into a Christian family, a quiet child in a household of busy committed parents and bright, outgoing siblings with whom she felt unable to compete. She early convinced herself that the way to be appreciated in this family was to be what people wanted and needed, to be "the perfect child: good, kind, forgiving, loving and caring, always thinking about other people – and never, never angry". She grew up codependent and married a man with a big problem.

Alan's homosexuality was well disguised when he married Willa. He only became homosexually active again as family and career pressures built, putting pressure on his fragile masculinity. As his marriage deteriorated he remained outwardly "a solid churchman, a stable respectable man" though he began drinking heavily and became progressively unable to function sexually with Willa. Willa fathomed the problem but told no one for five years. Her pain pushed her towards a personal Christian commitment and she began to hear God for herself.

That was when she heard one word: relinquishment. She was sitting alone at the piano when it came so loud and clear it was almost audible: "Stop playing God with Alan. I can't help him unless you let him go." Says Willa:

> I really couldn't understand why God would say a thing like that because I thought I had only been what God wanted me to be in our marriage: loving, forgiving and kind. Whatever I thought Alan needed I did, because that's what I thought a good wife did. Then I began to realize that I had been really nice all my life: trying to keep him, never showing him my bad side, trying to understand and take care of him. God said, "I've been trying to talk to Alan for many, many years and the only way I have left to help him is through pain. But every time I get him in pain, you come and stop the pain." And I said, "Well, no-one can love him like I do." And God said, "And that's not playing God?" He said, "I want him on my altar and you're to take your hands off him."

Willa obeyed and took her hands off.

> But I was quite convinced that when I withdrew my support of him and started being me, taking care of me, and

starting to react in a normal way to the treatment I was receiving, that my anger and bitchiness would drive him out of the house. I saw him leaving the family, the children and going out on the street and never coming back.

In fact the opposite happened. A spiritual revolution occurred in Alan's life that has gone down in the annals of homosexual healing, and their marriage blooms today, 30 years later. Alan was one addicted man who *did* decide to pursue healing once his wife stopped trying to do it for him.

Willa relinquished her husband and saved her marriage. Others relinquish their husbands and lose them, like Carrie (Chapter 10). Unlike Alan, Tait was not interested in healing. If Carrie hadn't finally pushed him out – after 18 years of marriage – he would never have gone. Tait wanted marriage and homosexuality too. That wasn't the way God planned it. I reproduce some of Carrie's diary as she struggled to relinquish Tait to God and resist the temptation to go after him and make it all better.

Lord, I will not carry shame or guilt for Tait's lifestyle. If he mucks up his life entirely, that's his fault, his problem. He is unhappy because of his own decisions. I cannot waste my emotional energy on feeling sorry for him. Hands off, Carrie. There is no way you're a failure because you cannot help Tait. Tait and God are the only ones who can help Tait. The prodigal son decided to help *himself.* No one pleaded and coerced, so don't bother. Don't plead with him at the pigsty. There is a large part of me that is finding it very hard to let him go because I want to have him back and I can't have him because he's not mine. So Carrie, let go. You can't fix or rescue him. He can only do that for himself with God's help. You're emotionally addicted to Tait, Carrie. It's very bad for you and you'll get hurt if you play this game. So don't play it. Lord, I've mentally wrapped Tait back up in green paper and silver ribbon and put him in a high-up cupboard with the door shut. Tait is the present I give you, Lord. He was yours before you gave him to me, and now he's yours again. Goodbye my dear,

dear Tait. I will keep away from you. Lord, I let him go. I leave him at the foot of the cross. HE'S ALL YOURS, LORD. My marriage is my offering to you, Lord. Tait is my offering to you. May your will be done.

Relinquishment is not giving up on someone, it's giving someone up – to God. It's to stop being *protective*, and to permit another to face *reality* and experience the natural consequences of his behaviour. It's to admit *powerlessness*: the *outcome* is not in *my* hands. For the codependent, to let go doesn't mean to *stop caring*; it means you can't *do it* for someone else. To let go is to stop trying to change *another*; you can only change *yourself*. It is not to *cut yourself off*, it's to realize you can't *control* another. It's stopping the games and being honest.

ANGER AND BEING REAL

The relationship addict who is being healed will find she is angry: angry that she was abused or unloved as a child; angry that she has had no identity for so long; angry that she deserted herself for the strong persona in the attempt to gain love; angry at the abuse she has put up with in her relationships. Often the relationship addict does not feel able to admit her anger: "Being a good girl had been one of my life's goals since childhood," says one codependent. "It was not 'good or nice' to be angry. I felt like I would die if I allowed myself to be angry." The Christian relationship addict feels it even more. Christians are not meant to be angry; anger is "a sin". Particularly where anger has early roots and Christians are anxious to "honour" parents, they will feel it is unchristian and unloving to own up to anger towards parents.

But God is not wanting automatons who make the right religious noises. We cannot deal with what we will not own up to. Wherever there has been injury there will be anger. It's alright to be angry. God was also angry when we were unloved or abused. He is our friend as we come to grips with how angry we are and express it to him. He knows, he understands and he doesn't hold it against us. *Out the other side of anger is forgiveness of our offender.*

Vaughan (Chapters 3 and 14), relating obsessively with his wife, had a significant breakthrough when he realized he was allowed to take the lid off his anger against his father, asking Jesus to take it all. He swore, hit the wall and kicked tree stumps and wept as he said God seemed to be saying to him: "That's right Vaughan, I've been wanting you to do that for a long time."

When Willa finally expressed her anger it exploded over Alan. The good little girl who was never, never angry beat him with her fists, broke chairs and screamed, "I hate you, I hate you", till she was exhausted. (God meantime baptized Alan with supernatural grace.) Like Vaughan she found God was pleased when she expressed her anger.

Jesus was very responsive to the angry little girl. I had a very hard time accepting and loving that angry part of me, but I finally did because I could feel Jesus' love for that angry person far more than I ever felt it for the good person. He took that angry little child and just held it to him and had very little to say to the good girl.

One codependent who finally "allowed" herself to express her anger out loud said she felt as if "someone who had been lying down inside of me stood up. I didn't have to be a victim. I'm somebody important because that's who God made me."

Carrie's anger erupted into her diary – helped by Tait's latest affair – after weeks of remonstrations that were reasonably gentle as long as it looked as if he might come back. But when it became clear that Tait was not going to rise to the challenge, and that the marriage was over, she let it out into her journal – not at the children, not at Tait. It ended in forgiveness.

... you dirty, rotten, sodding, disgusting, appalling bastard. Your heart is rotten to the core, no good thing can come out of it. Your motives are tainted. You have no morals, no values, no opinions, no integrity, no honesty. You are rude and arrogant. Your mouth is a sewer and the rubbish that comes out stinks. You are a non-person. You're an emotional dependent. You will look for love in increasingly hungry ways and you will never be satisfied. You are a pervert. Your brains are in your pants; you have a depraved mind and a rotten heart. You are a lousy, double-crossing bastard, an evil man. You have no conscience. I HATE what you have done to me and the children. Drop dead.

… I would love to tie that precious penis of yours into a great big knot so it withers and dies and falls off. I would love to push you off a cliff, dig a hole and bury you alive, push you into a cauldron of boiling water. I hope all your hair falls out and you become bald and you get fat. That feels much better. Much better to get all this anger on paper than inflict it on everyone else.

Goodness, it feels great to be honest. To really feel some honest anger without placating it all away and putting on my NICE mask. I loathe and detest what you have done. You deserve every rotten thing that is going to happen to you. I am glad I am telling you as it is. Lord, I feel so very, very angry about the horrid marriage I was in, how I was so gullible and taken for such a long devious ride. Tait, you are becoming an apathetic, unreliable, irresponsible father, just like you were a husband to me. Good riddance. Wow, do I feel much better! I can see this deep anger needs venting and facing up to. I am committed to the process of forgiving and letting go, but I am now convinced these processes do not happen overnight, that they need working through and are on-going.

ANCIENT ANGER

Says Willa,

In the codependent, when you've never been accepted or wanted for who you know yourself to be, when you've had to desert your real self in order to be loved, when that pain starts to come up – there is a great, great anger in you; in some people it's a scream of anger.

The relationship addict invariably finds herself heading back to her early years to resolve her anger. Carrie and Vaughan both discovered that they bore repressed anger against one particular individual in their early lives that was now being unleashed against the person in their present who was hurting them most.

Carrie's anger against Tait went on and on until it frightened her. She only began to get the better of it when she made the discovery that she had been "angry since childhood", in particular with her mother: a Christian but a perfectionist and efficiency fanatic, an undemonstrative woman who ran the house and drilled her children like a sergeant major and was injured if they did not reflect well on her. Carrie felt "victimized" by her mother and "wounded" by her inability to earn her mother's love by measuring up to her expectations of the perfect child. She learned to wear a "jolly, coping, happy-face mask" so her mother "wouldn't have the pleasure of knowing she had hurt me". Of all seven children she was known as "the happy one". Her mask became the strong codependent persona that Tait was attracted to while Carrie "loved him to bits", sure her love for him would "conquer all". As she resolved her anger against her mother Carrie found her anger against Tait also began to subside.

Willa eventually traced her anger back to early childhood, to her father who was "never there when I needed him". Although she hated herself for hating her father, and wanted to love him, "no amount of repentance on my part, of saying sorry, of forgiving, would do it. I told myself, 'My father has done nothing wrong; it's all me. He was a good man.'" The breakthrough came when she woke up in the middle of the night with the words running round her head, "If you ask your father for bread, will he give you a stone?" As she sat up in bed wondering what it meant she "saw" her father – by then deceased.

> My father just looked at me and said, "Would you ever forgive me for what I did, it was so wrong. There were so many times you reached out to me and I either told you I was too busy or I was doing God's work, and you were given a stone."

With that, said Willa, "it seemed like a tremendous thing inside of me broke – which was just a total inability to love my father and believe that I was loveable. All I could say over and over was, 'It's not my fault!'" "Anger often overlies fear and pain. The inner healing experience that enters fear and pain and heals it, also helps dissipate anger and make it manageable. "You start to be able to say, 'What you said or did then really hurt me,' instead of exploding all over people," says Willa.

No-one struggling with a well-established, stubborn problem of a compulsive nature will get very far against it if he feels it is not permissible as a Christian to own up to the anger that will invariably underlie it.

It's OK to express to God our anger towards someone else no matter how florid it is. God is not surprised by it, or fazed by it. Jesus took it 2000 years ago, and he takes it today. But anger should not be indulged for its own sake. The object is to be able to give it up at some point.

Jesus entering our deepest fears helps us to do that. When he has begun to pervade those places we begin to be less self-protective and controlling and freer to relinquish and to forgive – another important step on the way to freedom.

FORGIVENESS

Forgiveness is something we set our face towards, though it can take us a while to get there. Forgiveness – *genuine* forgiveness – lies out the other side of anger owned up to. Carrie's diary recorded the results of her eventual triumph over her anger:

> Lord, at last my feelings for Tait are neutral. What a relief. What a wonderful load of useless baggage to get rid of! Today I was able to pray compassionately for all the gay men who have walked through my life and for the gay community – without any feeling of bitterness or anger. I really pray Lord, that you will give me a deep love and compassion for gay men.

Two years after she pushed Tait out, Carrie was able – as she had always intended – without malice, to tell Tait how much she had loved him and how much he had hurt her. At the end they hugged each other, Tait returned to his gay lover and several weeks later Carrie filed for divorce. Five years later she remarried. As she had always wanted to, she was finally able to "close the door gently".

Sometimes "inner healing" has to happen before we are able to forgive. It was Merrell's unsuccessful attempts to forgive her father that released repressed memories of sexual abuse and led to her healing encounters with Jesus in those memories (Chapter 14).

Alan noticed a big change in Willa's attitude to him from the time she forgave him. "I literally took half an hour to form the words: I FORGIVE YOU," says Willa.

> I fought it inside my stomach. I screamed up all my rights to feel and to keep what I felt, and all the injustices, and they were like puffs of air; my rights to be angry, they meant nothing to God. He just zeroed in and I knew I had to get it out of me.

THE TRIGGERS

In the same way any addict has to identify and avoid his triggers, the relationship addict has to know the kinds of men or situations that attract her, and back away. For Leone it only needed to be a fatherly figure who showed a warm personal interest, for Gina something about a man that promised emotional interaction and sensitivity. If you sense magnetism, infatuation, charm; find yourself trying to bind him to you, of trying to impress him and of preoccupied thinking, you're getting hooked; something destructive for you will be lurking there somewhere. Stay out of his company. According to Nita Tucker (cited in *Beyond Codependency* by Melody Beattie) 80% of happily married couples did not feel an immediate attraction to each other when they first met.

Confrontation, separation and divorce for the wife of a gay man

Heather

Heather's husband, Mike, was a pillar in the church and community, and father of their two children when Heather discovered he was homosexual. She says she had to "work through her own codependency issues" for three years, slowly relinquishing Mike "in her heart" before God put her through "the hardest test of her obedience and faith" by showing her they were to separate while Mike decided "whether to overcome homosexuality, or continue in the gay life and sacrifice his family". One very difficult year passed and then Mike chose Christ and healing and returned to his family. Heather now gives thanks for the "godly man God chose for me".

Obviously a woman will only be able to confront her husband or make the decision to separate when, like Heather, she is strong enough to relinquish her husband and trust a loving God to meet her needs for love.

"If she separates following someone's else's orders, she risks in nine cases out of ten running right back because she can't live without him, or running into another equally disastrous relationship," says Willa. Willa says she never counsels separation; she never has to. Women leave when they're ready.

> When such a woman begins to know the love of Christ and know how deeply he adores her, she will begin to love herself and believe she is worthy of being treated properly: inhuman treatment of her will no longer find a home, a comfortable place in her.

Wives of gay men have scriptural grounds for divorce where there has been adultery: gay sex is adultery. Carrie was quite within her rights to push Tait out. But God is for healing and forgiveness and reconciliation; he wants us to make the choices that will heal ourselves and our marriages.

Confrontation

"Let's say a couple have been married 11 years," says Anita, who counsels a lot of wives of gay men:

> but he's acting out sexually and lying to her; just telling her enough to keep her happy and get her off his back. He's masturbating and fantasizing, reading porn, and cruising (looking for casual homosexual sex). But he's covering his tracks. OK, she's entitled to evidence that her husband is doing something about his homosexuality. I tell her it's time to make a list of the things she would want to see him doing if he wants healing: things like going to an ex-gay group in his area, getting a good counsellor, becoming accountable to his pastor, letting her know where he's going when he goes out. It's not to manipulate him, or force him to go straight. It's to show her he's going to come through with what he's promised her.

Separation

If he doesn't come up with evidence that he's committed to change, separation is the next step. "The married homosexual man has the best of both worlds," says Anita.

> He goes out to get his needs met then comes home to his wife and family. She doesn't separate to shock him, but sometimes he needs to feel the results of his choices; that he hasn't got home life or his kids any more. The negative side of the gay lifestyle is loneliness and isolation: you can't be out there having it all the time.

If separation is used as a threat, it is merely another form of manipulation. "Don't say it unless you can still say it and mean it when everything is good between you," says Willa. "Either you stay with your husband and make every effort to help him, or you leave him," says ex-gay man, Frank Worthen. "There is no middle ground. To stay and nag only gives him justification for his behaviour." Obviously if your husband is honestly seeking help and wanting to change, separation is not even an issue. The ex-gay movement appears to have above average success in using separation to galvanize gay men into choosing between their orientation and their marriages: one ex-gay group reported more than 50% success.

It's up to you

Whether a woman makes a decision to divorce or not, she has to be willing to live with the consequences, says Sy:

> God hates divorce but God also hates wife abuse and gay men can put their wives through hell on earth. What you don't know is, will he ever change? You might be missing out on that opportunity if you say goodbye. I know women whose gay husbands have got saved after 10-15 years and their marriages are now better than they ever dreamed they could be. Then again you have no guarantee that he will ever repent. You have to do what God tells you.

ESSENTIAL STEPS OUT

Robin Norwood in *Women Who Love Too Much* lists ten steps she believes are essential in the recovery of the codependent:

- Going for help. You will back away from this for several reasons: fear that the relationship may end, fear that now everyone will know the worst, and because you still think you can work this thing out yourself, even though none of your best efforts have worked so far.
- Making your own recovery first priority: The same extremes you went to to help *him* recover you must now lavish on yourself. It takes that amount of time and self-focus and effort to get well.
- Join a support group.
- Develop your spirituality. For Norwood this means surrendering self-will to a force higher than yourself, letting go the "what ifs" and "if onlys", and leaving the consequences there. This frees you from the "overwhelming responsibility of fixing (controlling) everything".

- Stop caretaking, that is: managing and controlling him. Stop being helpful. Don't solve his problems, no longer encourage or praise (manipulate), stop watching, leave him to deal with the consequences of his own behaviour, say and do nothing.
- Don't get hooked into the games: the rescuer, persecutor, victim scenario.
- Courageously face your own problems and pain. Do a lot of thinking and writing about your own life, past and present. The problem is not him, it's you.
- Cultivate whatever needs to be developed in you. That is, stop waiting for him to change before you get on with life.
- Become selfish: for the codependent this only means letting go martyrdom; it does not mean indifference, thoughtlessness or self-centredness. It means you matter. It means being able to say "No".
- Share with others.

In a lecture on codependency, Willa lists these steps toward recovery for the codependent woman.

- Express your feelings openly.
- Don't be afraid to show the bad side of yourself.
- Start to communicate directly not through messengers.
- Try to find what's normal, because you don't know.
- Shed perfectionist expectations of yourself.
- Allow yourself to be "selfish". Buy a dress, style your hair, go to the movies. "Whenever codependent women do anything that brings them an ounce of joy they feel it is selfish and not Christian," says Willa. "Satan plays on that every chance he gets. But look at Jesus' face, look at his joy when you do something for yourself. When you get a new dress look at him watching you spin around."
- Learn how to play and have fun. Codependents are usually overly responsible.
- Put to death dreams of a perfect marriage and allow yourself to grieve.

- Get with people who are going to love you and accept all of you. Coax your frightened child out of hiding and make sure she gets lots of praise and positive strokes.
- Settle it that you are intelligent; it's just that your confidence has been annihilated. You're not crazy.
- Determine to be ruthlessly honest with yourself about your relationships: no cheating.

Willa says:

> At the end of my healing, at a conference where everyone was saying, "I'm healed from homosexuality", I got up and said, "I'm healed from codependency and I love me." It just came from really knowing how much God loved me. I had looked so Christian and so loving for so long, but I had never really known the love of God. Now I really love me. I wouldn't trade me for anything in the world – not one hair.

Chapter Eighteen

THE RESPECTABLE CHURCH

Some people make the mistake of thinking that the church is meant to be filled with respectable people. In the respectable church:

- things and reputations are meant to *look* good.
- people in the church do not admit to *unrespectable* personal problems.
- other people get flustered or judgmental if they do.
- the church is not getting training in handling deep-seated personal problems.

The church stays respectable *because* people will not own up to their problems and its respectability *stops* people owning up to their problems.

In the respectable church holiness has become confused with morality. We are expected to be moral rather than holy. To be holy is to be thoroughly washed, thoroughly loved by God and thoroughly acceptable to him, though I am still having an uphill struggle against my addiction. It means I will be understood and accepted by other struggling holy people. To be holy is the beginning of healing. To be moral in the respectable church means I don't admit to myself or anyone else that I am sexually abusing my daughter because respectable people don't do those sorts of things.

As Dietrich Bonhoeffer says in *Life Together*:

> The pious fellowship permits no one to be a sinner. So everybody must conceal his sin from himself and from the

fellowship. We dare not be sinners. Many Christians are unthinkably horrified when a real sinner is suddenly discovered among the righteous. So we remain alone in our sin, living in lies and hypocrisy. The fact is we are all sinners!

When Chad (Chapter 6) was looking for a church that would allow him to be honest about his homosexual struggle, two people had visions in the Sunday morning service Chad was attending for the first time. The first person saw a roll of paper towels. All the sins in the person's life were rolled up and God wanted to peel off the sins one by one and deal with them, he said. A second person spoke up: he had seen the same roll of paper towels, but every time the person tried to tear one off and talk about it with anyone, all he got was "condemnation, misunderstanding and finger-pointing". Chad owned up to the picture, the church service stopped and everyone gathered round Chad. "I opened up that morning in the church service," says Chad. "They got me involved in a kinship group. Every time I was tempted, I could go and talk to someone." Chad made the place his home church.

CHURCH – NOT A SAFE PLACE

Because we all bring all our raw material to conversion, we should not be surprised that the rate of child sexual abuse, wife battering, and secret homosexuality in the church is so high or that one evangelical pastor in four admits to "sexually inappropriate behaviour"[1]. What *should* upset us is that these people have so obviously found the church is *not* a safe or helpful place to open up and get answers.

Of those pastors who responded to the *Christianity Today*[1] survey on sexual indiscretion, almost half said they had nowhere to turn with sexual problems. Commenting on the survey Dr Larry Crabb remarked: "Pastors aren't allowed to admit their vulnerability. It's rare for a pastor to feel comfortable as anything other than a model Christian. Most churches require their pastors to live in denial."

People who are unable to share because they fear ostracism

if they aren't respectable, struggle alone. But isolation makes the problem worse. Bonhoeffer again:

> The more isolated a person is, the more destructive will be the power of sin over him, and the more deeply he becomes involved in it, the more disastrous is his isolation. Sin wants to remain unknown. It shuns the light. In the darkness of the unexpressed it poisons the whole being of a person. This can happen even in the midst of a pious community.

While the church remains respectable, many of us will remain hypocrites, people who look good on the outside but keep our compulsions hidden on the inside.

RESPECTABILITY AND EVIL

There is another side to respectability. Where a Christian will not own up to himself and God (and preferably someone else), about his private compulsion, he closes Christ out – because Christ is the Truth and the Light. The more we close Christ out, the deeper our darkness grows and the more evil finds a home within us.

Jenny

From about the age of four Jenny was sexually abused by her Christian father, usually after he had been drinking. He told her she was "Daddy's little girl", and what they did was "our special secret". She learned early on that it only made things worse if she cried or asked him not to do it. Her mother knew what was happening but never did anything about it.

Jenny repressed the memories of her sexual abuse. They only came flooding back when she sought counselling as an adult because she was chronically depressed. When the memories began "flooding back, like a movie screen playing in my head", her first reaction was denial. "I denied it emphatically. It shattered my concept of a loving father. It was easier to blame God than blame my father." But she slowly came to terms with it and decided to confront her father. When she did he violently denied it. Jenny wanted to keep the issue one between herself and her father, but his denial was so vehement the rest of the family became involved. Her mother took her father's side, her brother didn't want to know, and her sister believed her. Jenny's only contact with her father now is abusive letters from him.

> I needed to confront him for my own healing; it had become impossible for me to continue the lie. I still pray for a miracle in my father's heart though it does not seem likely. I grieve for the father I do not have, and often feel pain for the hell he lives in.

Respectability? Yes, Jenny's family was concerned to preserve appearances. "We appeared to be a happy, well-adjusted, average Christian family," said Jenny. "No-one believed this could be happening and to date most family friends do not believe it." But it was more than respectability. Jenny's father was unable to open himself to the Truth and the Light. Everyone who does evil hates the light, and will not come to the light for fear that his deeds will be exposed (John 3:20).

Collusion

Something else happens when people refuse to face the Truth and the Light. A conspiracy of lies and darkness develops; respectable people with the same sorts of secret problems shield each other. Jenny was also approached sexually by her pastor. So the pastor shielded her father and her father shielded the pastor. In the same way Blackstone sprang to the defence of those who felt got at by Buchman's mild comments on "absorbing friend-ships" (Chapter 1). In the respectable church, people protect each other from too much Light. Sometimes they will point the finger at "worse" sinners – like homosexuals – instead.

The person who refuses to take an inside look, who refuses to admit, like Keith (Chapters 1,16) and Jenny's father, that there is a problem, is a person who is saying "No" to the Truth and the Light. He is a person who refuses to change. According to psychiatrist, Dr M. Scott Peck, in his book *People of the Lie*, evil is synonymous with refusal to change. He says the person who refuses to acknowledge or change a destructive behaviour is an evil person.

> Evil human beings are those who refuse to change, who see no reason to change, who have built layer on layer of self-deception. We are led to believe that real evil does not have anything to do with the mother of three next door, or the deacon in the church down the street, but my own experience is that evil human beings are quite common and usually appear quite ordinary to the superficial observer.

Martin Buber goes further in *Good and Evil*:

> Since the primary motive of the evil is *disguise*, one of the places evil people are most likely to be found is within the church... I do not mean to imply that the religious motives of most people are in any way spurious... only that *evil people* tend to gravitate towards piety for the disguise and *concealment it can offer them* (my italics).

The alcoholic denies he has a drinking problem, the adult incest victim denies she was raped by Daddy and Daddy denies he ever did it. Homosexuals parade their homosexuality, he-men their machismo, relationship addicts deny there is anything wrong with their relationships, and workaholics deny they work too hard. Keith had convinced himself he was respectable, that his marriage was problem-free even though his anger was out of control and he was sexually obsessed. We do it to avoid facing our original pain, our empty or unbearable place. Life without the mask, without the addiction, is too hard. But behind the mask, hiding from Truth and Light, our darkness deepens and evil begins to make its home.

With this result – as Jesus himself said in an amazing statement:

> For this people's heart has become calloused; they hardly hear with their ears, and they have closed their eyes. *Otherwise* they might see with their eyes, hear with their

ears, *understand with their hearts and turn, and I would heal them* (Matthew 13:15).

It is probably the classic statement, from the Truth himself, on our addictions and personae. They become all we need. They close our eyes and block our ears and harden our hearts to any other Saviour. They reject Christ. We remain religious and respectable but unhealed. We become Pharisees: Jesus' sworn enemies. Our addictions sabotage our healing. "God waits for us to recognize this 'survival kit' as a fabrication of the flesh and therefore something to be repented of," says Mary Pytches in *A Child No More*.

It is in letting Christ reach behind our personae and addictions to heal us that we stop being Pharisees and respectable people and start being real. It is in being prepared to face up to what really *is* in there, that we find we are no different from anyone else underneath it all. The sexually promiscuous person is no different from the man who is driven to succeed, who is no different from the homosexual, who is no different from a person with an eating disorder, who is no different from the woman who is obsessed with some man, who is no different from a lesbian. We cease believing anyone else's sin smells worse to God than our own. We begin to teach each other and learn from each other. We begin to join hands as a holy, healing community.

And, when we can bring ourselves to be honest with ourselves, God and someone else, Jesus Christ the Truth, the Light, the Healer, begins to penetrate our original pain to remove the poisoned dart. He becomes the Lover of our souls. He takes us in his arms and bind up our wounds. He heals us.

And then he sends us out, *unrespectable* people, free of our judgmentalism, to heal others. And he will expect us to love as he has loved us: *in compassion and mercy refuse to interact with people's personae, but instead help them face up to their original pain, because that is the only way they will be healed.*

It can become a call to love our enemies, because people may become implacable enemies if evil has found a home in their hearts and they *refuse* to take an inside look. But it is, nevertheless, our calling.

How does the respectable church get real?

Ken

Ken's black eyes are bitter. He is an ex-gay with AIDS who became a Christian several years ago but he's having a tough time at church: conservative evangelical, "heavily into marriage and children". He was up front from the beginning about his gay background and AIDS so no one could say later he hadn't told them. In the following year he said he was ignored and passed over. He underwent three months of membership training but wasn't invited up front with all the other new members to be introduced to the church on graduation night. He doesn't think it was accidental. People rarely get his first name right. He is often exhausted from AIDS but no-one offers to come over and push a vacuum, though "if Sister Suzy has a hang nail they'll go over and cook her dinner and clean her yard". They know the progression of the disease and that AIDS is fatal but no-one has called him up to ask if he is OK, though he has received a couple of sympathy cards.

Ken reckons he has become something of "a barometer of hypocrisy" in the church – "showing what people are made of". His pastors have never mentioned homosexuality or AIDS from the pulpit. Ken is convinced that at the bottom line the church's attitude to him is not an ignorance problem but a "heart" problem. "It sounds nicer to say, 'If only I had more education', but there's too much on television, the radio, and in newspapers and magazines for that to cut it with me," he says. "Everyone knows you can't get AIDS through casual contact." He's leaving the church soon partly because as he deteriorates he can see he won't be able to count on it for support, partly because he wants to return home and heal the rift with his parents. He believes God wanted him there to "shake them up a little" and he thinks attitudes have shifted "quite a bit".

Cedar

Cedar, Maryland[2], is a wealthy upper class suburban church whose first response to the AIDS epidemic was a satisfied sense that God was judging homosexuals, and that the "gay plague" was cleansing society of an unwanted perversion. When a homosexual man privately owned up to the pastor, also revealing he had AIDS, members of the pastoral team agreed to meet with him in a car in the parking lot once a week to pray with him. He was not invited into the church; they were afraid and angry. Some time later the young man rented a motel room and was found lying dead in his own vomit 48 hours after an overdose. A few months later a male 16-year-old attending Cedar and also struggling homosexually, committed suicide; he was afraid to confide in anyone because of the church's attitude to homosexuality.

The pastors decided something had to be done. The senior pastor preached on John 4: Jesus went to Samaria, so that he could quench the thirst of a woman at a well who was living in adultery. They turned the regular morning adult Sunday school classes (well over 1000 people) into a question-and-answer session on AIDS before a panel of health-care professionals. "If you're still having a hard time with homosexuality and AIDS after all your questions are answered, then you're up against a spiritual problem and you may need to make an appointment with our counsellors," said the pastor. "If you still have a problem after that you may have to find a new church."

Six months later a man called Wayne, the church's pride and joy: Christian college student president, Christian youth worker and soul-winner par excellence, stood up before the congregation to announce he was struggling with homosexuality, had AIDS and needed their help and forgiveness. There was a dead silence. Then one of the pastors rose to his feet to say he also had a personal problem and needed the church's prayers. (He was specific later to a small group.) Then an elder rose, then several parents saying, in essence, if Wayne can be honest about his problems then we need to be too, we're needing help as well. Then a son of one of the parents stood up, "If my Dad can open up and talk like that in front of you and ask for help then I need help too. I'm on drugs."

Cedar began changing. In the following months several families left but 200 more arrived.

Becky

Becky was a church-raised southern girl. She "always struggled to please God and try to be whatever anybody told her good was" – her Sunday School teachers, school teachers, parents, friends. She was an adult practising law when she was appointed to defend a 16-year-old youth on a charge of breaking and entering. "I went to his cell and he had all the hallmarks of a homosexual: feminine mannerisms, high voice. I thought, *Ugh*, got the facts and got out. He was repugnant to me." Back in her office she said God "laid her low". "I heard it. God said, 'I called you to love him, but you judged him.'" Becky returned to the cell. "The youth was as repugnant as ever but I knew God had spoken." She began to talk to him: found out he had no idea who his father was, that he had been homosexually raped. "I came away with a glimmer – just a glimmer of my own prejudice and God's call to love people." Later Becky resigned from law and joined the ministry team at Bladen Grove Presbyterian Church[2] in South Carolina. She got to know and love and respect the church's young youth worker, Bryce. Then Bryce confided to her that he had homosexual desires. Bryce was the first homosexual man to surface at Bladen Grove and he was fortunate; the ministry team – and Becky – sought to help him. Becky learned. Paul and Joan, a married couple in the church with a lesbian daughter, decided to offer support to people in the area who were homosexual but didn't want to be and attended a national ex-gay conference to equip themselves. Referrals began coming their way. Paul and Joan needed support. "Knowing people were ignorant, prejudiced and didn't understand", they went to the pastoral team at Bladen Grove. "They stood behind us."

Pastoral attitudes on homosexuality and AIDS are important: congregations generally take their lead. At Bladen Grove the pastors were "real". "The way we get people to be real is to be real ourselves," says Kevin, one of the church's pastors. "We're not into fake spirituality. Homosexuality is just one type of brokenness from which all of us suffer. Sin takes 1000 different shapes. When you know your own brokenness you don't judge others for theirs."

Probably significantly, Bladen Grove was one of only two churches in the 77-church Presbytery that was growing.

MAKE HASTE SLOWLY

Then came the business of educating the church about homosexuality. Bearing in mind the area's conservatism the ministry team decided to proceed slowly. They passed over the more flamboyant Sy for the academic approach, and Dr Moberly ran a seminar for the church leadership and interested individuals which left a good nucleus of the church well-informed and supportive. Then Paul and Joan formally set up an ex-gay support group, and Bladen Grove offered to take responsibility for it, granting functional autonomy in return for accountability. The following year the church sponsored a second seminar for the church's leaders, led by a mature couple in the ex-gay movement; and some time later a third, this time an all-church seminar taken by ex-gay leaders. In the following five years Paul and Joan's mother ministry gave birth to five other ex-gay ministries in the state, all working with local churches.

Bladen Grove did it cautiously in America's conservative Bible belt and it worked: in a church of 1500 no-one left.

It also takes someone to get the ball rolling. At Bladen Grove it was Bryce – courageous enough to risk rejection and criticism and dismissal. At Cedar it took the lives of two young men – but at least it was not in vain. At Ken's church it took Ken and apparently not much was achieved; it may be easier for the next catalyst. In some places it has been struggling parents starting a parents' support group. Interestingly the greatest catalyst of change in the attitude of the conservative church has been the number of good boys from respectable Christian homes who started coming home sick with AIDS.

When we have owned up to our addictions and let Christ into our original pain, we know from experience that none of us is any worse or any better than anyone else. Judgmentalism is replaced with compassion. Once we have realized that our compulsions and addictions are just our misguided attempts to find value, love, and significance, and that we can find it in the arms of God, we become healers. We understand that we are all somewhere on the continuum – taking refuge from our pain in behaviours we don't want to be parted from. We live in a world covering its pain and nakedness and shame with poor, ragged substitutes for God's love.

In seeking to heal others we will sometimes succeed in getting behind their masks, sometimes not. It depends how much they want to keep their masks. But our commitment as healers must always be to the person behind the mask. We are called to it: Jesus was.

BILL

Bill's story was told to me by an ex-gay man, Jake, who works with men dying of AIDS. He kept breaking down in the telling. It shows what can happen when we commit ourselves to bringing Light and Truth into someone's pain.

Bill was a dying AIDS patient who came into Jake's life because his family called Jake. Bill was slowly committing suicide under hospital supervision: totally unresponsive to medical staff, family, friends, treatment; even refusing food.

Jake picks up the story as he enters the hospital room. "Bill had obviously once been a handsome man, but he was now thin and haggard. He received me in a depressed but cordial way, but turned away when he found I was connected to a church ministering to people with AIDS," said Jake:

It was that sort of physical gesture that said to me, "You can get lost". I took the hint and said, "Thank you for letting me introduce myself and I'm glad to have made the contact. If you want me to I'll come back to visit you at some other time." He never said "Yes", he never said "No". I stayed a while then put my hand on his forehead and said, "Bill, would you look at me." He did, and it was the expression in his eyes that changed my life forever. The colour of his eyes was really blue but when I looked at them they were black. I have never seen in any human face such depths of unrecordable, incredible torment; it was not physical pain. It was ultimately pain and spiritual conflict of a profound and overwhelming kind. They were black literally with despair. And it was as if – almost behind the pain in his eyes – there was this pleading, this flash of yearning. I don't think he even knew what he was asking for or looking for. But it shocked me so much that I reacted physically. It was so powerful I stepped back from the bed. And at that moment in time it was as if God laid a 50-pound weight on my shoulders and said to me, "Jake, you stick with this man either until there is a breakthrough or he is dead."

I returned several days later. Bill grunted a couple of non-committal responses and then shut his eyes again. But as I left I did the same as I did before: put my hand on his forehead and said, "Bill, would you look at me", and he did. Again it was the same dual message but with this difference: on the top layer there was still the torment, but at the lower layer it was as if Satan was looking at me through his eyes and saying, "Forget it, I've got him." And all of my superficial enthusiasm evaporated. I went home and cried uncontrollably all the way.

I kept going back and in the weeks before he died it was a kind of a warfare thing – back and forth: at one level he was rejecting, but at another level I always sensed this undercurrent of need. There were actually times when I tried to disengage because of his hostile responses. At one point I decided I wouldn't go back. I asked him specifically, "Do you want me to come back?" He said, "No." But then his mother phoned me and begged me to go back. It was as if we were stuck together in spite of everything. I continued to visit him regularly and I got nowhere. Sometimes he would tell me to shut up, other times to get out of the room. Other times he would lie very, very quietly. I never harassed him, I never Bible-thumped him, I was never provocative. I never prayed with him unless he specifically asked me to. I would talk, and often sit – just sit.

But there was one thing he allowed me to do every time – one link we had. It was the one thing that kept me going back even against my own feelings at times. He would always take a drink of water from me – always –

even when he told me to shut up or get out of the room, or never come back again. As I was leaving I would say, "Your mouth looks dry, Bill, take a drink." And he would.

From Bill's family Jake was able to piece together something of Bill's life. He was in his forties, divorced with teenage sons. His background was devout Roman Catholic – at one time. No one knew for sure but it seemed his sexual orientation was heterosexual but that he had experimented homosexually and become HIV+. His hostility and rejection of people seemed to stem from guilt, self-loathing, and shame. But it was hard to know. And Bill wouldn't say anything.

On the afternoon of the day Bill died I went to see him again. I knew this would be it. Basically I just sat by the bed and quietly prayed. I didn't talk. He was incapable of talking at this point anyway. When I felt it was time to go, I helped him clean his mouth and gave him a drink of water. As I left the room I went to the other side of the bed; Bill was turned away from me clinging rather desperately and despairingly to the bedrails. I stooped down so that his face was level with mine but again, his eyes were closed and there was no visual interaction. I put my hand on his and I said, "Bill, I'm going now but I want you to know that I'm still praying for you and I'm asking above all else that God will give you his peace." He never said "Goodbye", or "Thank you", there was no response whatever that I could sense other than this feeling of sad resignation under my hand. He didn't pull his hand away, he didn't reject me either.

It was as I was standing there trying to say goodbye that a physical sensation swept over me three times, so powerfully that it registered emotionally. I can only describe it as three distinct but identical waves of sorrowful tenderness. As the last wave passed – there was no vision, no voice, nothing mystical, just the sense of this thing physically ebbing away from me – it was as if Jesus said to me, "Jake, this is what I feel for Bill". And that physical burden I had felt for him all those weeks I was visiting him, lifted. It just disappeared. There was this inner sense that whatever I was supposed to do for him was over.

In terms of your classical evangelical conversion and nice things happening, there was nothing nice that happened – there were no answers to any of my questions, none. And as I cried and reflected on the whole relationship and the unproductiveness of it, I began to understand something. I think in our limited human way we have assumed that hell is linked to vindictiveness. What I learned through Bill about the character of God in a really life-changing and unforgettable way was that, even if – and I don't know, and I'm glad I don't know – Bill was lost, there was no hate and vindictiveness in God. The only biblical truth I can hook into that helps me explain it, is Jesus looking over Jerusalem: how often I would have gathered you as a hen gathers its brood under its wings – but you *would not*. In the face of their doom his compassion was still extended, he still loved them. That's the Father heart of God, and it is that emotion taken to an infinitely perfect degree in God's heart that sent Jesus.

And I realized that our call was to serve, just serve, whether we get thanks or not, whether we have to love in the face of provocation that emotionally is driving us in exactly the opposite direction. It doesn't mean you're a doormat, or weak or manipulated. You do it because they matter to God. You bother for Jesus' sake.

JO

Jo was a 26-year-old man dying of AIDS in a hospital in Washington DC. Doctors had taken him off AZT and suggested he return to his parents in Harlem to die. Chad (Chapter 6) visited Jo, heard his story, held and prayed for him. As he left Jo called after him, "Chad, please come back, come back alone."

Chad returned 30 minutes later to find Jo sitting in the corner of the room banging his head against the wall and sobbing. He was by him in an instant his arms around him: "Jo, what's happening in your mind?" Frantically Jo clung to him,

"Chad, just hold me, I'm so afraid to die." Chad clasped him and prayed.

What followed for Chad was a revelation. The passage in Matthew 25 burst into meaning. "I suddenly understood for the first time in my life what Jesus meant when he said, 'I was sick and you looked after me.'" Holding Jo, Chad realized it was Jesus he had in his arms. With Jo's arms tight about him he realized he was being embraced by Christ – a suffering Christ. He also realized the contrary and still cannot recount it without breaking down: to refuse to minister to people like Jo was to reject Jesus – the very Lord he claimed to serve.

In the 1870s Gustave Flaubert wrote his own version of the medieval legend of St Julian the Hospitaller. Julian was called out one wild night to ferry a hideous, ulcerated leper across a river. After the crossing he took the man to his own hut and gave him food and drink and tried to warm him first by a fire, then in his own bed. The leper closed his eyes.

> "It is like ice in my bones! Come close to me."
>
> And Julian… lay down on the dry leaves near him, side by side.
>
> The leper turned his head. "Undress so that I can have the warmth of your body."
>
> Julian took off his clothes; then, naked as on the day of his birth, got back into the bed. And he felt against his thigh the leper's skin, colder than a serpent and rough as a file.
>
> He tried to give him courage, and the other answered panting: "Ah! I am dying!… Come closer, warm me! Not with your hands! No with your whole body."
>
> Julian stretched out completely over him, mouth to mouth, chest to chest.
>
> Then the leper clasped him and his eyes suddenly took on the light of the stars. His hair became as long as the rays of the sun. The breath of his nostrils was as sweet as roses. A cloud of incense rose from the hearth and the waves sang… And the one whose arms still clasped him

grew and grew until he touched with his head and his feet the two walls of the hut. Then the roof disappeared, the firmament unrolled, and Julian ascended into heaven's blue reaches – in the embrace of Our Lord Jesus Christ.

And again and again Jesus said: It is I; it is I. It is I that am highest; it is I that you love; it is I you enjoy; it is I that you serve. It is I that you long for; it is I that you desire; it is I that you mean. It is I that am all... It is I that am enough for you. (Julian of Norwich)

Notes
1. See *Christianity Today* survey, Chapter 3.
2. Fictional name, true story.

SELECT BIBLIOGRAPHY

Recommended resources on the healing of disordered relationships and needs for love - whether homosexual or heterosexual:

On the Web: www.exodusnorthamerica.org/resources - Regeneration Books. One of the most comprehensive collections of publications, (incl tapes, videos) available anywhere on homosexuality, its roots and healing, much of it equally relevant to heterosexual relationships and behaviours. All reviewed. Simple searchable database titles. Online purchases and overseas posting.

www.narth.com A hugely-visited website run by NARTH, a US-based psychoanalytic and educational organisation dedicated to research, therapy and prevention of homosexuality. A browsable database of collected journal and conference papers, books and reviews, interviews and testimonies. Subscribable quarterly bulletin.

www.exodusnorthamerica.org How to find a ministry near you, testimonies, speakers, links. FAQs.

The most reliable materials are those written by former gay men and women who lives show stable, long-term evidence of change. Into this category fall authors such as Frank Worthen, Alan Medinger and Andy Comiskey. Leanne Payne and Dr Elizabeth Moberly have also written classics that were breakthrough titles in their time and remain in demand.
   These are:

Comiskey, A. (1989): *Pursuing Sexual Wholeness*. Creation House, Lake Mary, Florida. 207 pages. (Other titles available)

Medinger, A. (2000): *Growth into Manhood*. Shaw, Colorado Springs. 258 pages.

Moberly, E. R. (1983): *Homosexuality, a New Christian Ethic*. James Clarke & Co., Cambridge. 56 pages.

Payne, L. (1981): *The Broken Image*. Baker Books House, Grand Rapids, MI. 176 pages. (Other highly-recommended titles available)

Payne, L. (1985): *Crisis in Masculinity*. Crossway Books, Westchester, Illinois. 222 pages.

Worthen, F. (1984): *Steps out of homosexuality*. Love in Action, San Rafael, California. 171 pages. (Other Steps Out titles available)

One book exhaustively examines the claims that homosexuality is biologically based from a mainstream scientific point of view and concludes that any such effects are weak and indirect:

Whitehead, Dr N. E.; Whitehead, B. K. (1999): *My Genes Made Me Do It!* Huntington House, Layfayette, Louisiana. 233 pages.

Is homosexuality biologically fated? Can gays change their orientation? What does science really say? Taking a mainstream scientific position, this clear, accessible book concludes that the evidence does not support current views that homosexuality is genetically determined. Neil Whitehead, who has a PhD in biochemistry, joins forces with his wife Briar to check the facts. Available from: Whitehead Associates, 54 Redvers Drive, Belmont Hills, Lower Hutt, New Zealand (www.mygenes.co.nz).

A second book rejects from a scientific viewpoint claims that homosexuality is biologically hardwired and argues from a psychiatric viewpoint that change is possible:

Satinover, J. (1996): *Homosexuality and the Politics of Truth*. Baker, Grand Rapids, Michigan. 280 pages.

A very practical 400-page workbook dealing with homosexuality, child sexual abuse, sexual addiction, porn, masturbation, exhibitionism, voyeurism and much more:

Foster, D. K. (2000): *Sexual Healing*. Mastering Life Ministries, Jacksonville, Florida. 400 pages. www.gospelcom.net/mlm

Other titles:

Bergner, M. (1995): *Setting Love in Order*. Baker Book House, Grand Rapids, MI. 207 pages.
Hemfelt, R.; Minirth, F.; Meier, P. (1989): *Love is a Choice*. Thomas Nelson, Nashville, Tennessee. 284 pages. (2000): Monarch Books, UK.
Howard, J. (1991): *Out of Egypt*. Monarch Books, United Kingdom. 280 pages.
May, G. (1991): *Addiction and Grace*. Harper Collins, NY. 195 pages.
Nicolosi, J. (1991): *Reparative Therapy of Male Homosexuality*. Jason Aronson, Inc., Northvale, New Jersey. 355 pages.
Worthen, A.; Davies, B. (1996): *Someone I Love is Gay*. IVP, Downer's Grove, Illinois. 215 pages.